ANTON CORBIJN
STAR TRAK

ANTON CORBIJN

STAR TRAK

STEWART, TABORI & CHANG
NEW YORK, NEW YORK

INTRO

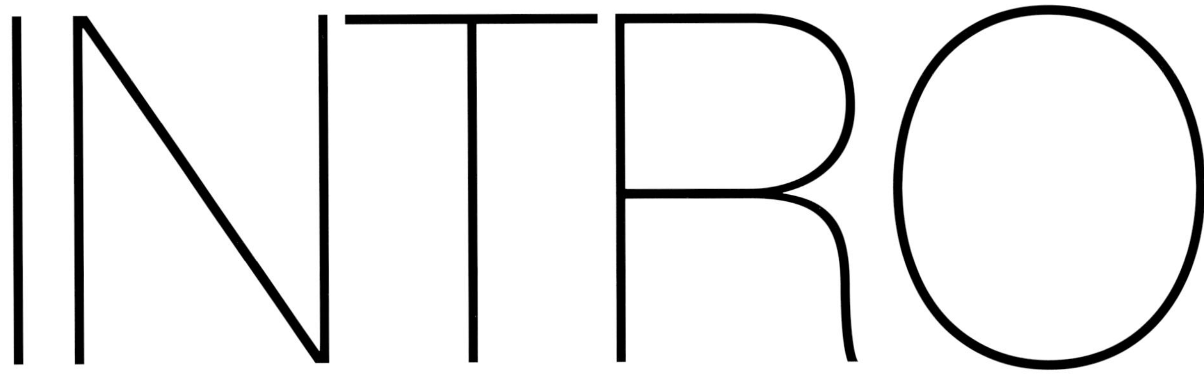

BRIAN ENO

February 1996

You sometimes hear something being dismissed because it's all image and no substance, as though these are completely separate, the first being ephemeral and lightweight, the second profound and permanent. But one of the messages of pop culture is that you can't usually separate them: 'image' is constantly turning into 'substance', and vice versa. The package is part of the contents. ★ This makes for a lot of confusion for people who want to pay their respects to pop culture by putting it into the same reference frame as High Culture. Fine Art distrusts what is seen as packaging – the art gallery and the concert hall are insulators intended to keep the work away from the transitory influences of the rest of life, to deliberately neutralize any possible 'package' effects. By thus neutralizing its presentation, Fine Art tries to say 'Look – just pure content'. ★ This represents a decision about where the edge of the work really is. What is being seen as the permissable site for creative work by the artist, and what is just 'the rest of the world'? What is 'inside' and what is 'outside'? ★ This problem – if you think it one – is particularly acute in pop music. When Madonna appeared, she was attacked for her concentration on everything other than the music – on the things that people called the package. Even if this had been true, would it have been so awful? Who said that pop music was ever just to do with melodies and lyrics and whatever else the word 'music' historically meant? For forty years, pop music and its culture have been at the center of the everyday conversation that our culture has with itself, and the talk is mostly about style: how you choose to *look* and to *look at* things, how you value what you are and what you have and what you do. Lifestyle, I suppose, is the word. ★ *Madonna,* they said, *is using sex to sell her work.* No, wrong: sex isn't the package – thinking about sex, and exercising different attitudes about it *is* the work, or, another way, if sex *is* the *package,* then designing the package has become the work. Or *Miles Davis is a real artist because he lived and died for his music without getting trapped in all this spurious image-stuff that bedevils pop music.* Are you kidding? Would Miles have sounded the same if he'd been a fat heating engineer from Oslo rather than a particularly glamorous member of a glamorous subterranean outsider culture? ★ Suppose you drew a diagram of a pop record. At the center, let's for convenience (and only for convenience) put the 'music' itself. Round that, there are lyrics – what's being said. Round those, the 'production', the kind of 'finish' the sound has been given. Round that, like layers on an onion, we could put the 'look' of the band – the fashion/lifestyle landscape with which they are associated. Now let's put the photographs, the videos, then the lifestyle stories leaked to the press by eager publicists, then the 'local conditions' of the scene in which they fall, then the bigger context of pop-history, and finally the culture at large. ★ Tradition would expect respectable artists to concentrate their attention on the center of that onion, treating the other layers as either trivial or uncontrollable. But what's to stop an artist working one of the other layers, and then moving 'out' and 'in' from there? There have been many bands who were primarily about 'production' (as opposed to 'music' in the traditional sense) so why not bands about look, but with some music to carry the look – so the music becomes, in a sense, the package? Why not? Who said developing an image wasn't a justifiable site for creative behavior? ★ This is all very well in theory, but in practice it hasn't quite worked out like that. The 'edges' have not generally been addressed with the same creative attention as the 'centre'. Most image-inventors are not Malcolm Maclaren or Shadow Morton. Most cover designers are not Russell Mills or Vaughan Oliver. And most photographers are not Anton Corbijn, a lively, if rather tall man with a camera. ★ 'Lively' is important: people holding cameras are normally dead. They are not in the same time as the rest of us. They are not here. They are already in the future, looking back at the now through their imagined picture *as if it is already history.* You think I'm making this up as I go along. But don't you remember those famous proofs? That cameraman at the Indianapolis 500 who filmed the wheel leaving a racing car at 160 mph, spinning towards him, spinning, spinning, until it smashed him to bits? And he never stopped filming it. Or that guy in Chile, filming the military bearing down on the demonstration of which he was a part, until, just a few yards away, we see (he saw) a soldier raising his rifle, taking careful aim at us – and shooting. The camera jerks up to sky and then black. Another dead cameraman. ★ Is this heroic commitment to duty? Or is it just forgetting that you are actually here, this is actually now, this is not a movie – yet. ★ That's what I think. It's being absent. You get the same effect with people piling off tour buses to take pictures of whatever they're told they ought to be interested in. They aren't experiencing it now, but collecting the thing for some hypothetical future experience. To experience something you must, to some extent, surrender to it, become part of it. And there just isn't the time. ★ So anyway, this is the problem with photography, from the point of view of the subject. This person walks in with lots of lights and lenses and reflectors and assistants, says 'Just act normal' and then immediately proceeds to go absent. You are supposed to just act normal but there is this sort of non-being in the room: 'Just pretend I'm not here...' floating around and looking back at you from the future. How do I do this? How do I act as if you're not here? You notice this if you're being interviewed for TV and you direct a comment to the camera person, who shrinks in mute terror, eyebrows raised to the director: 'Am I really here? Am I supposed to be here? Am I *allowed* to be here?' ★ Anton Corbijn is not at all dead when he's taking photos. He's actually a bit crazy, going all over the world to take pictures of people, but then acting as though it doesn't really matter in the least – sure, let's do a few pictures now we're here, but don't let it get in the way of anything. I think that's what everyone likes – his respect for whatever is going on at the time, his reluctance to impose, his sense of timing. He makes it light, lets you know that your life doesn't depend on it. In fact, when Anton turns up, the mood invariably becomes funnier, more pliable. He has a way of making you feel that you wouldn't mind experimentally making an arse of yourself – because he doesn't either. His life doesn't depend on it. ★ We were in The Supper Club in Amsterdam. It was one of those evenings when a lot of quite arty people were there, being a little reserved. Then this Sarajevan band – Riktur – started playing, the kind of music you couldn't really be reserved about. Instantly, Anton was up and dancing, looking like the result of one of those Department of Defense experiments – Stick Insect on LSD, or Amphetamine Conger Eel. All his limbs, and there seem to be a lot of them, spinning in asynchronous orbits, led by his nose (– this is very Dutch, to be led by one's nose). I've never seen dancing like this in my life, and it had a liberating effect. I thought 'Well, I certainly couldn't do worse' and joined him. Some people give other people license to take a chance. ★ However, we all occasionally lapse into pre-postmodernism, and Anton did, in an interview, saying something to the effect of 'I always thought that my job was to tell the truth'. This is confusing, because in fact there are few better and more interesting liars than he. The camera inevitably lies, so choosing the kind of lie you want to tell is actually the creative act of photography. And Anton invites his 'subject' to take part in that game – to create something new with him, to let go of the idea that the picture is going to show the real you, and say 'So what would I like to be?'. This is liberating – at the end of the process it doesn't feel like your soul has been stolen, but that you've tried on some other ones. And that is one of the central games of pop culture. It's the game that says 'So what else could I be?'. To do that, and to be seen doing that, is to take part in life in the carnival. It's possibly the source of our empathy, because by putting ourselves in other minds we begin to understand what it is like to be *of another mind.* ★ That's one end of the process – the context of play and experiment that Anton inspires and out of which he makes his pictures. The other end is what he does with them after he's taken them, and that too is a process of further falsification (aka creative behavior). The way he works the images in the darkroom makes photography look like one of the most interesting things anyone could do for a living. He discovers (makes) nuances of light that are just plain beautiful, that create an enchanted sculptural stillness – like in those Maya Deren films where time seems to have become viscous. It looks so easy: you sense that here is something that relied on keen judgement more than stubborn drudgery. You think you could have done it – if only you'd thought to try.

PHOTO GRAPHS

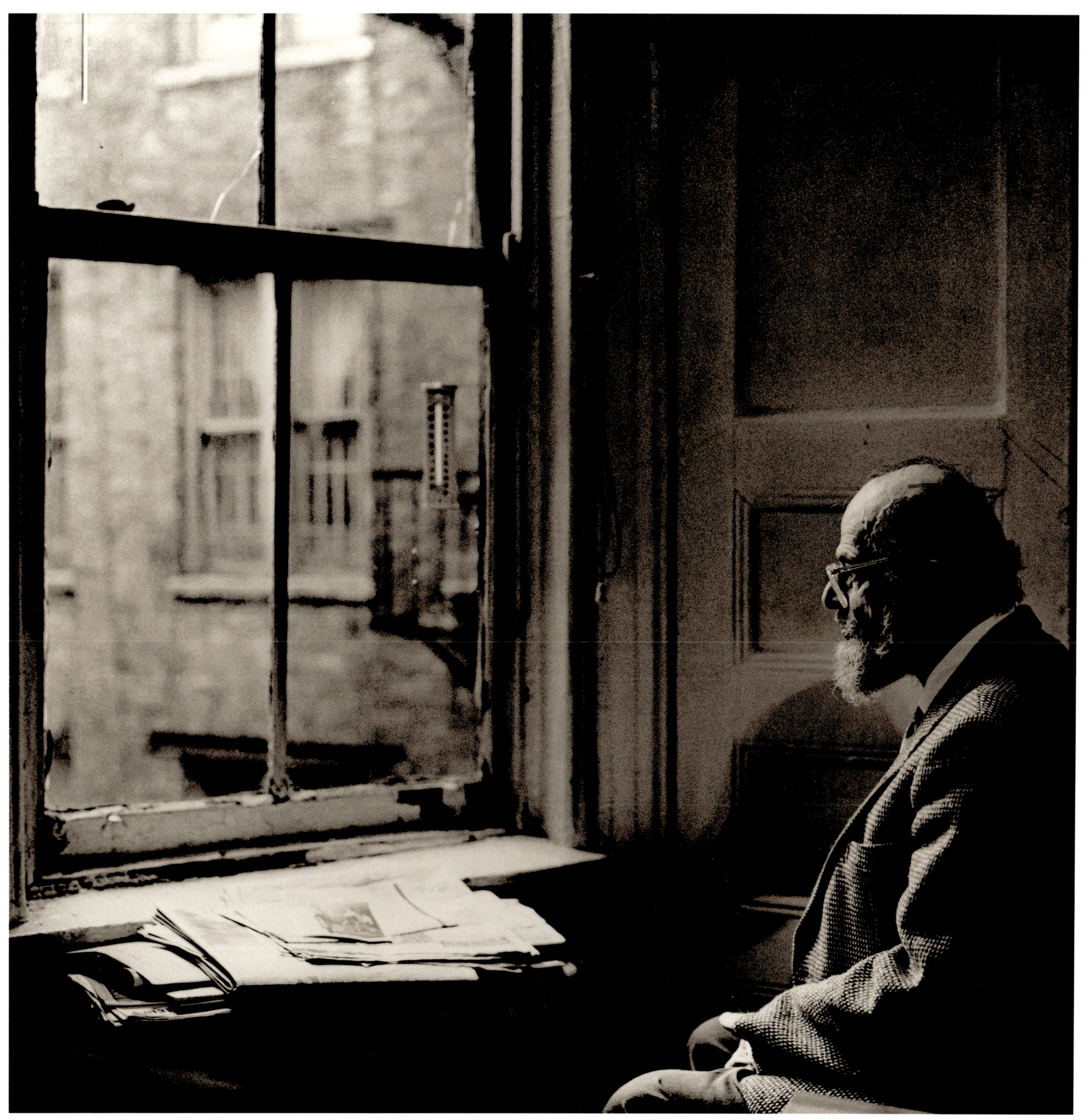

allen ginsberg

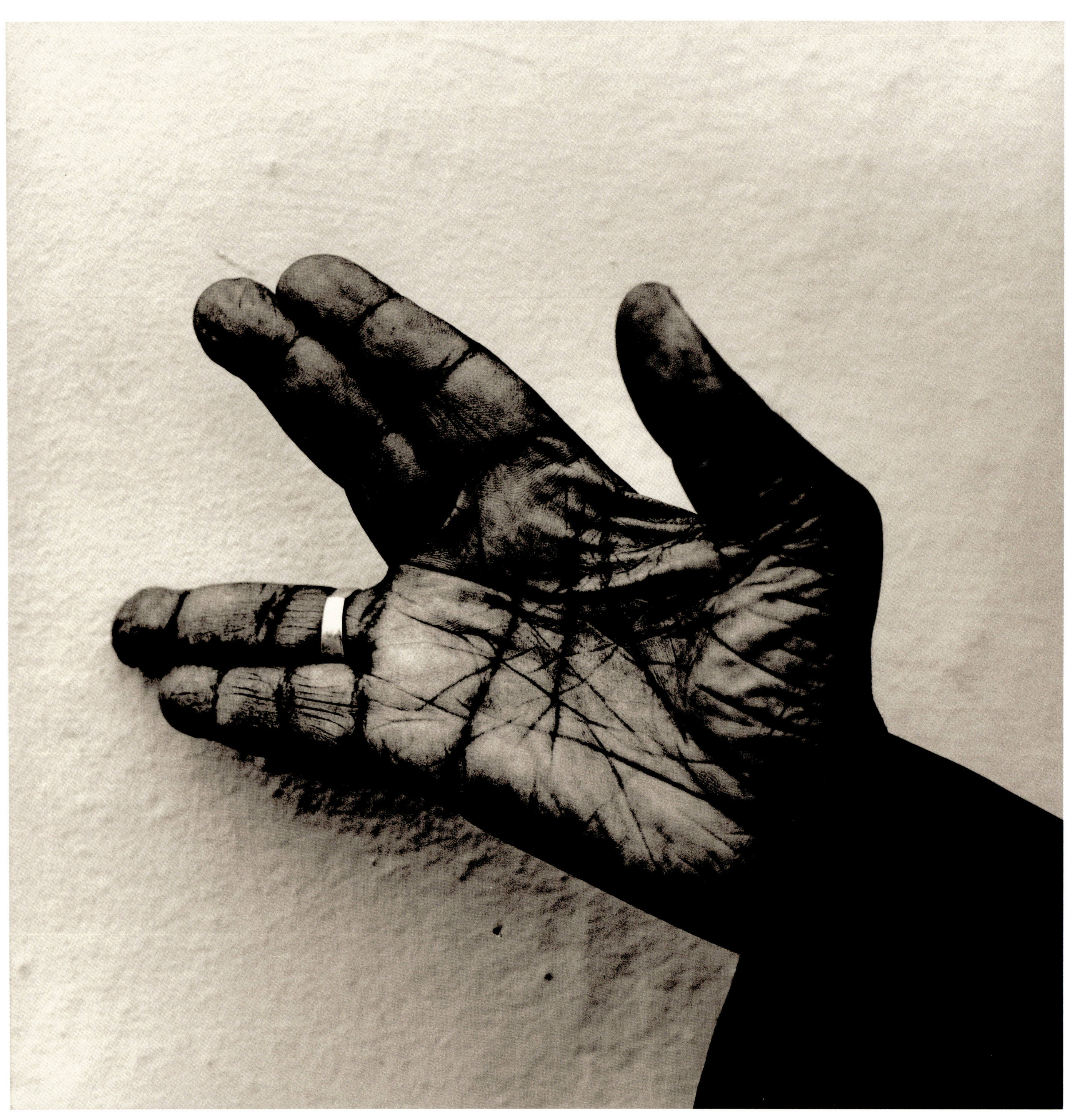

john lee's hand

2

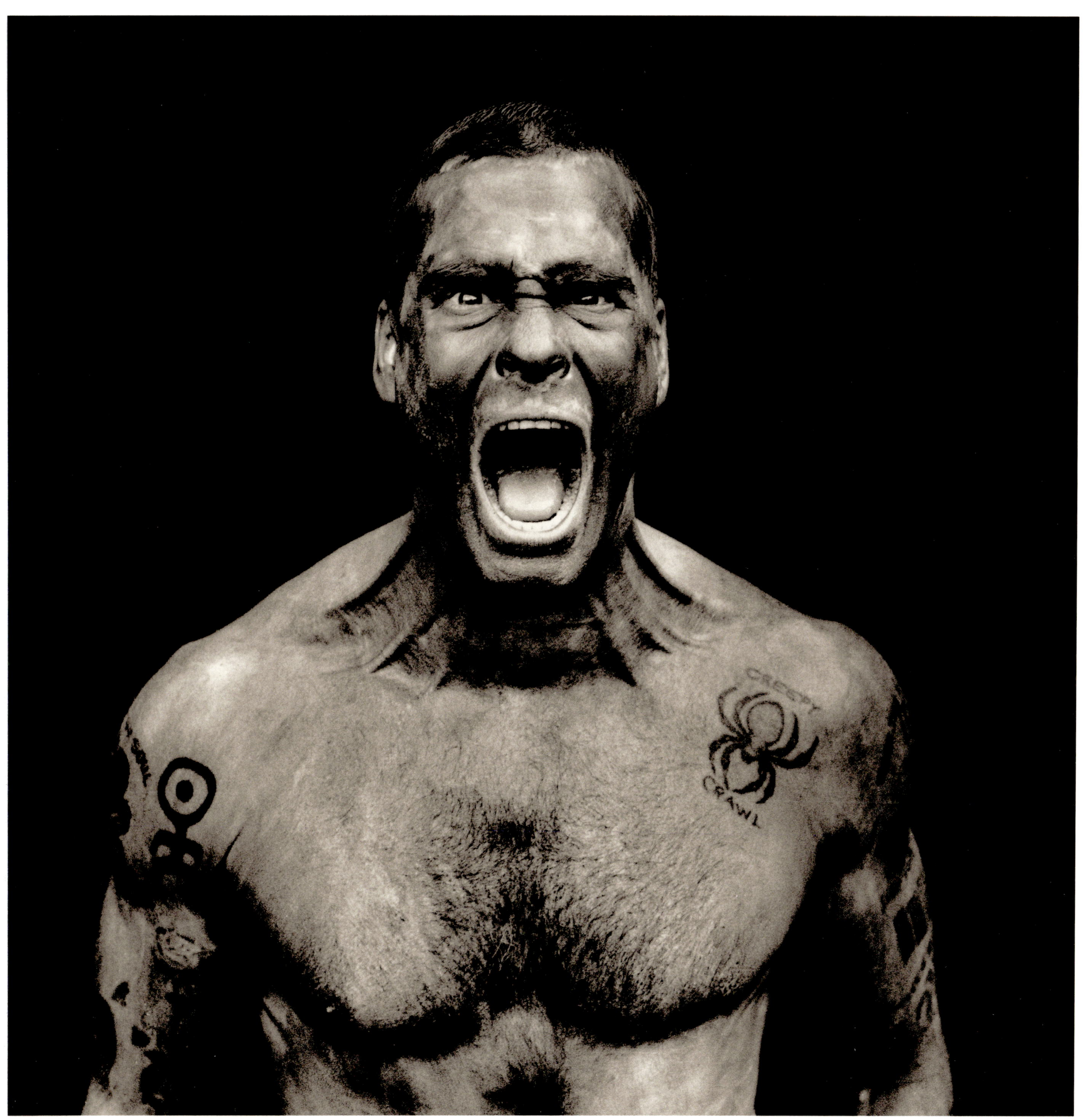

henry rollins

3

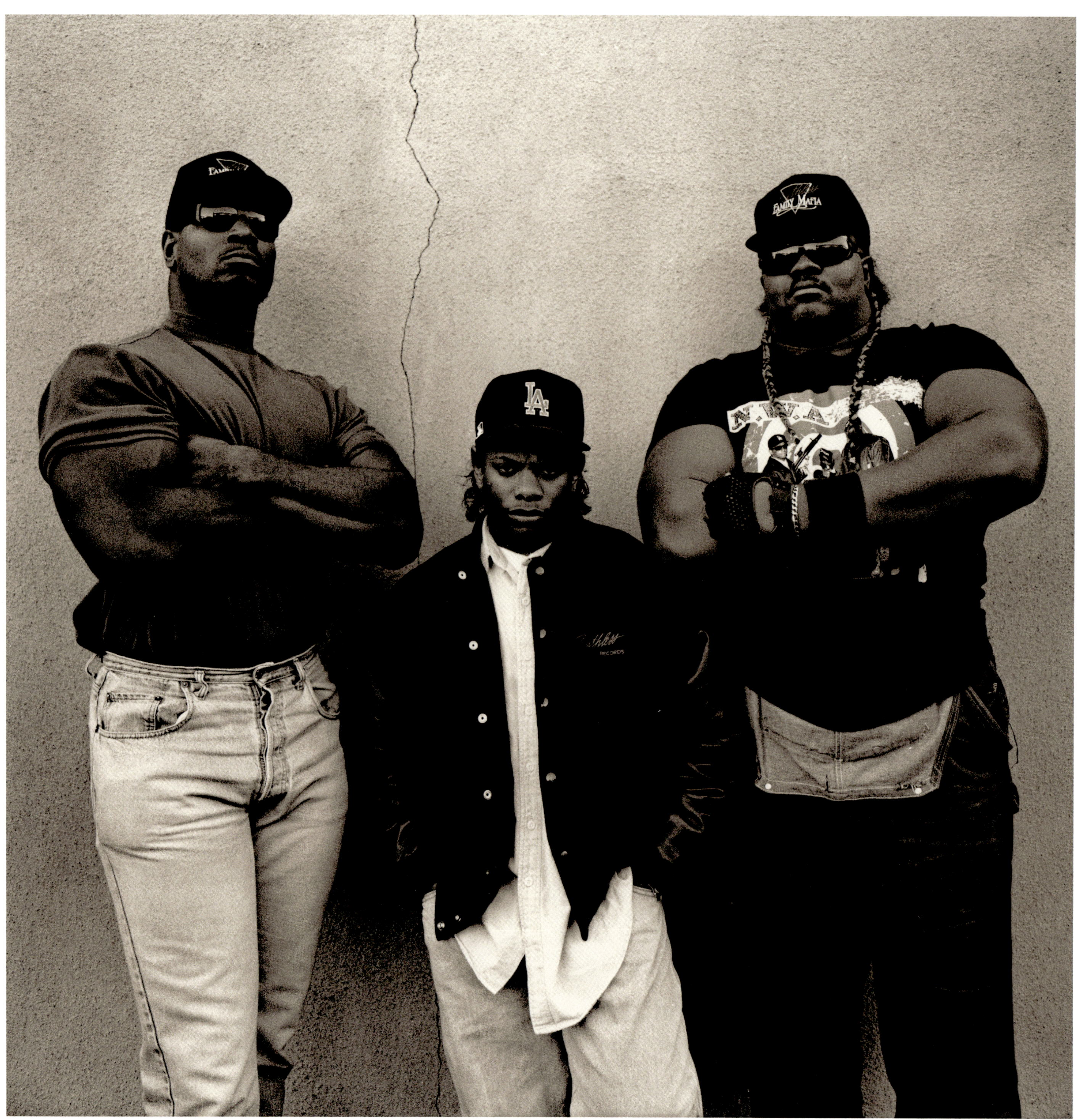

eazy-e

4

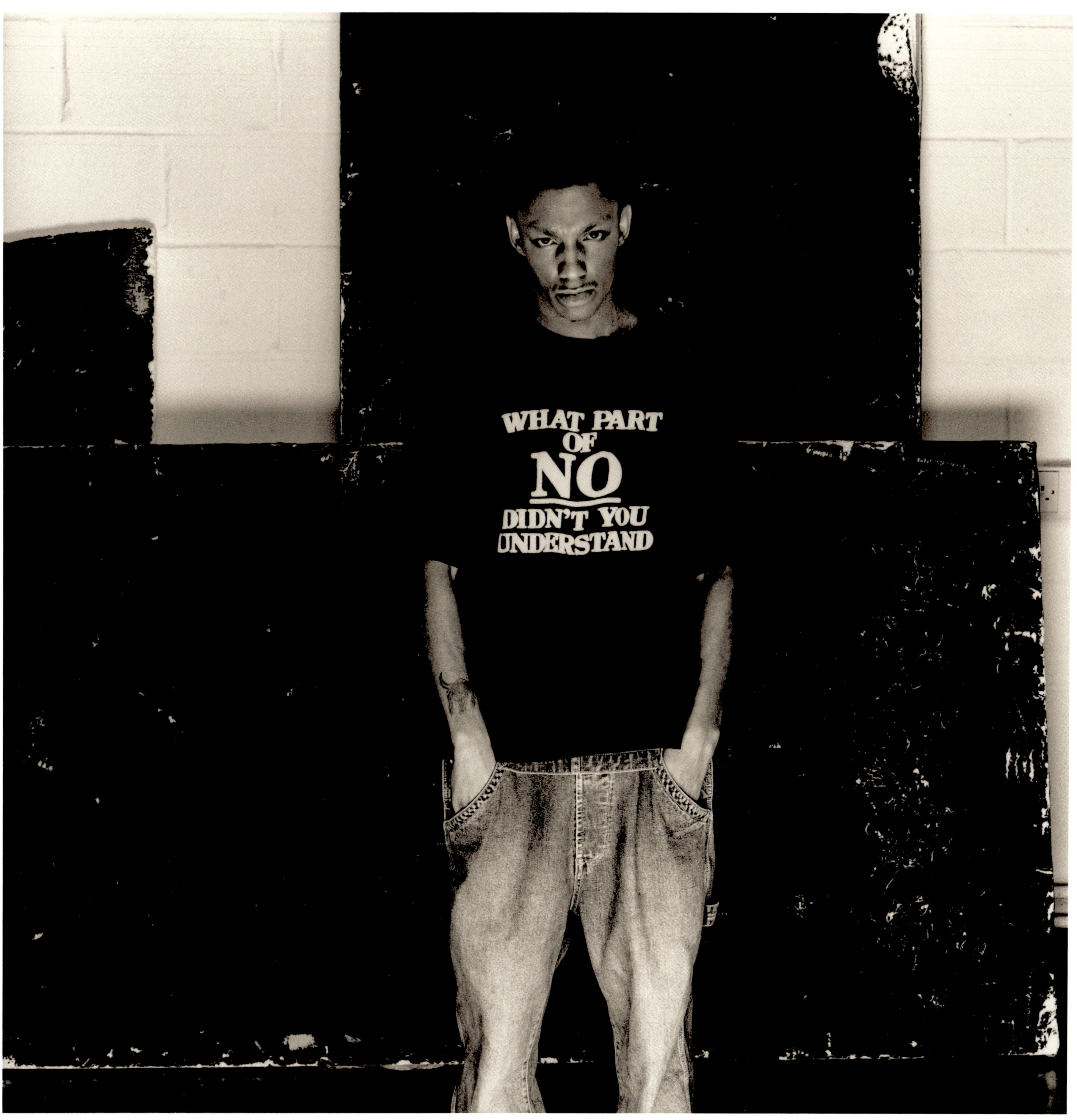

tricky

5

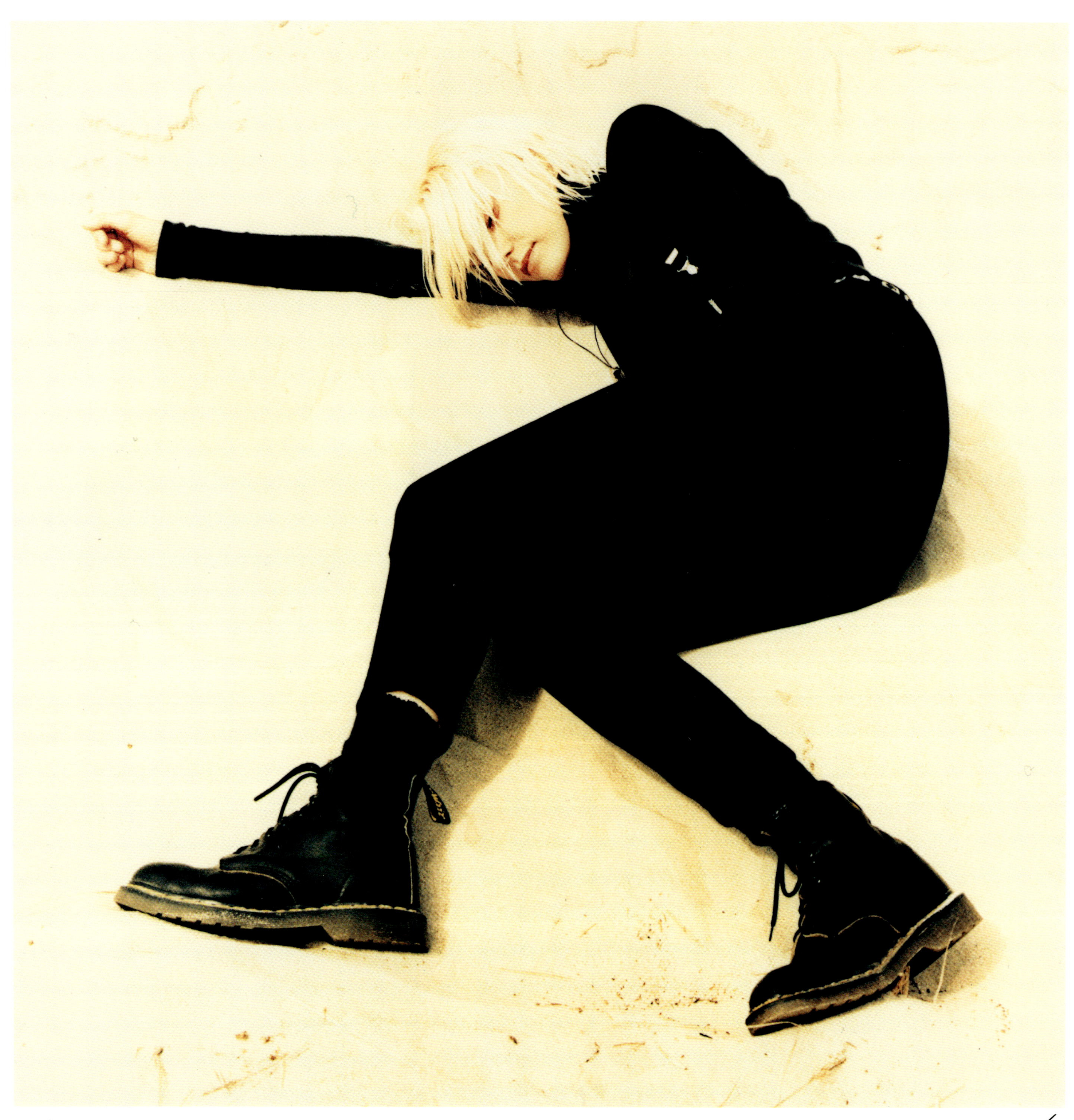

aimee mann

6

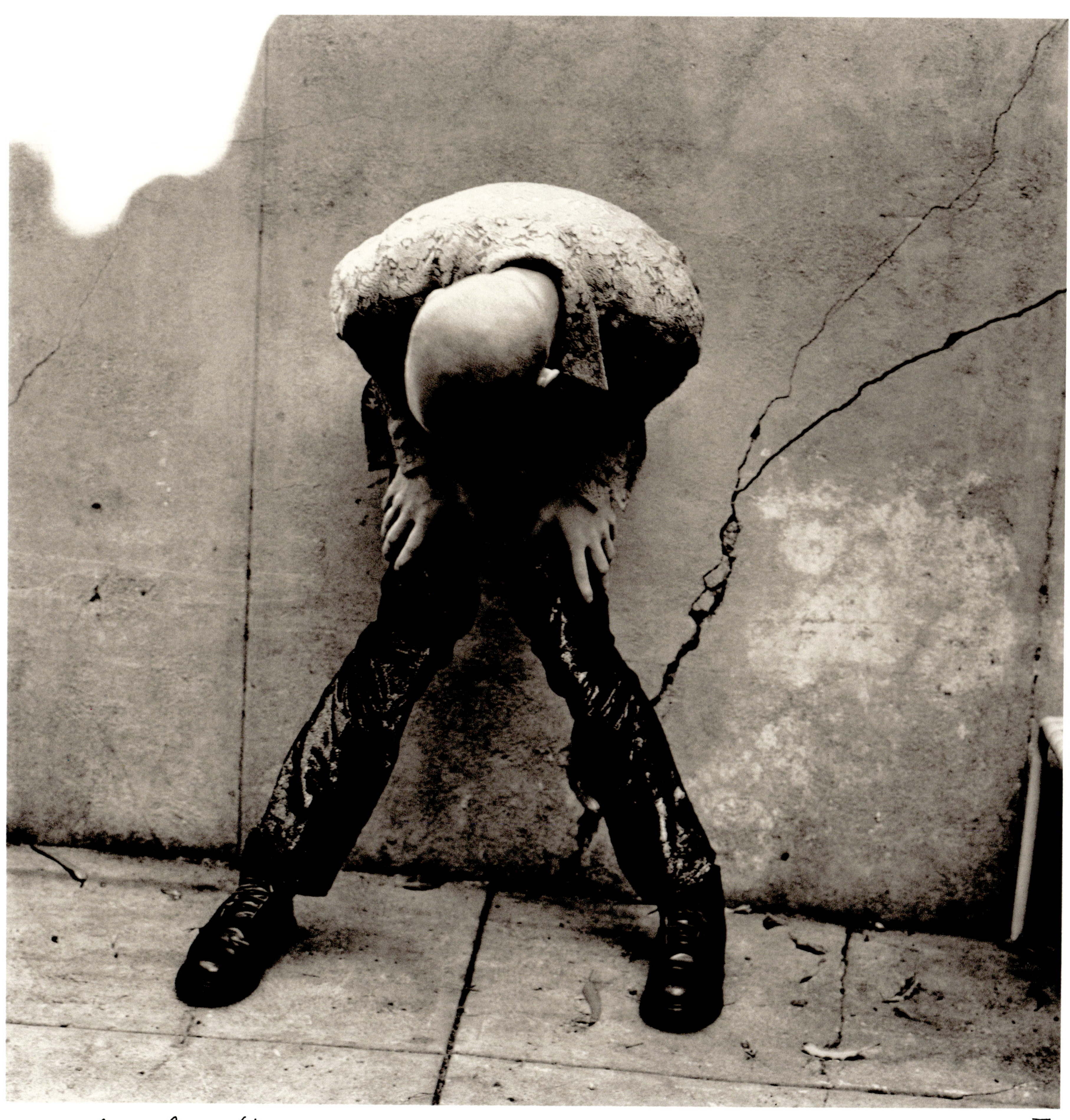

michael stipe

7

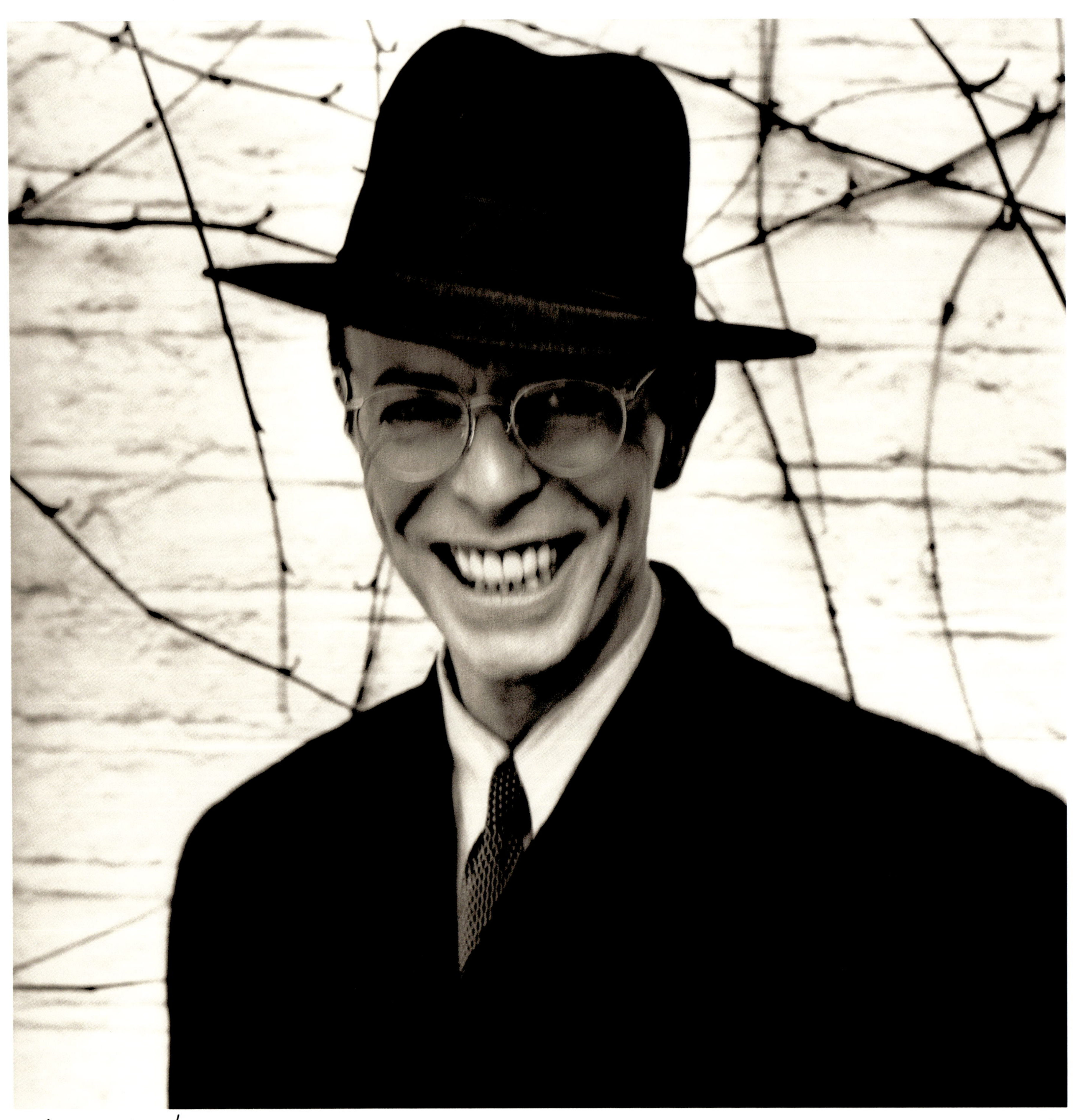

david bowie

8

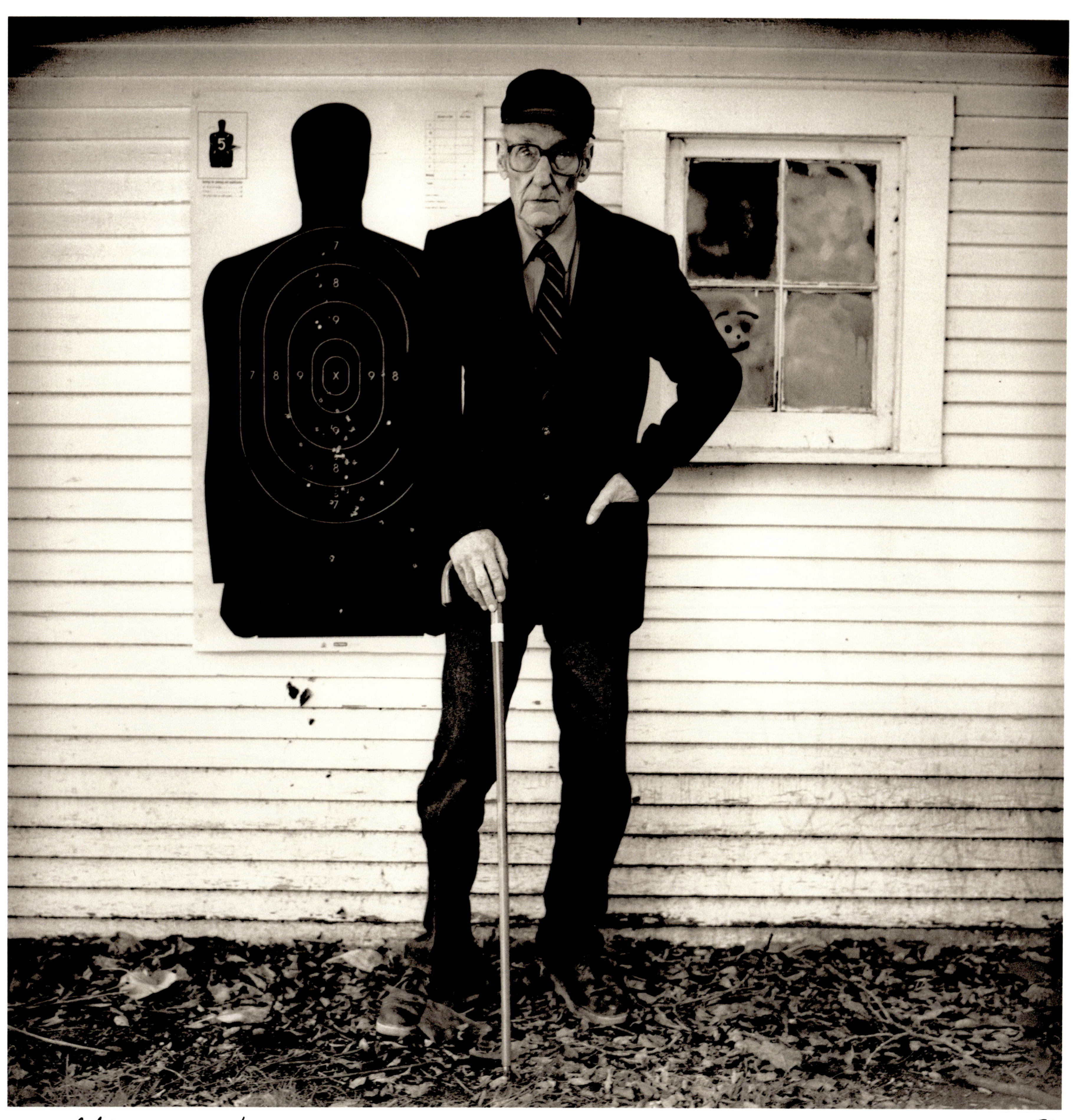

william s. burroughs

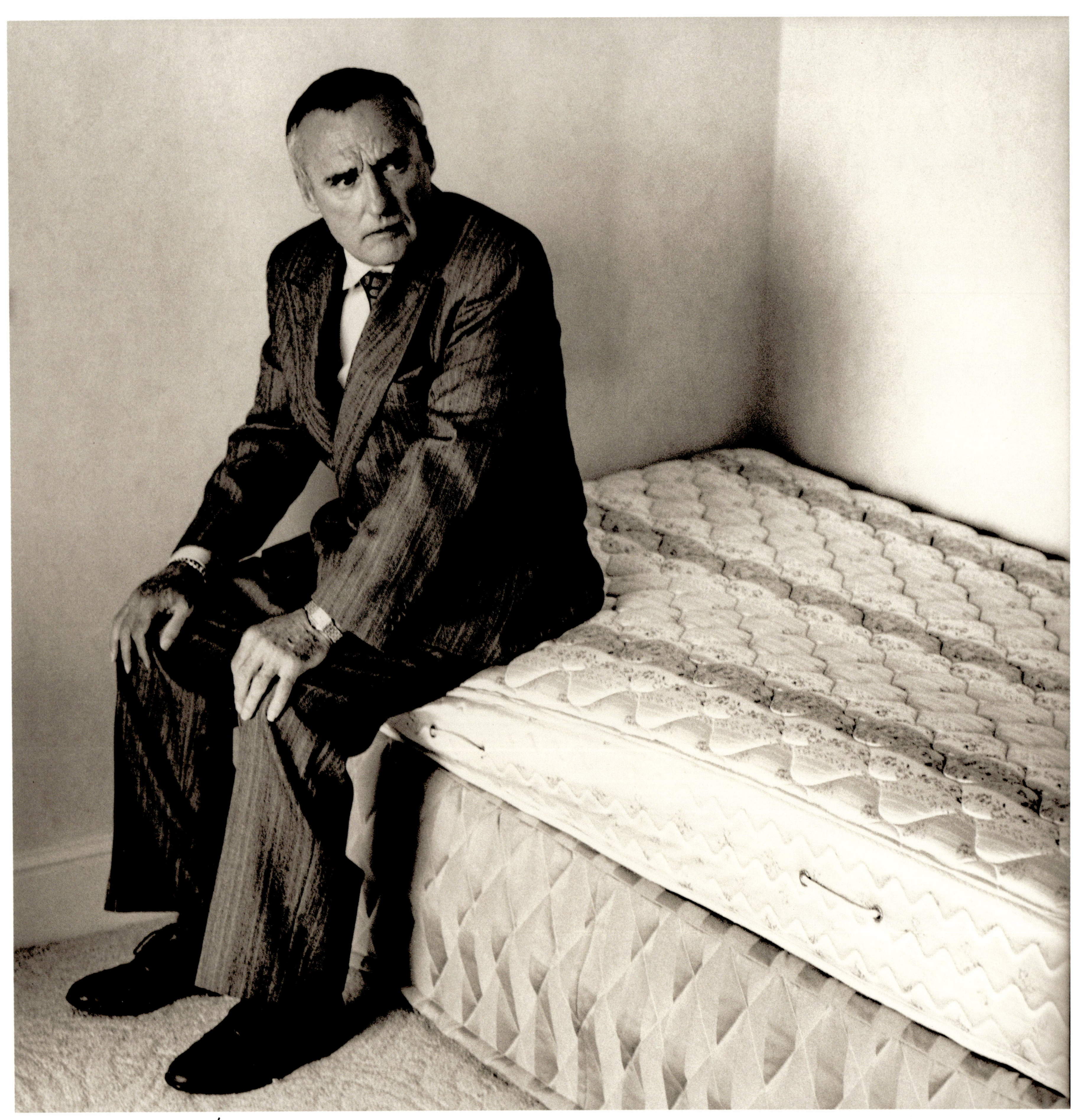

dennis hopper

10

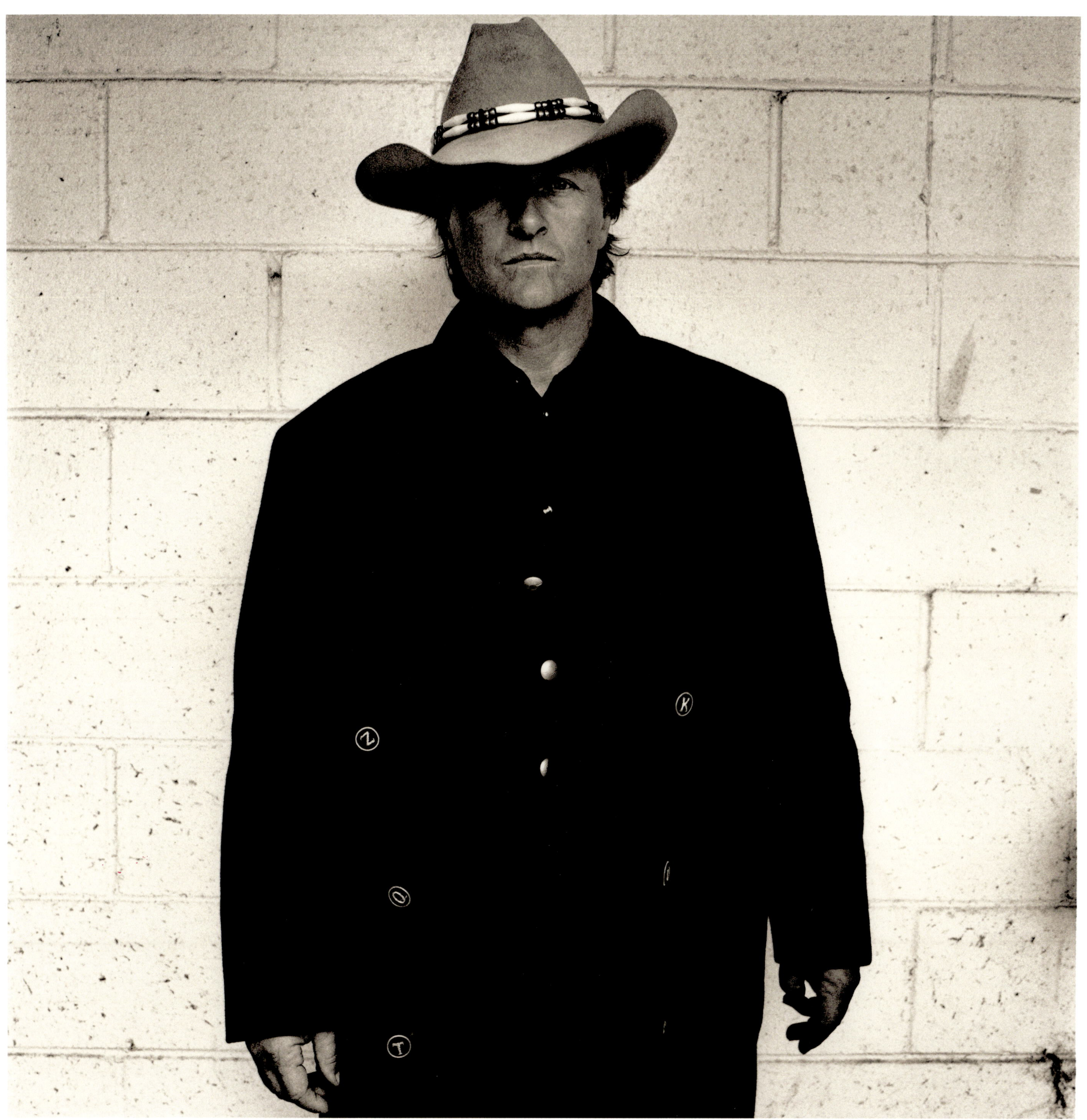

rutger hauer

11

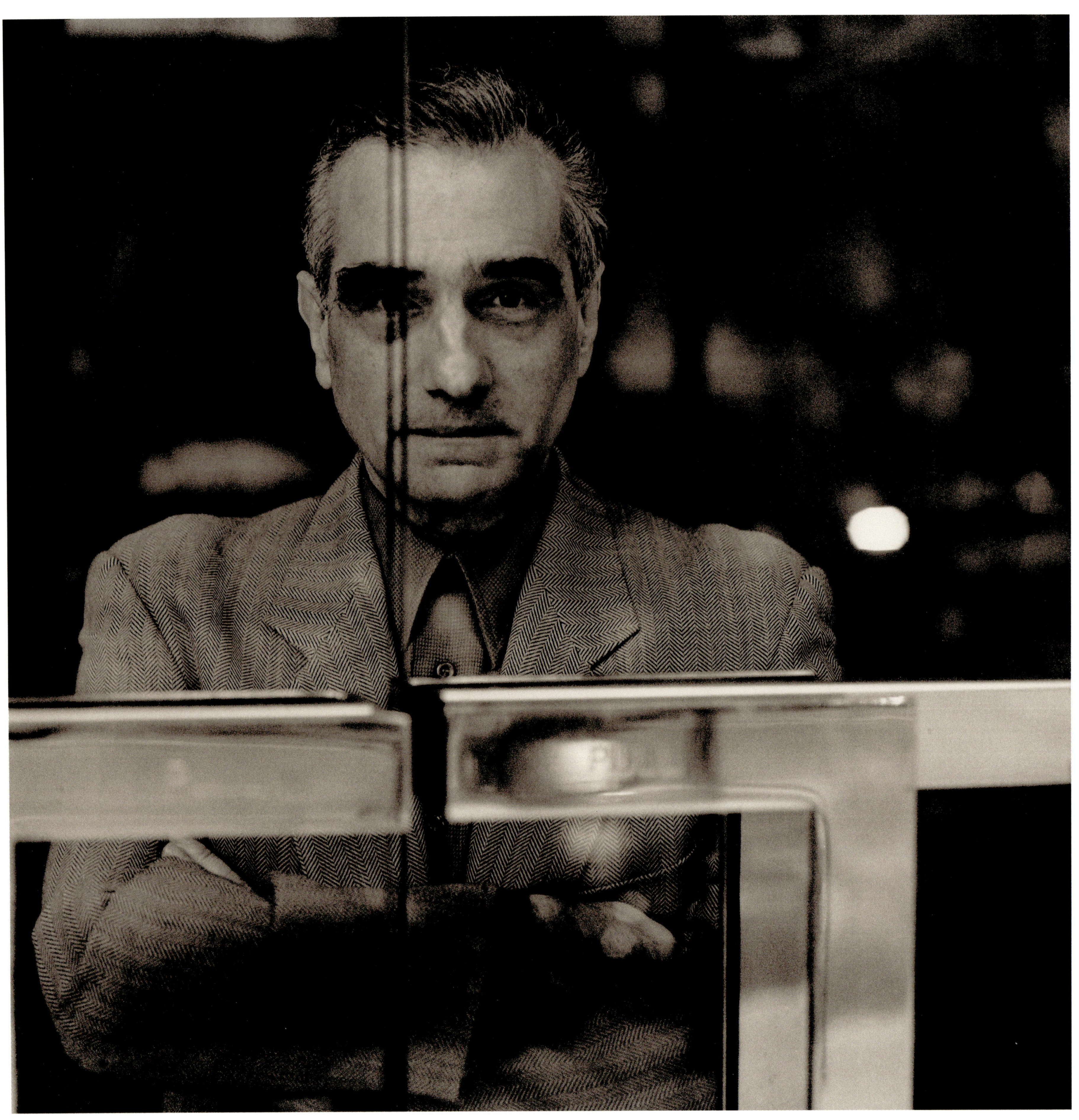

martin scorsese

12

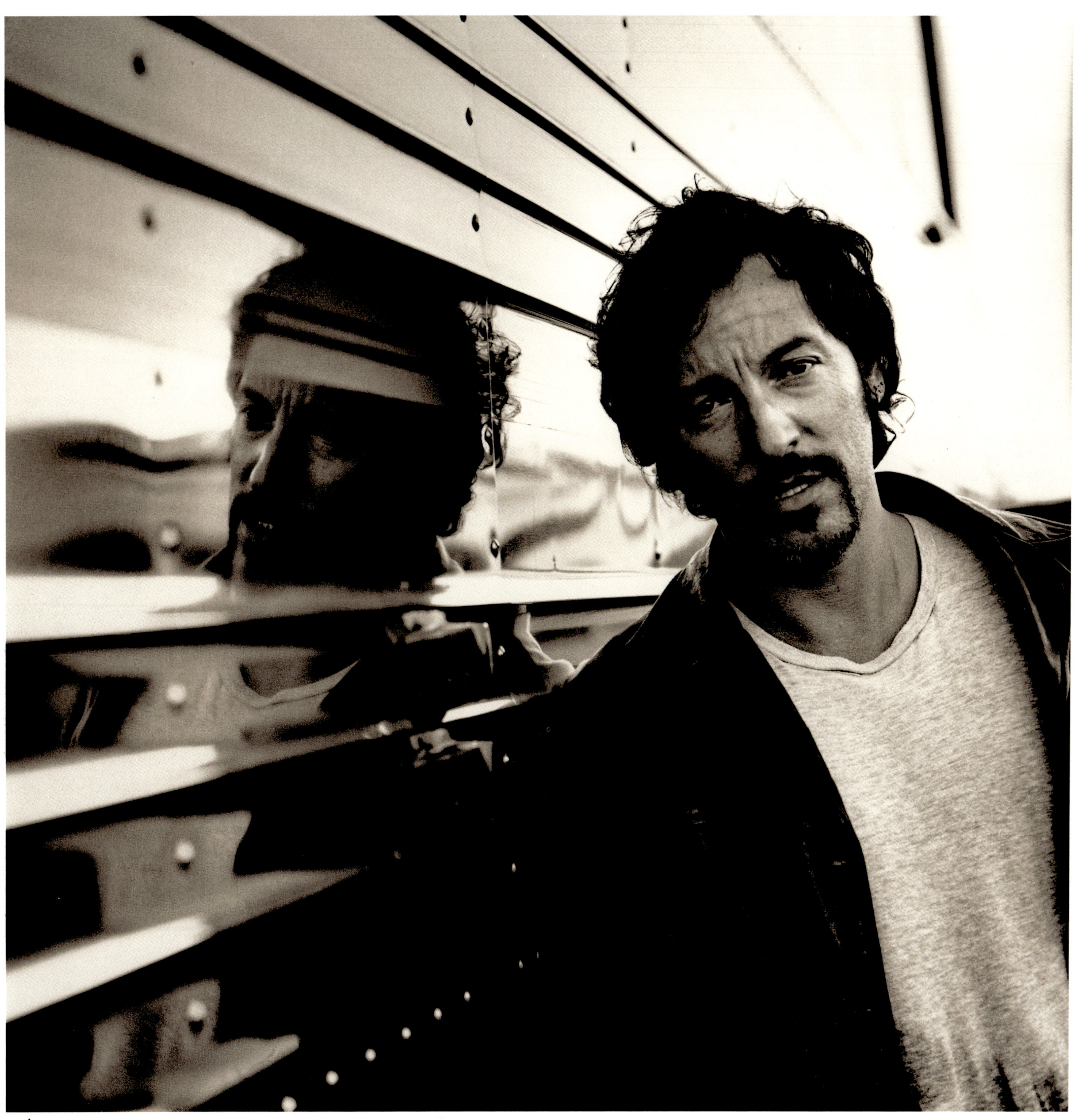

bruce springsteen

13

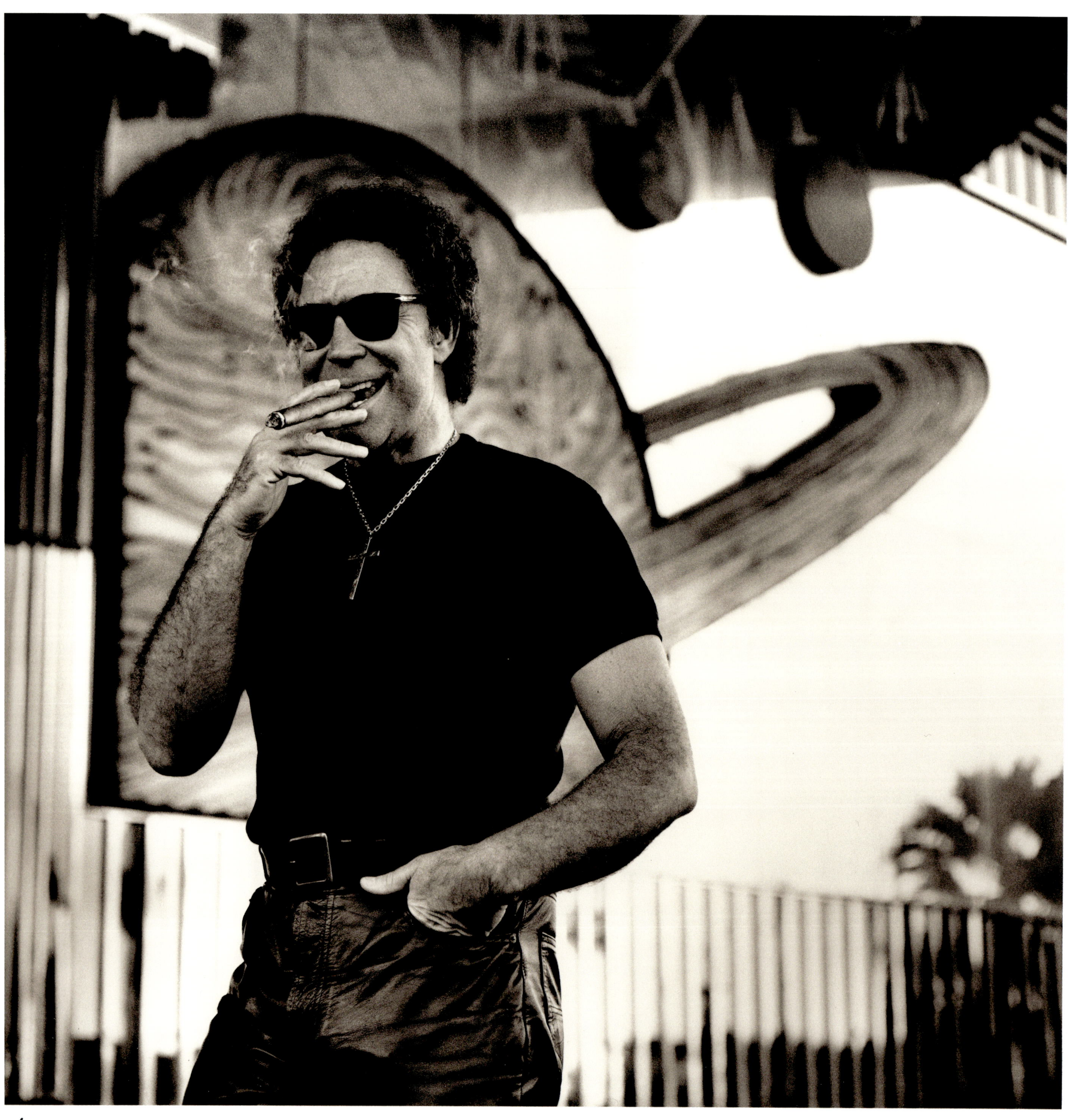

tom jones

14

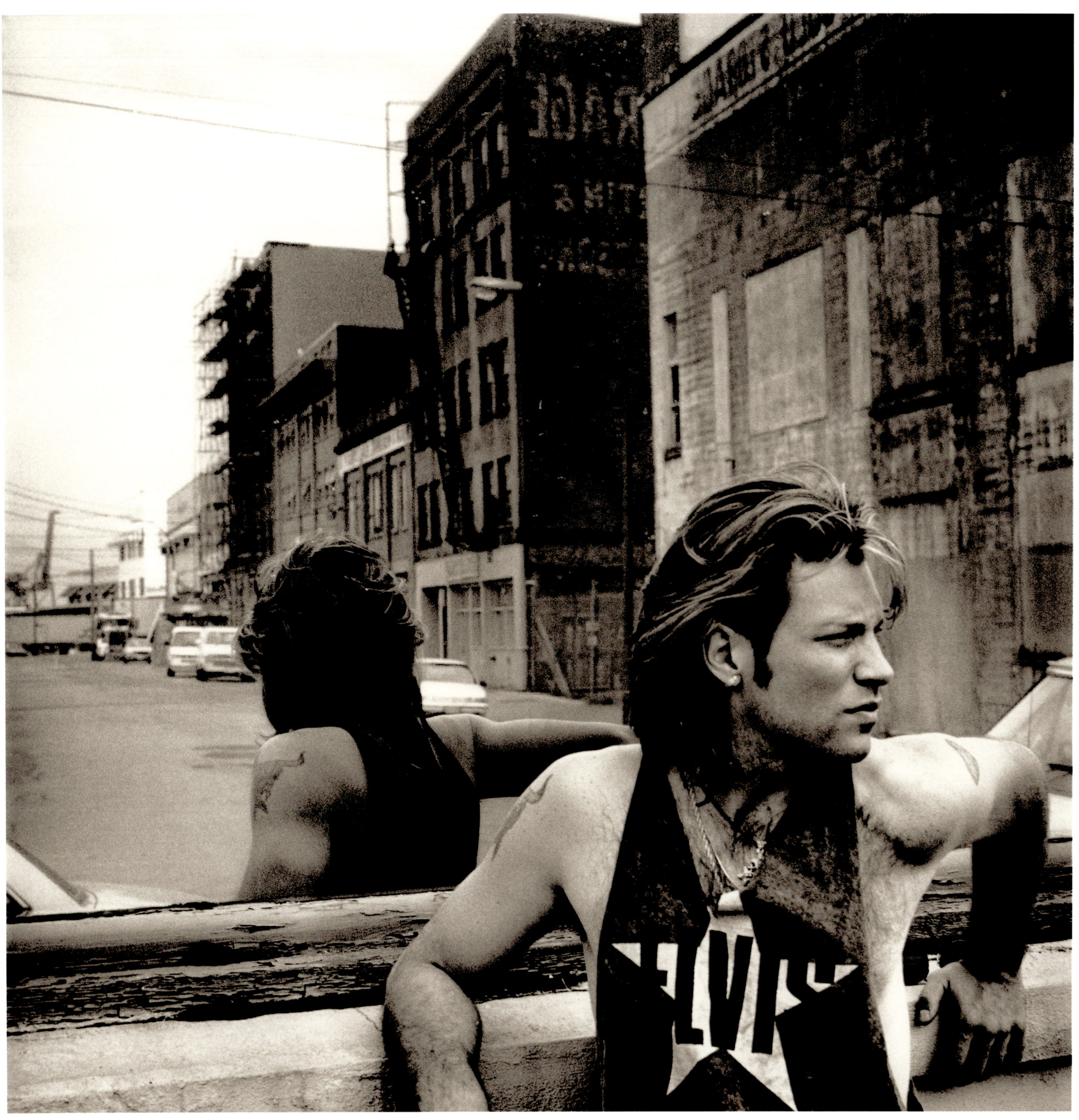

jon bon jovi

15

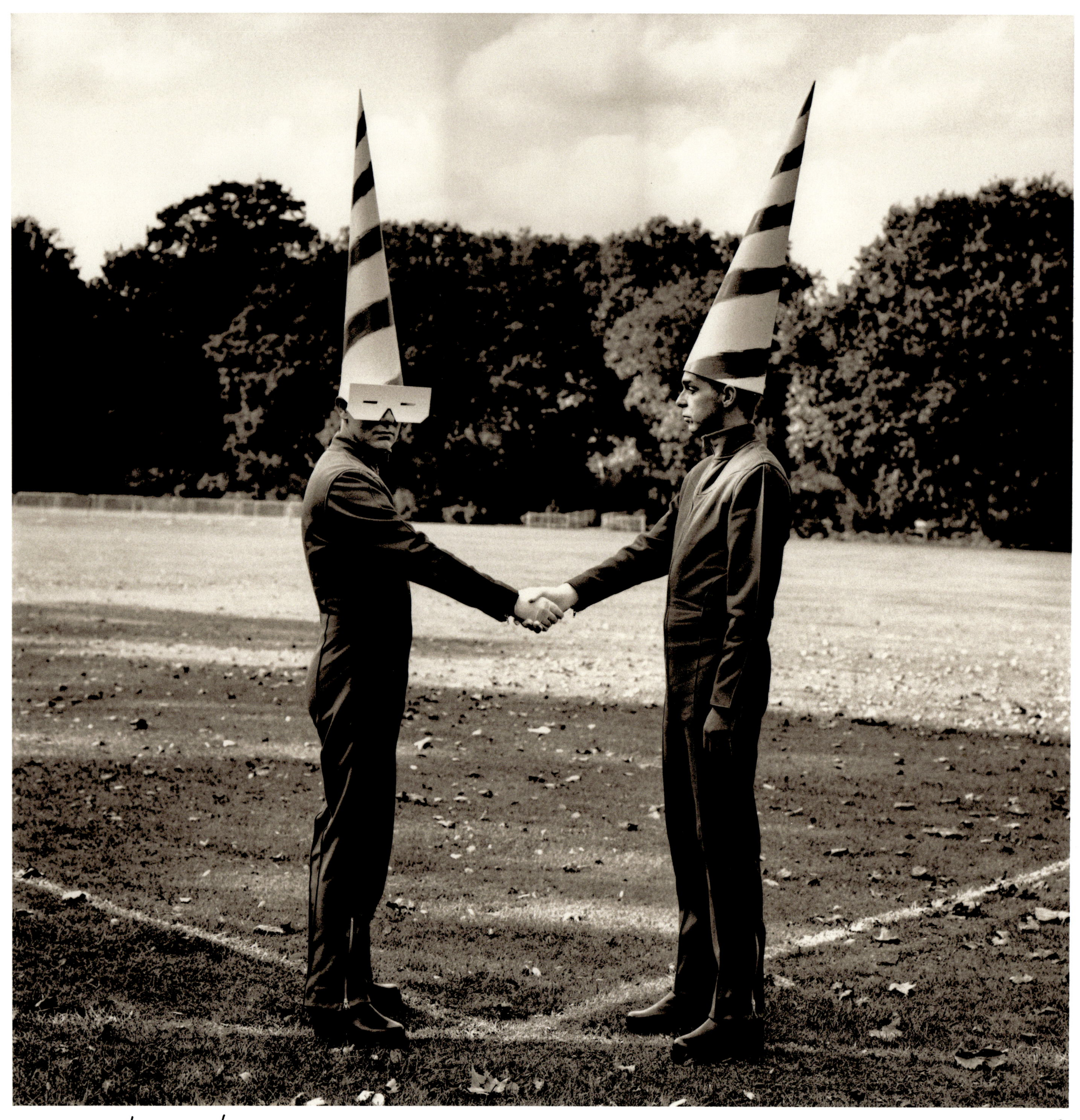

pet shop boys

16

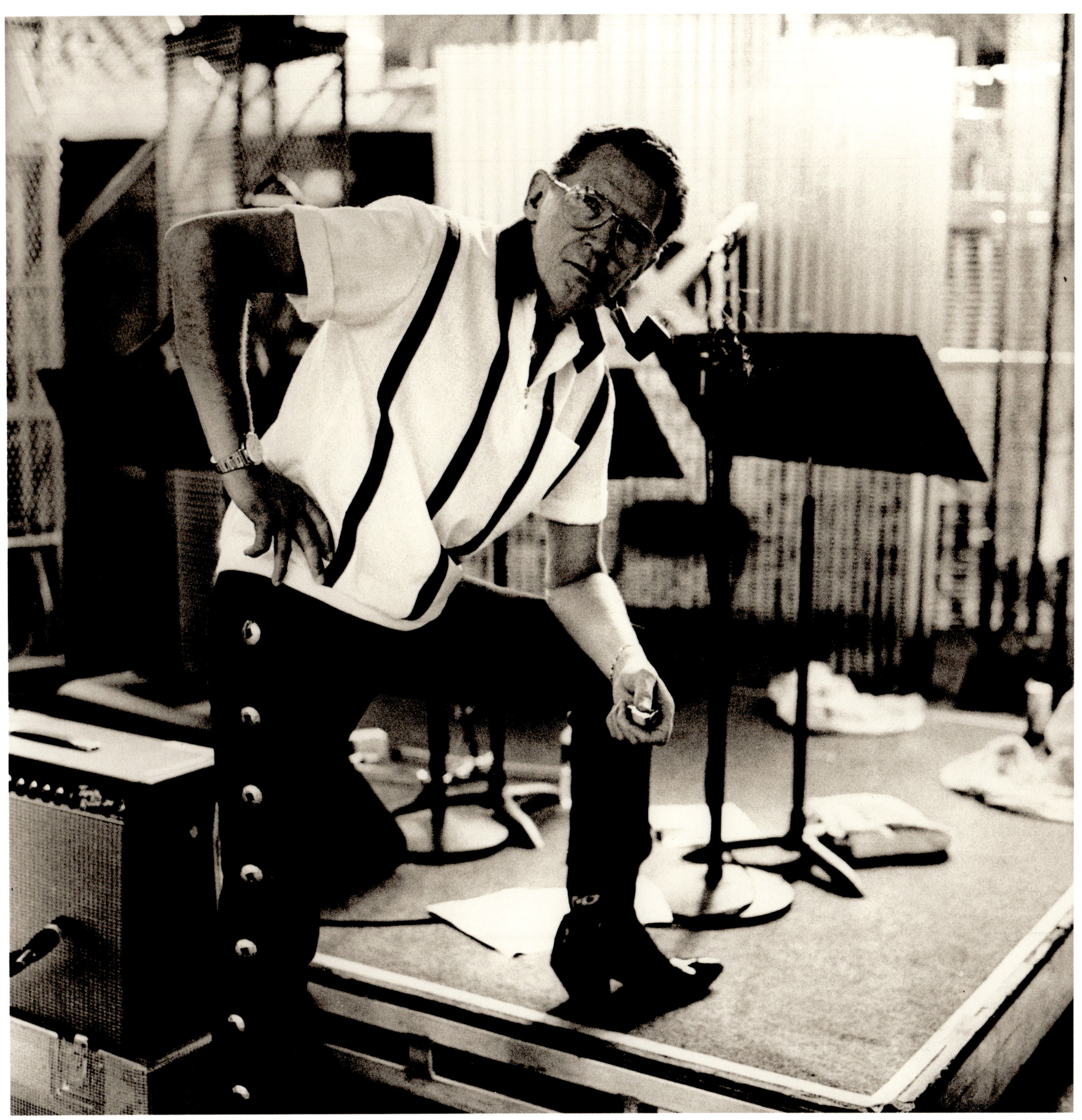

jerry lee lewis
17

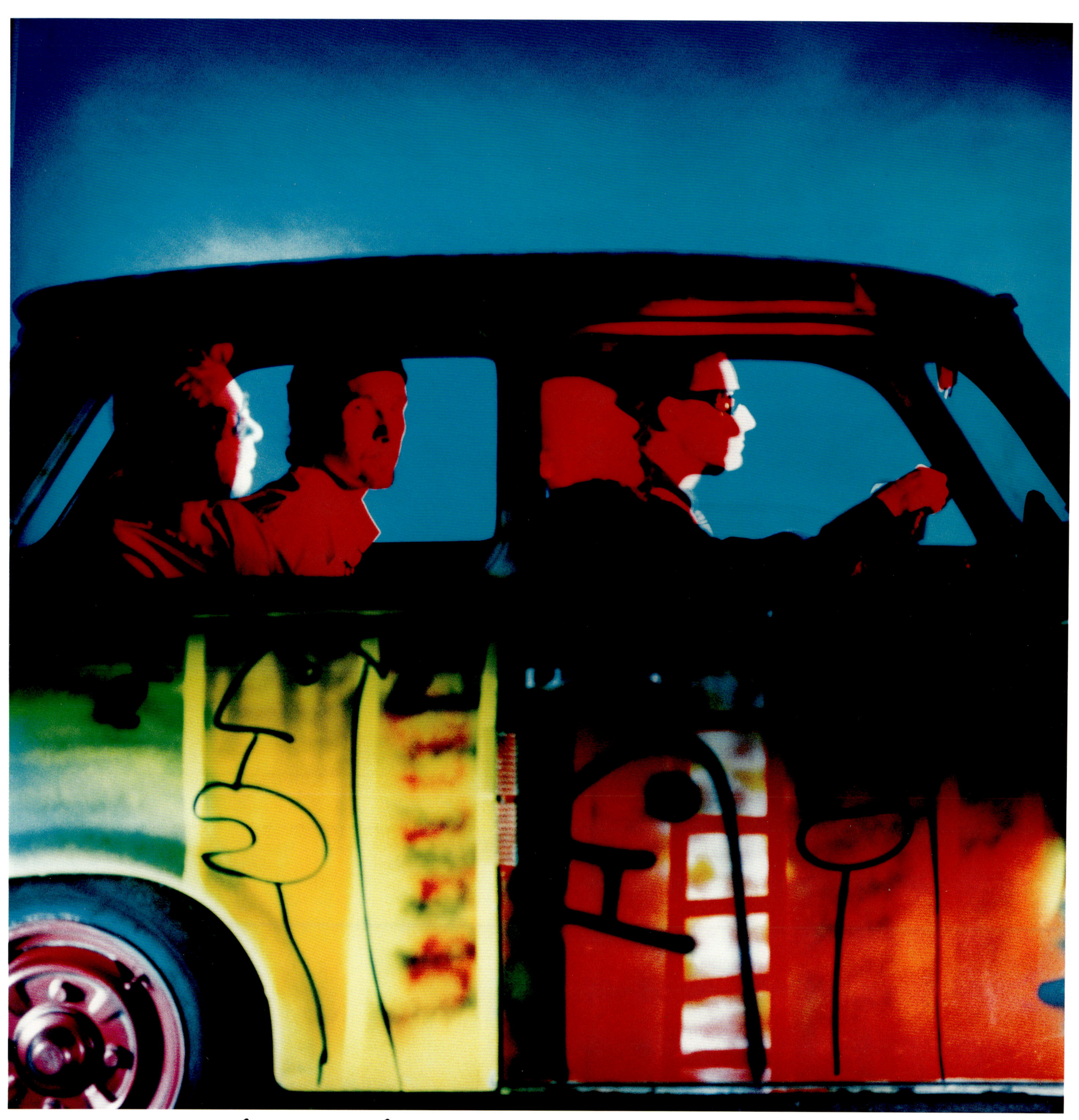

adam, edge, larry & bono

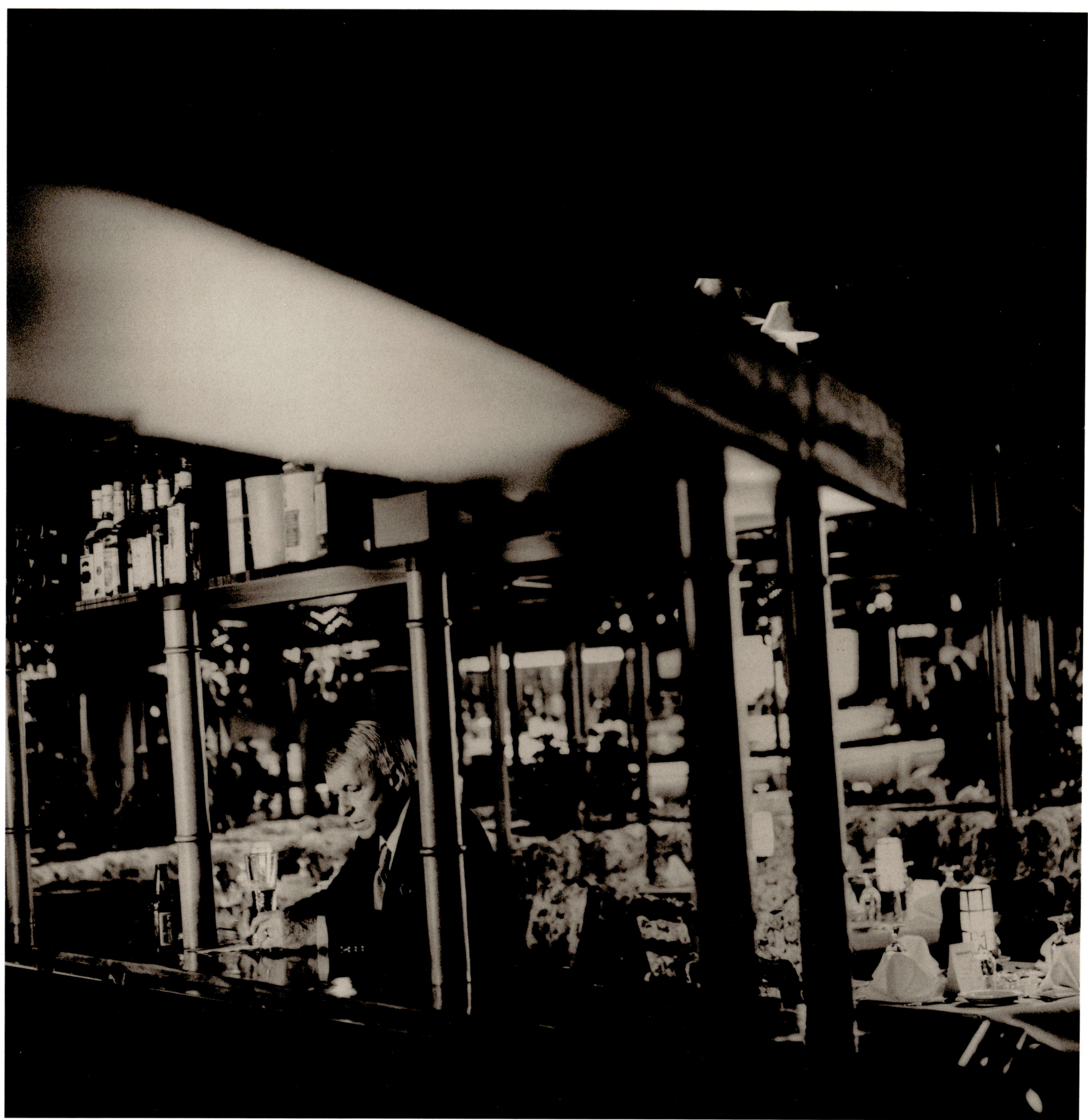

frank sinatra

19

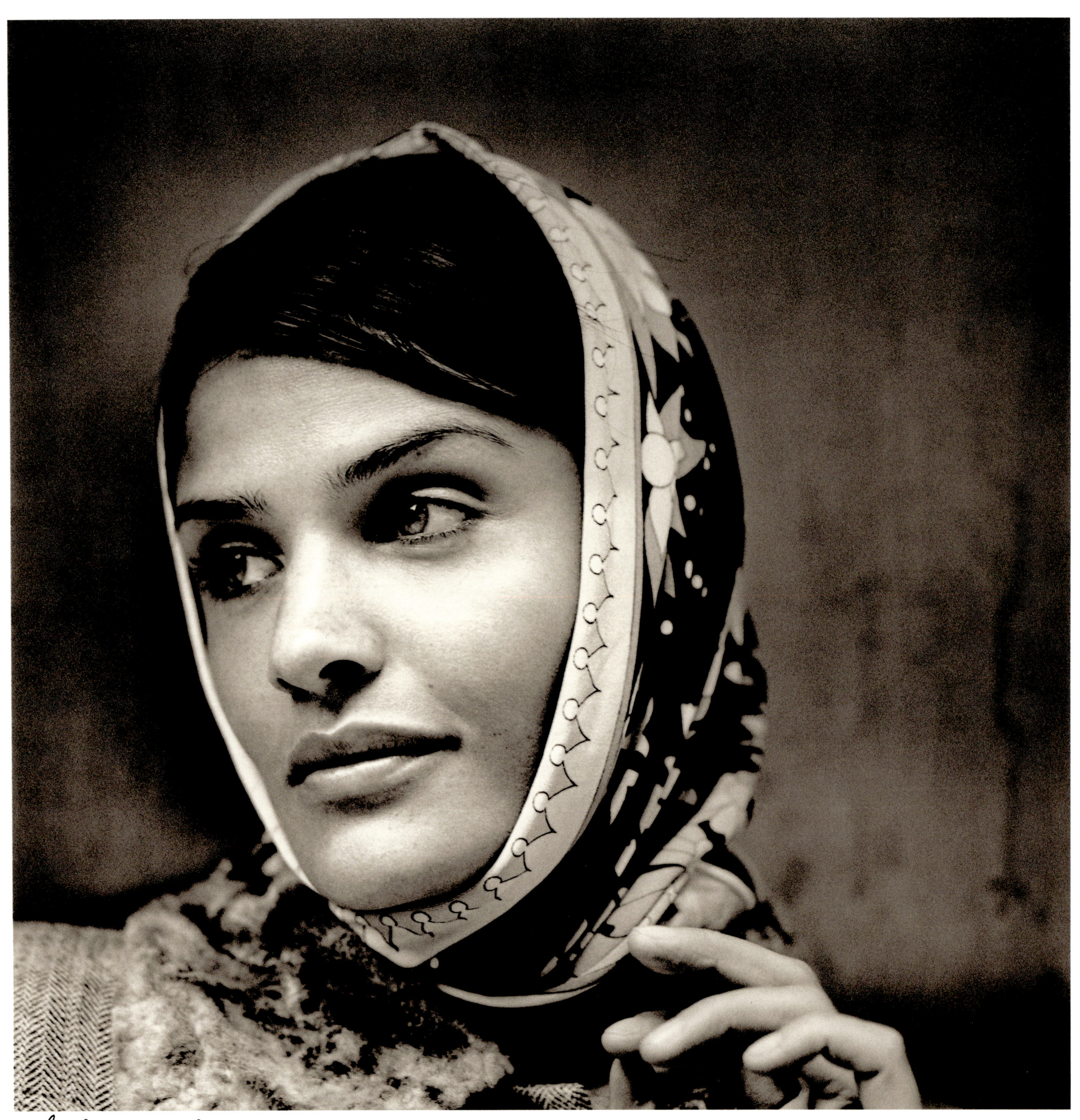

20

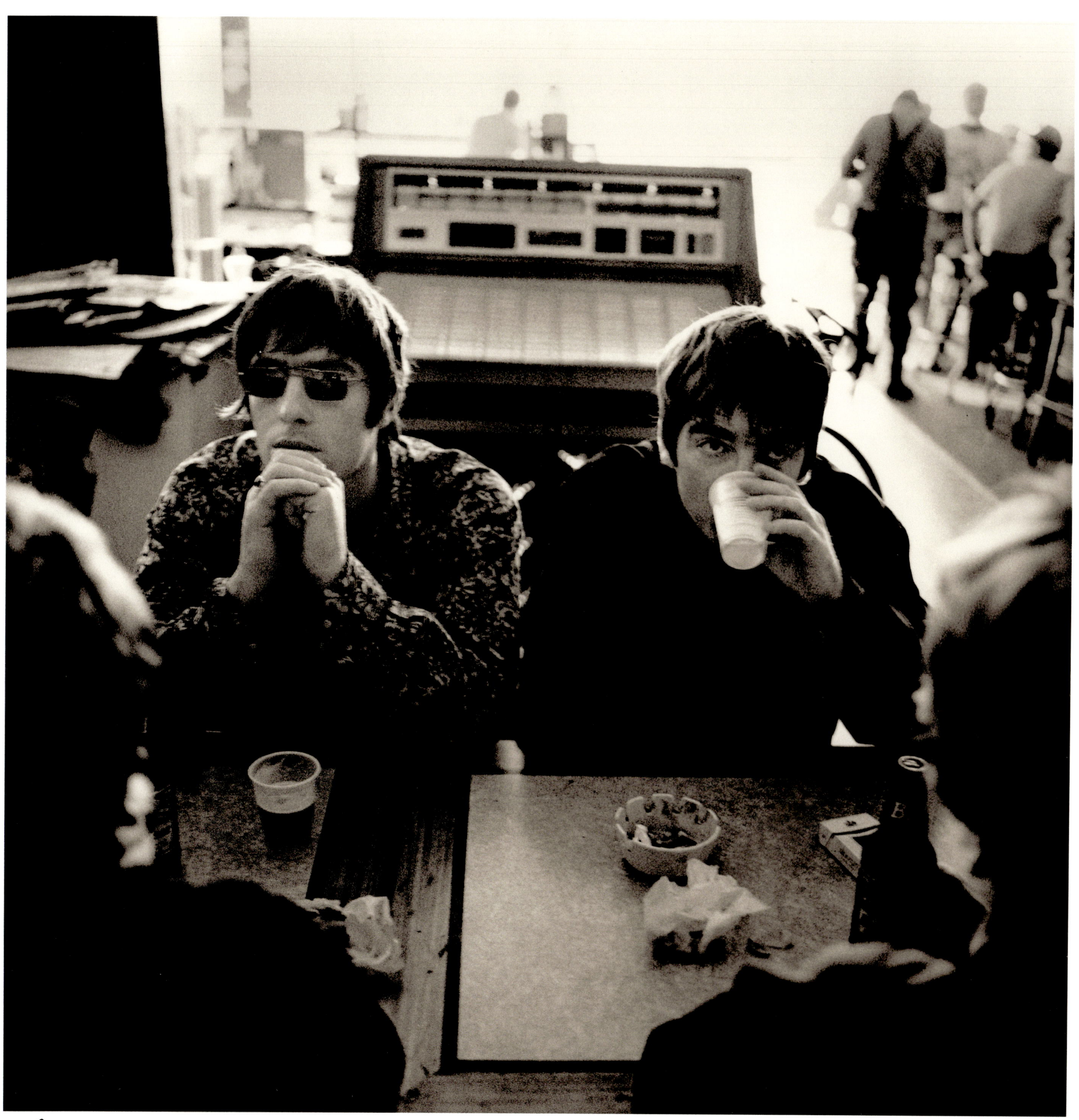

liam and noel

21

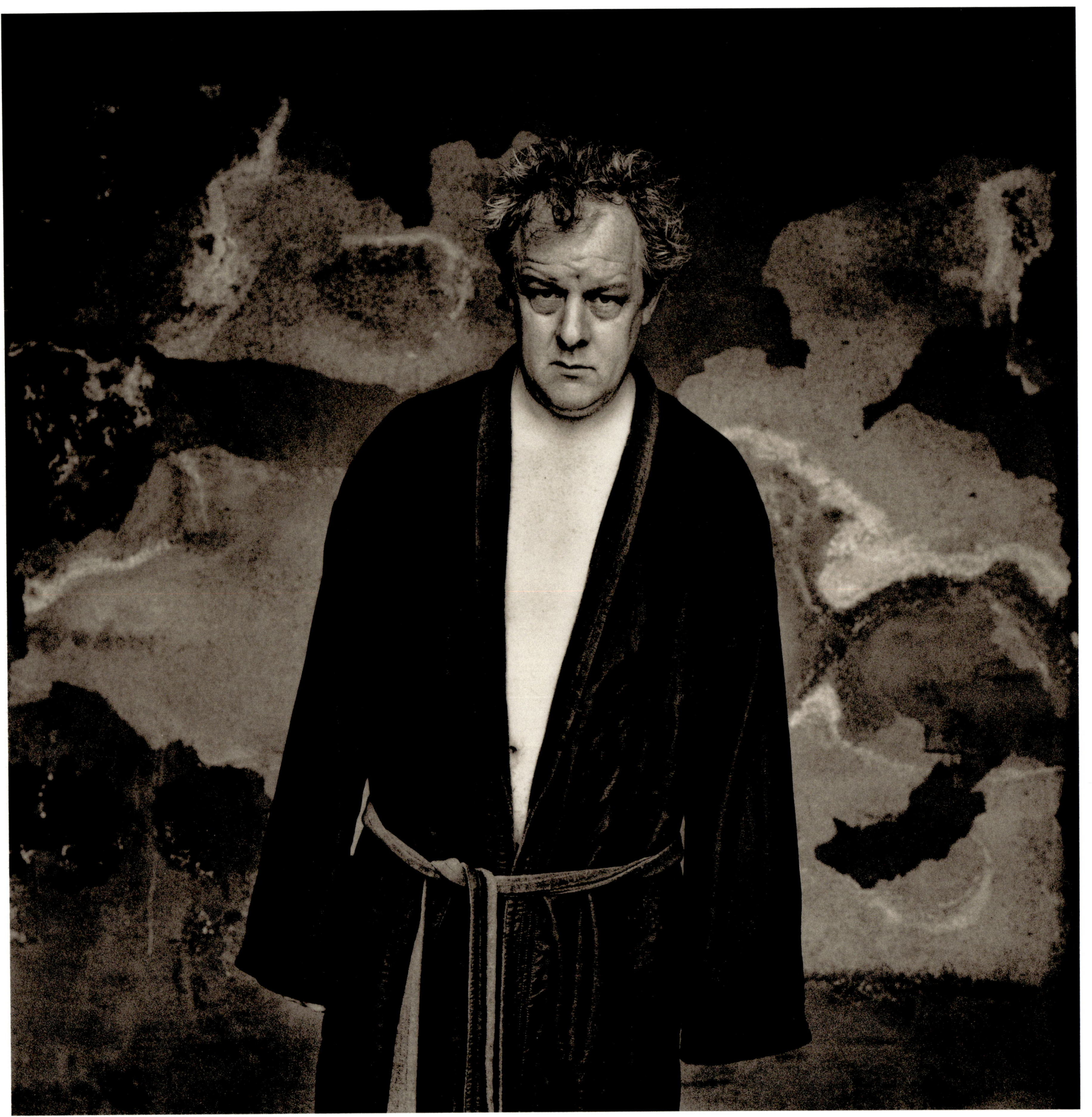

jim sheridan

22

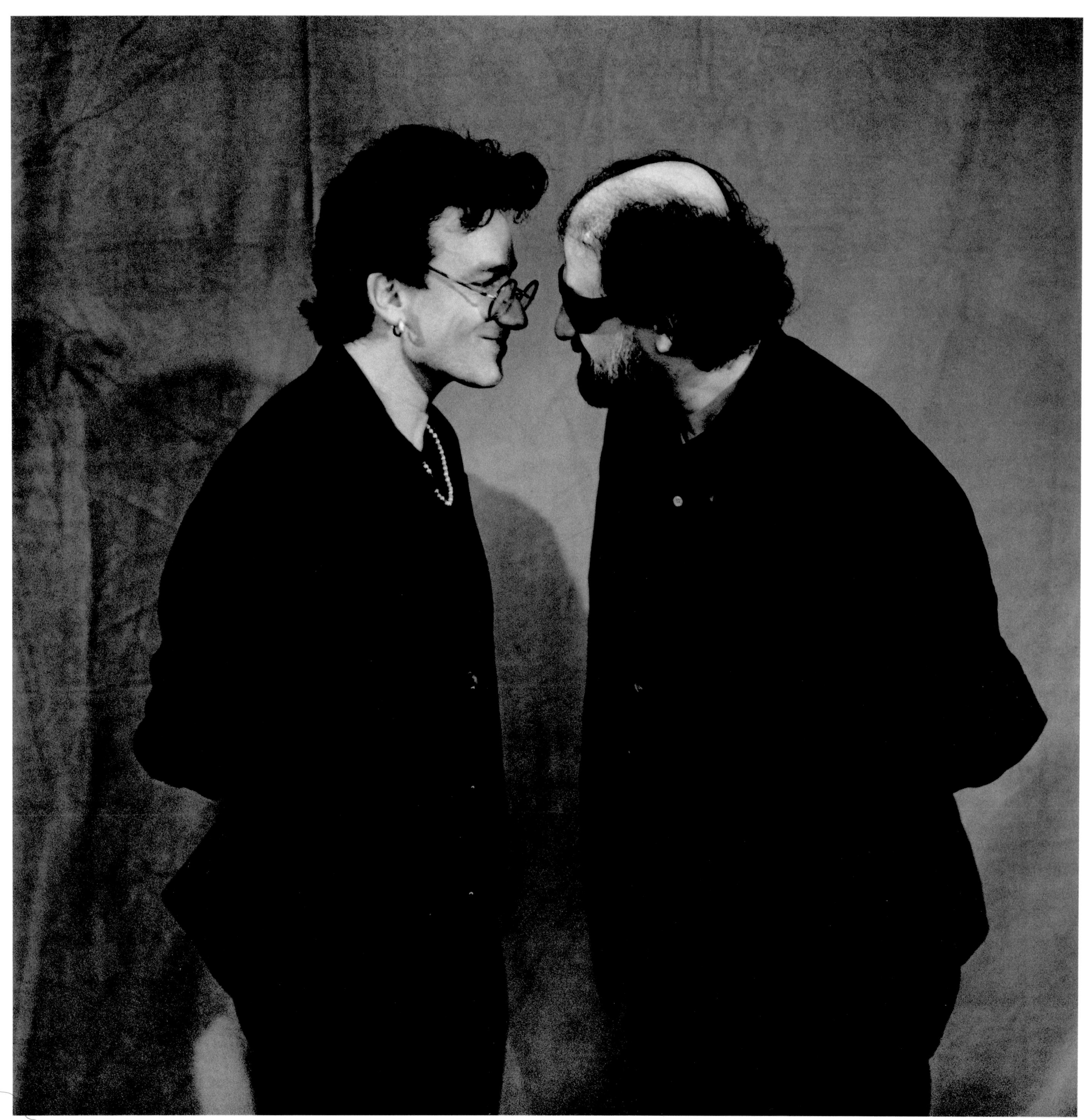

bono and salman rushdie

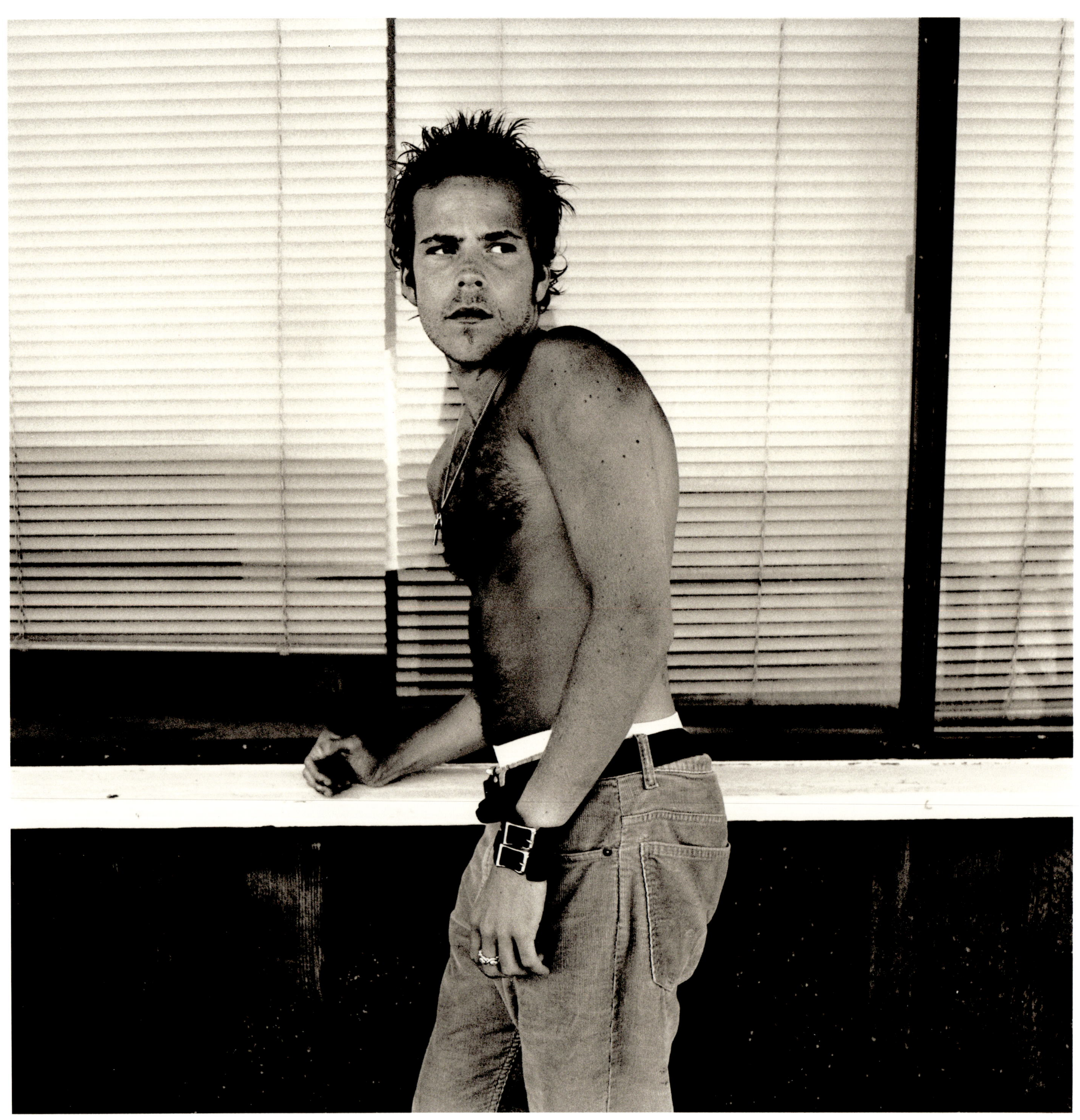

stephen dorff

24

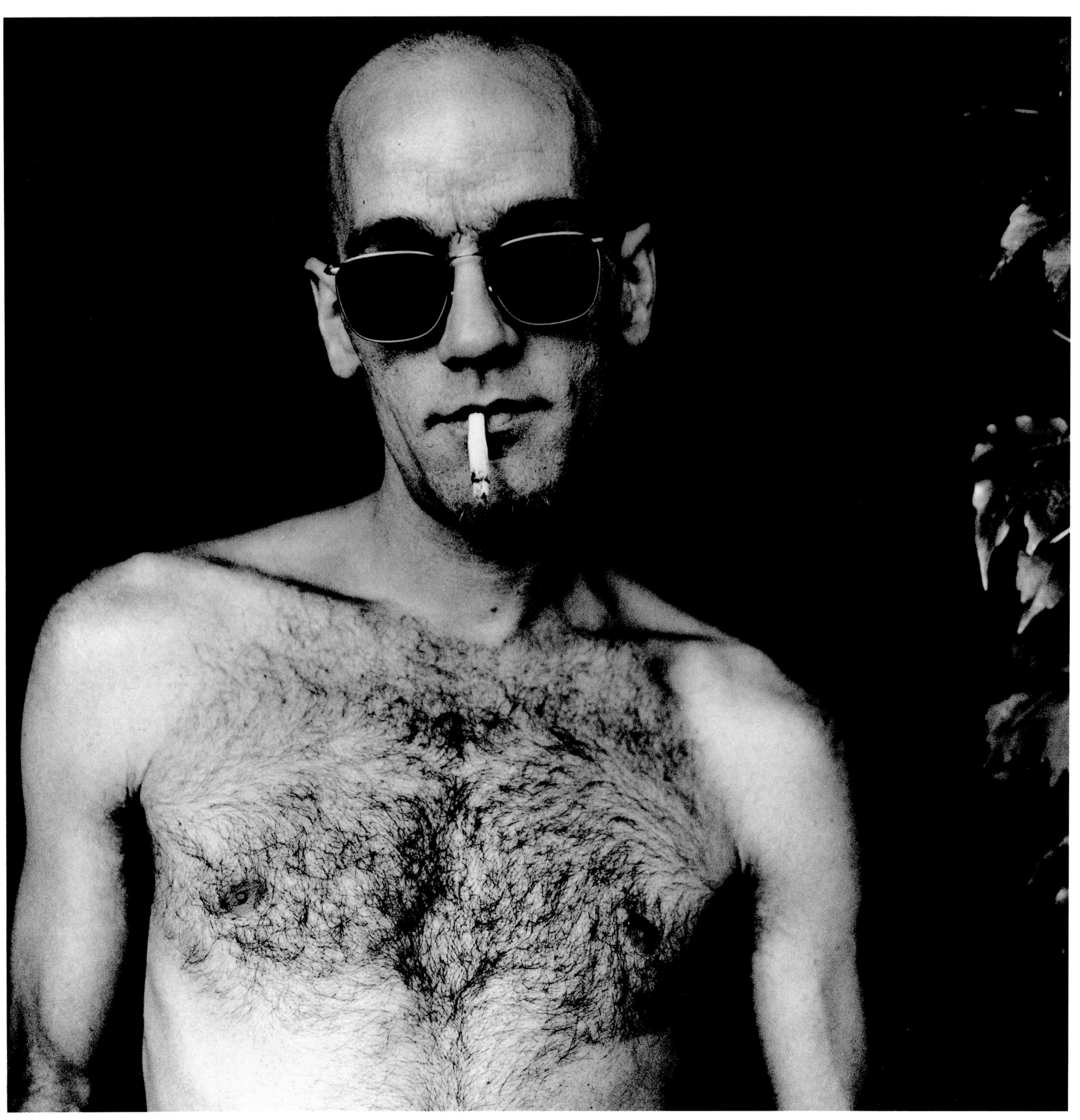

michael stipe   25

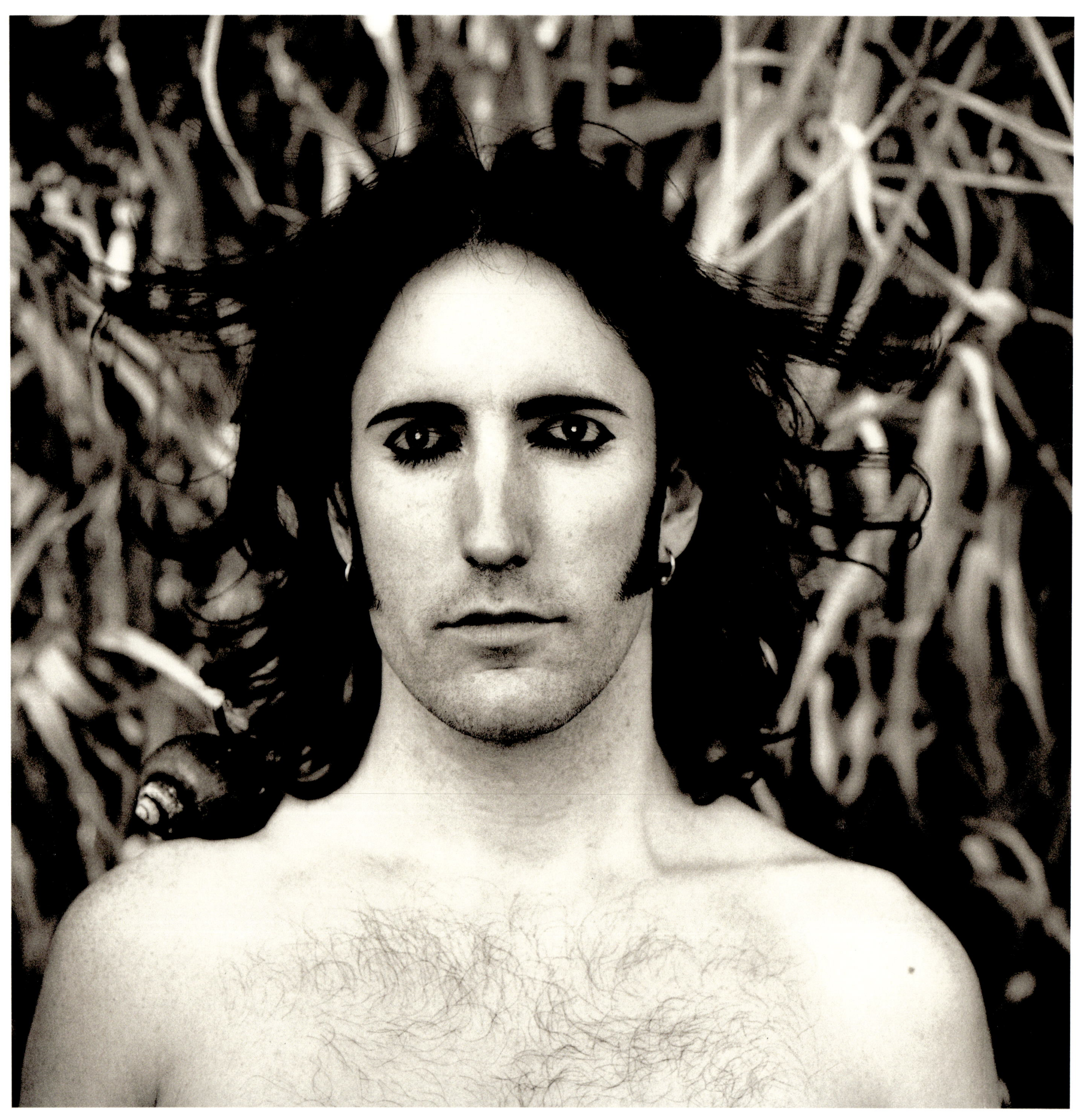

trent reznor

26

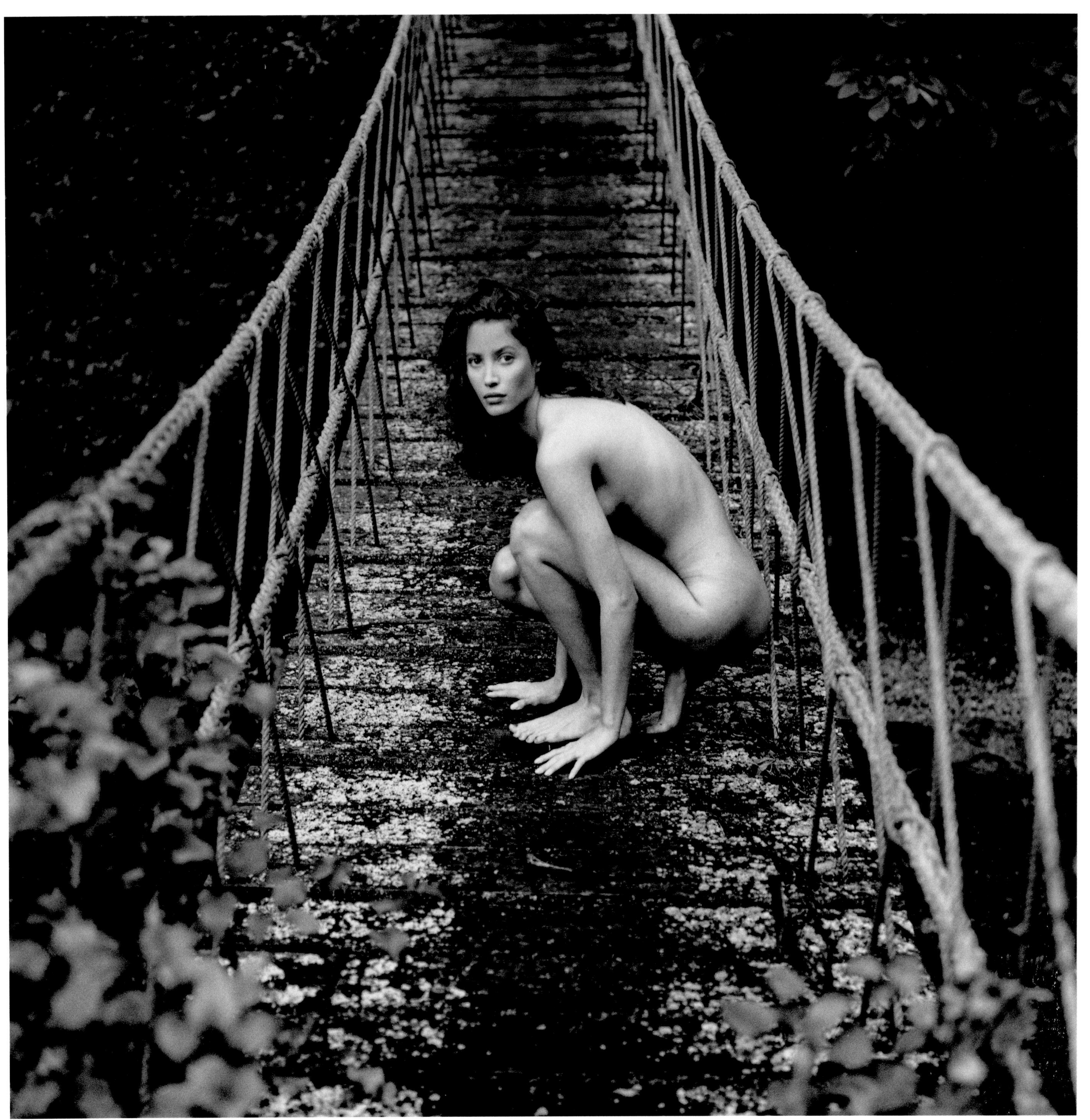

27

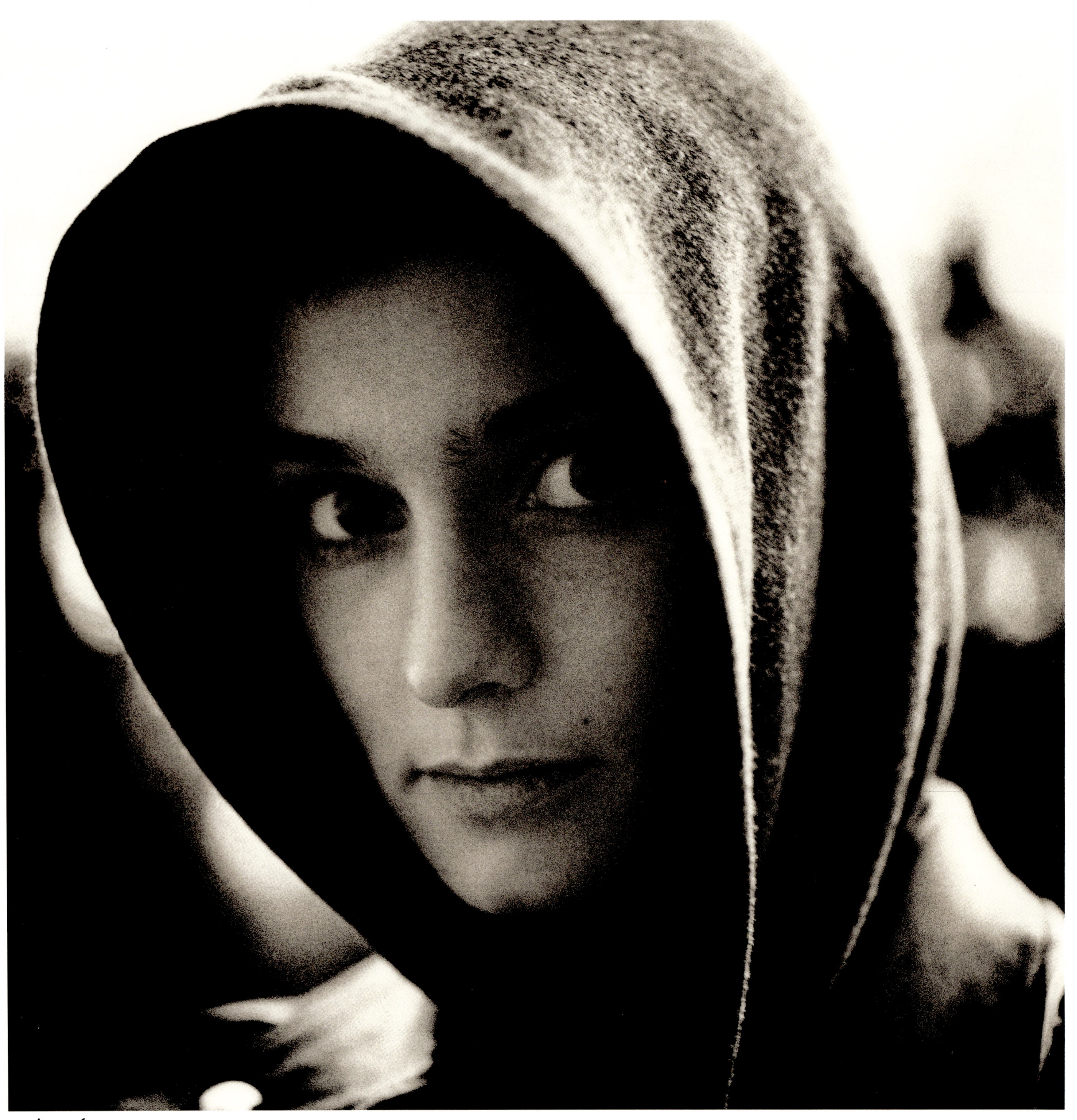

Sinéad O'Connor

28

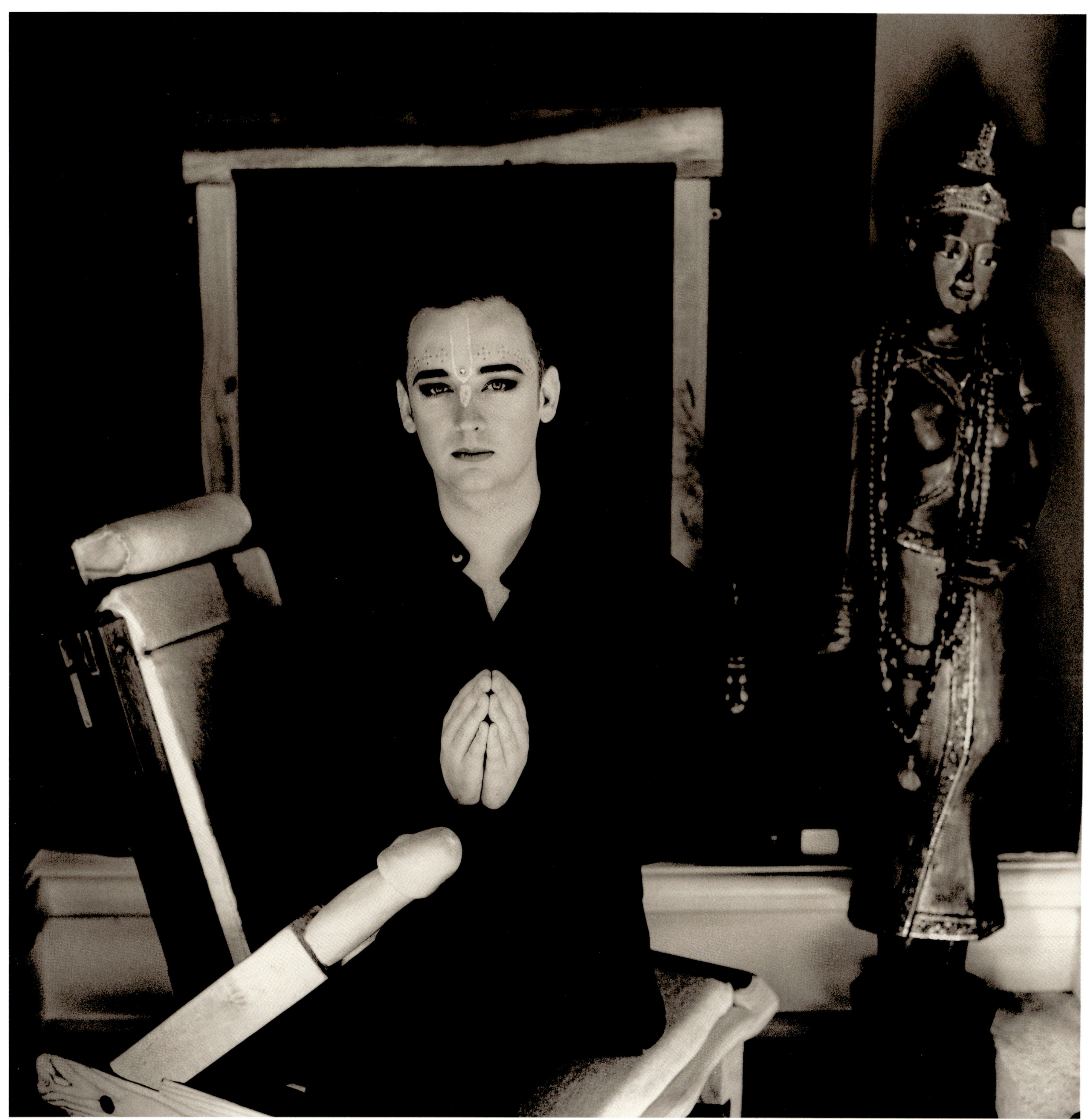

boy george

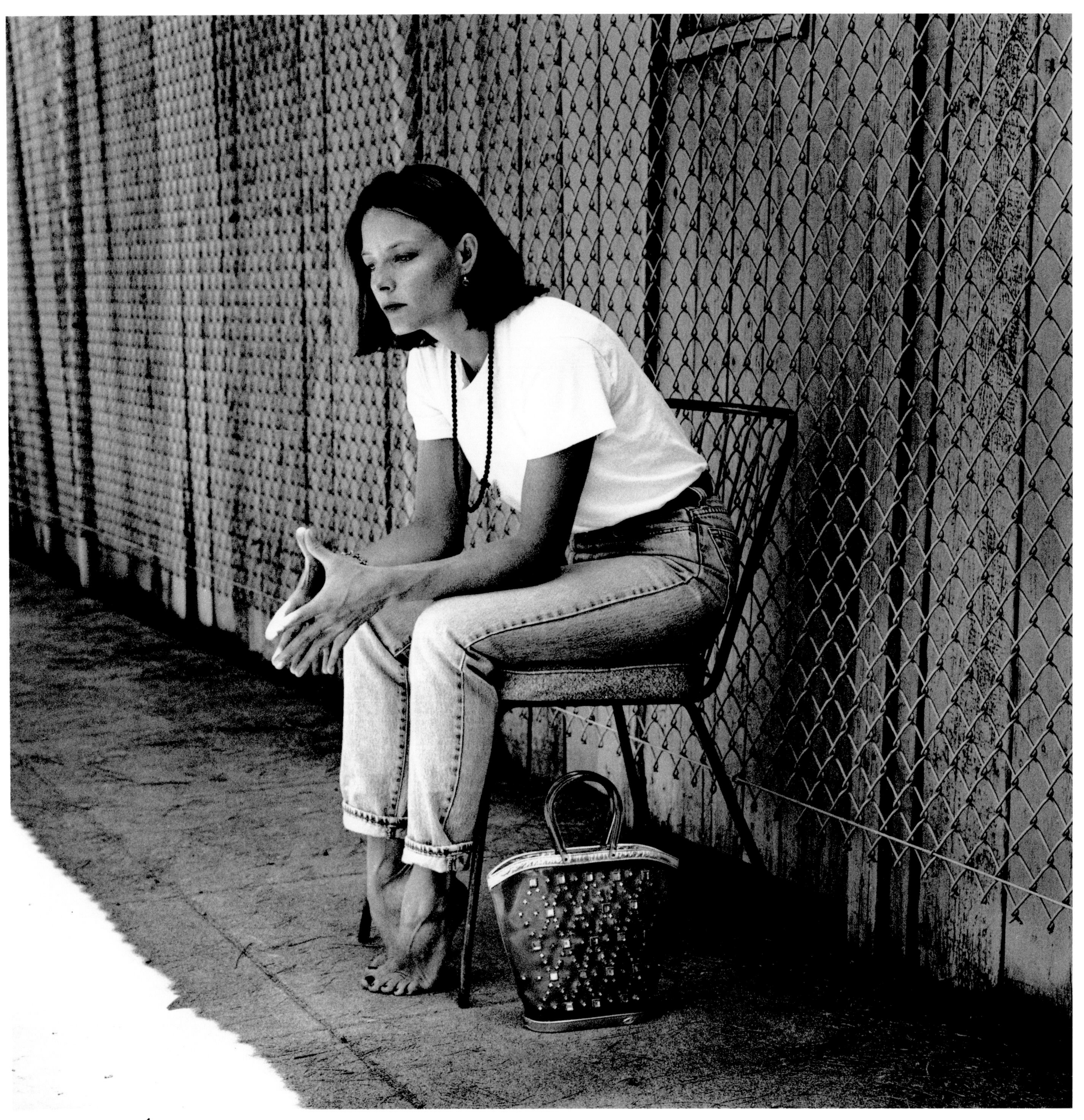

jodie foster

30

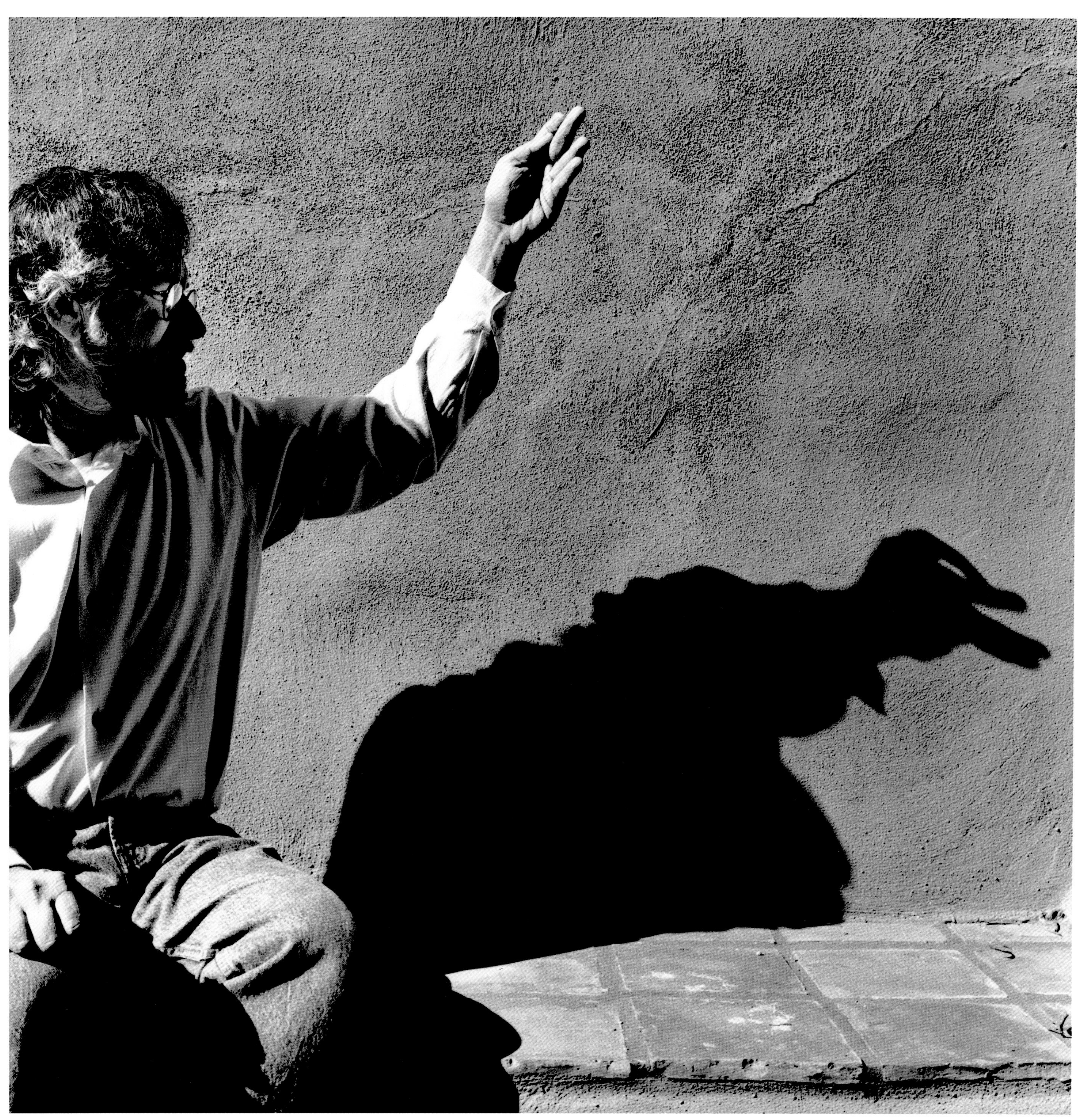

steven spielberg

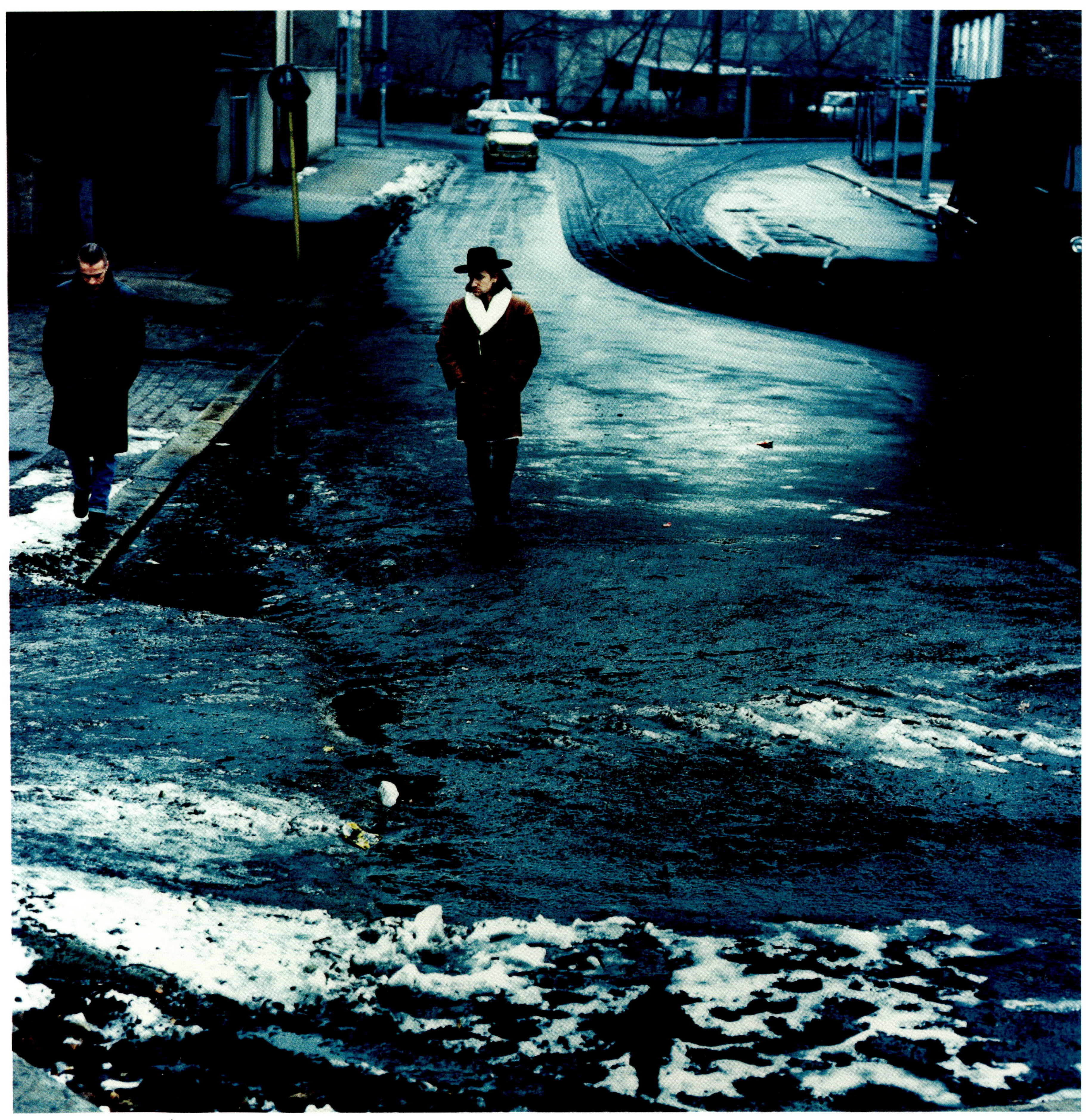

larry & bono

32

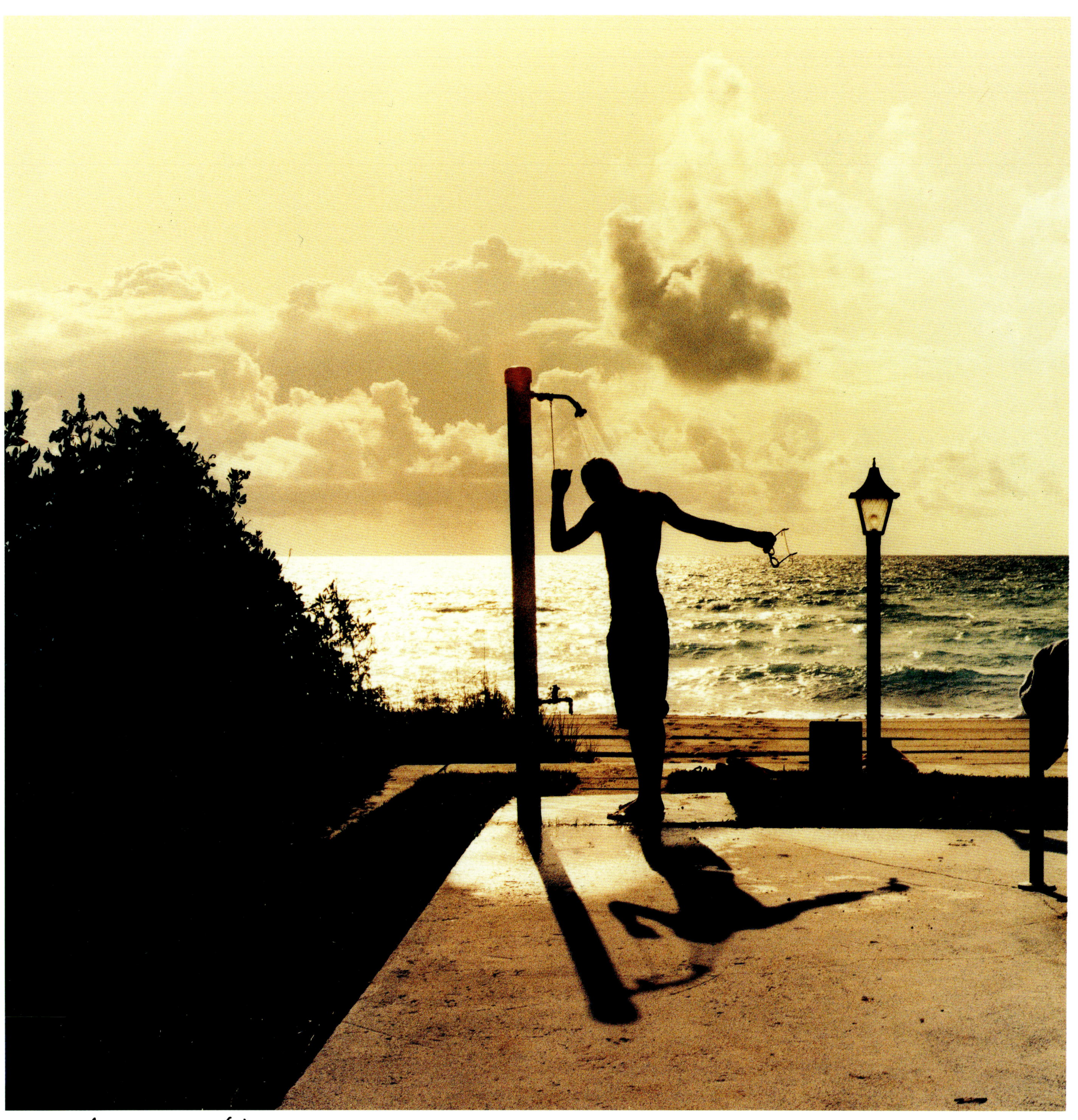

michael stipe

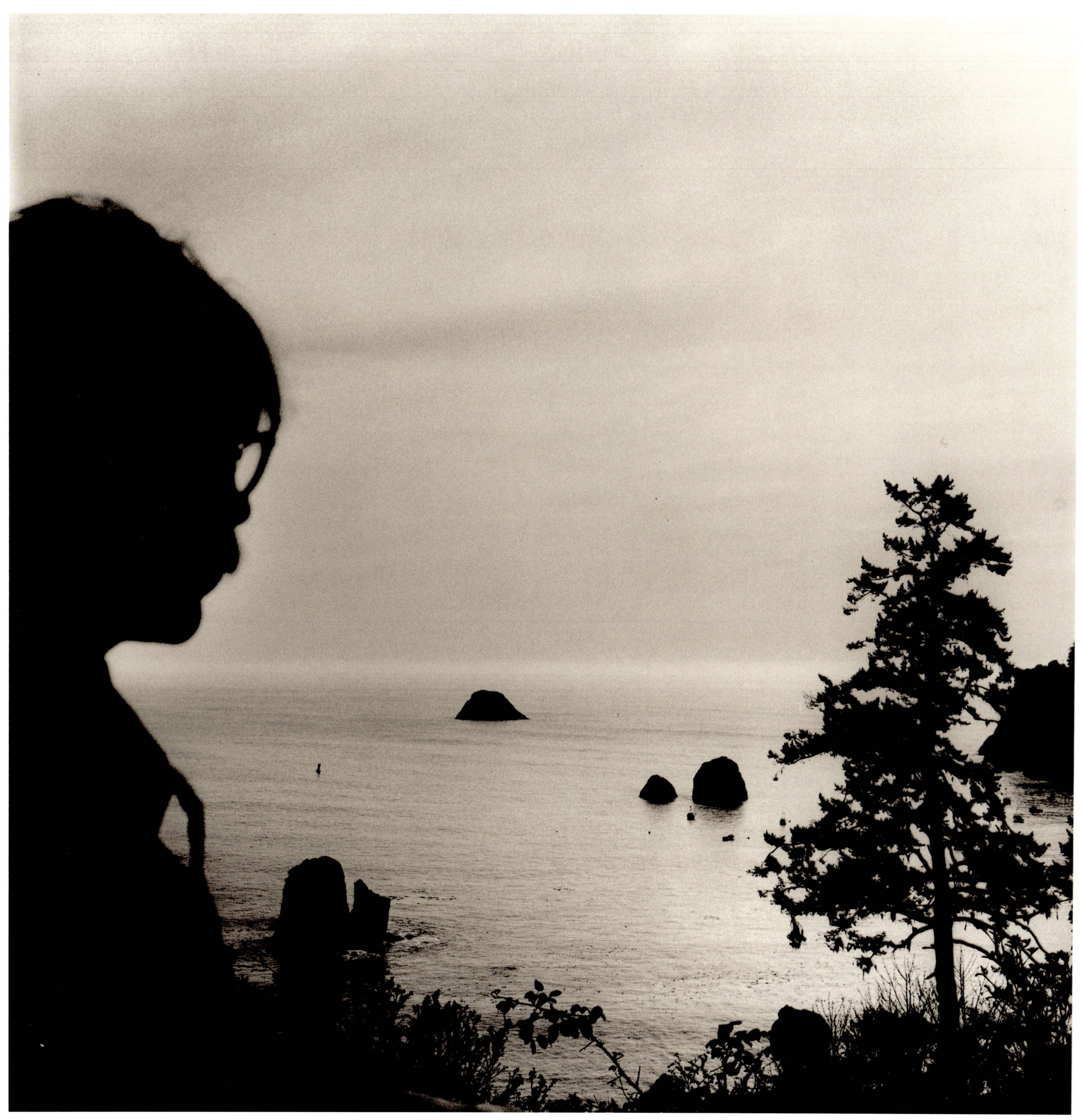

don van vliet

34

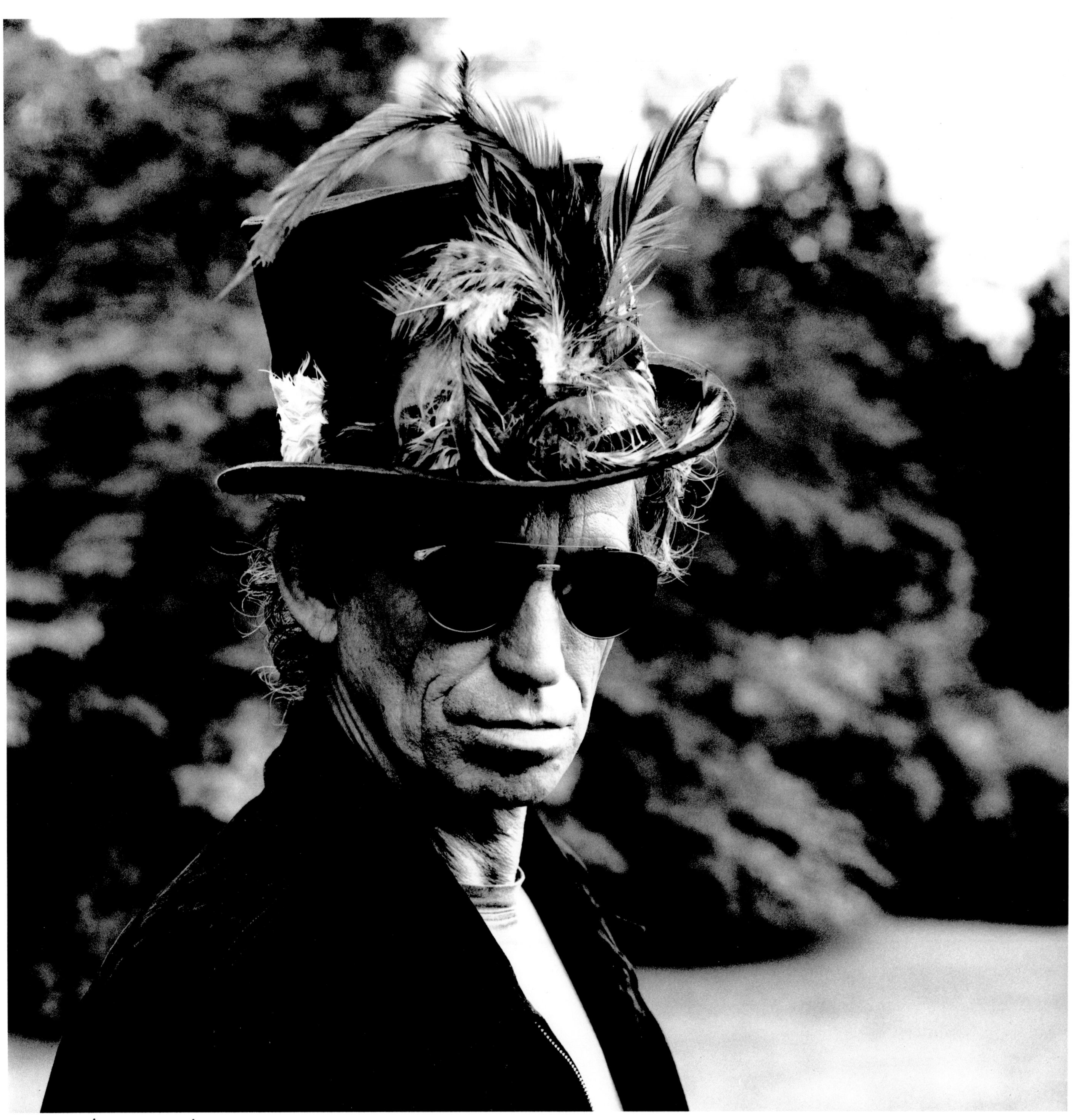

35

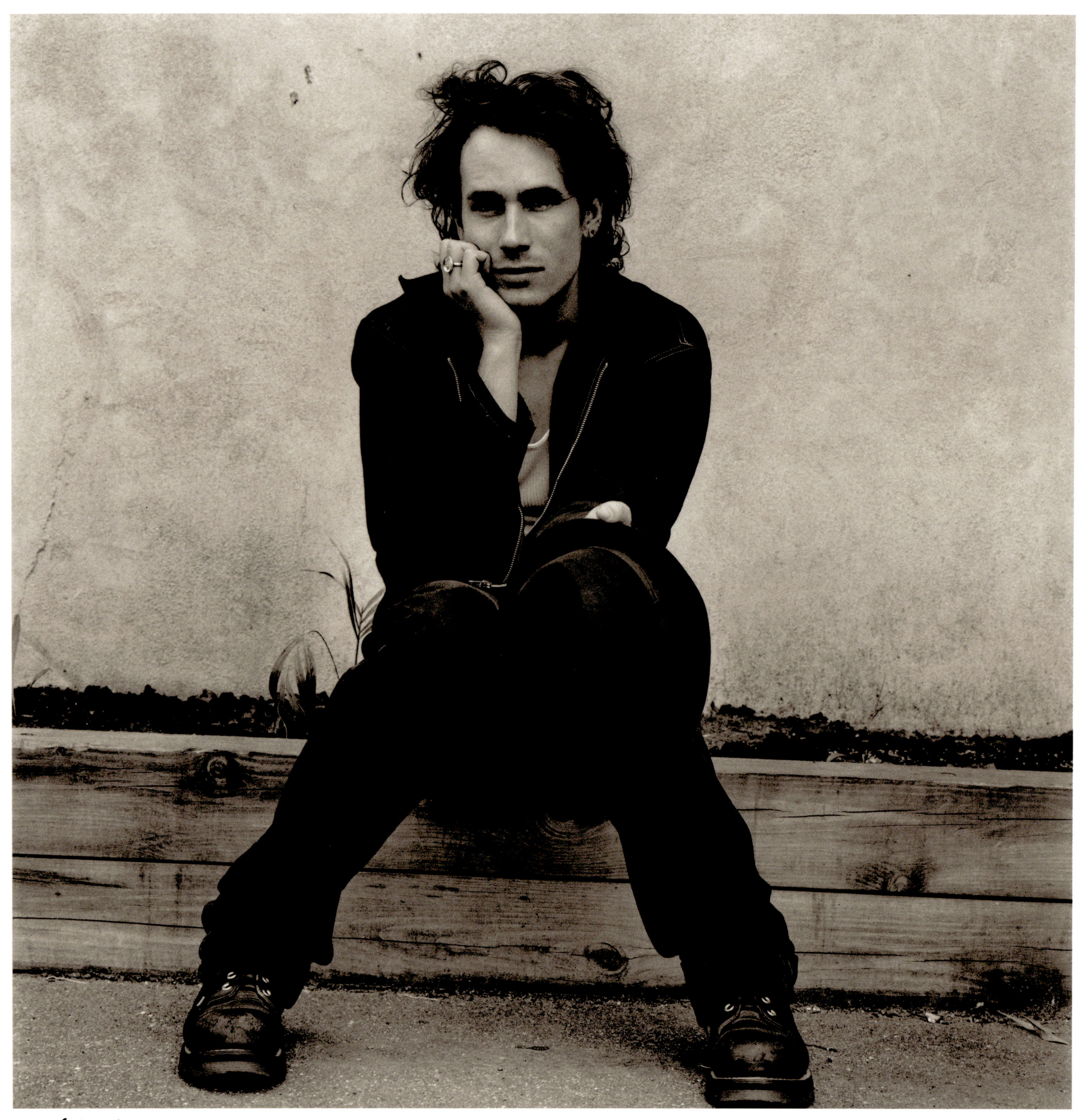

jeff buckley

36

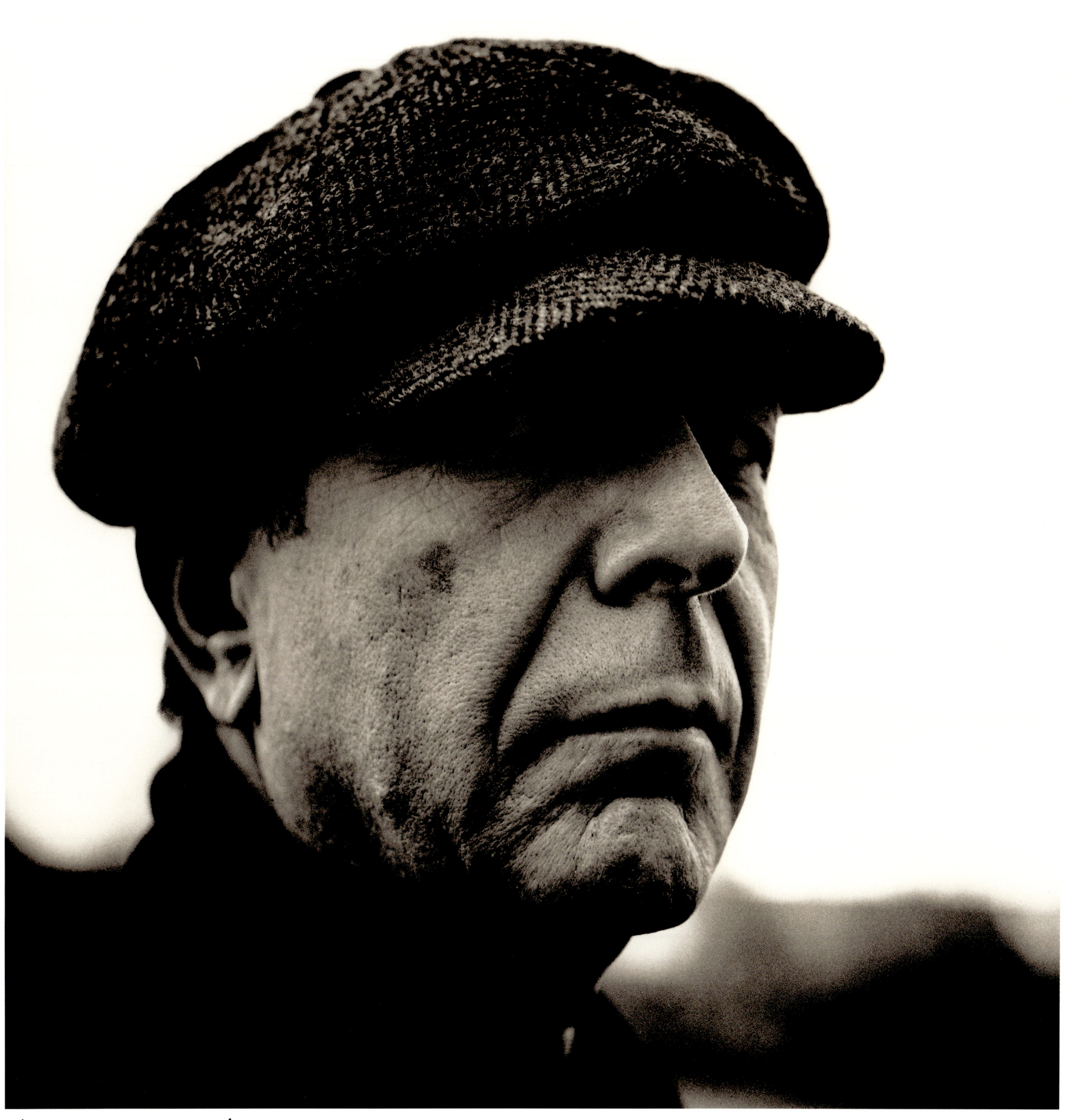

leonard cohen

37

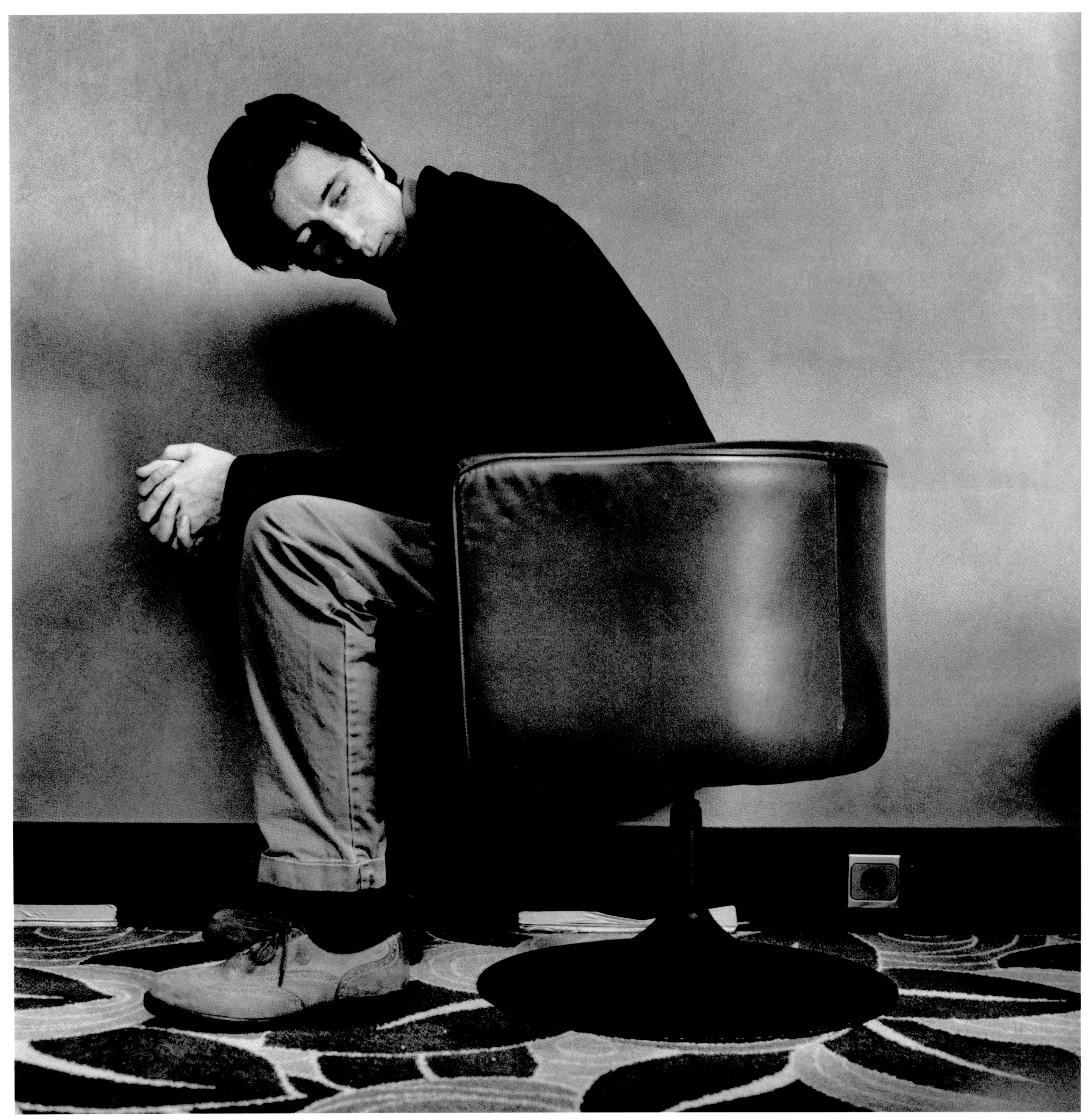

hal hartley

38

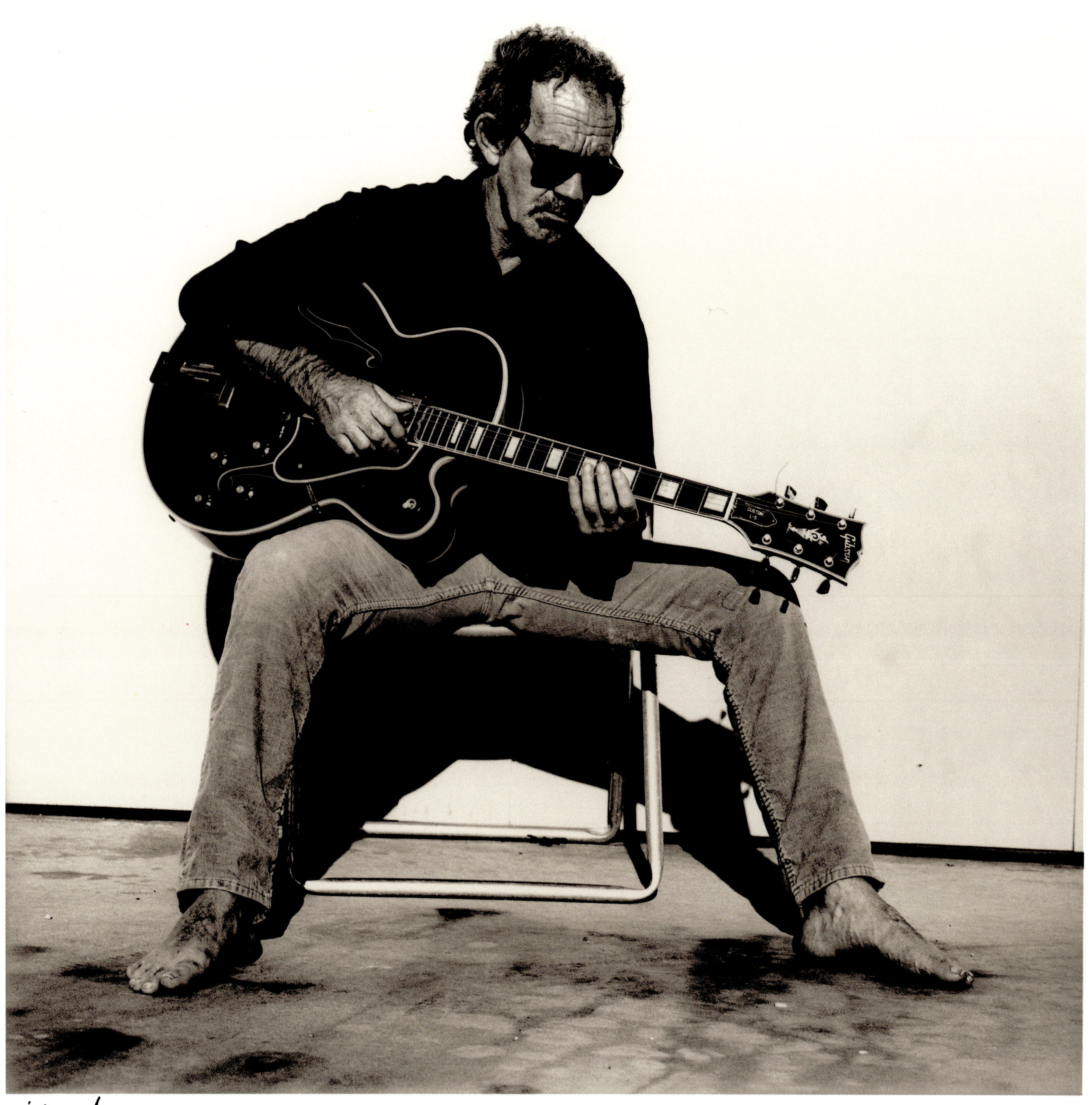

jj cale.

39

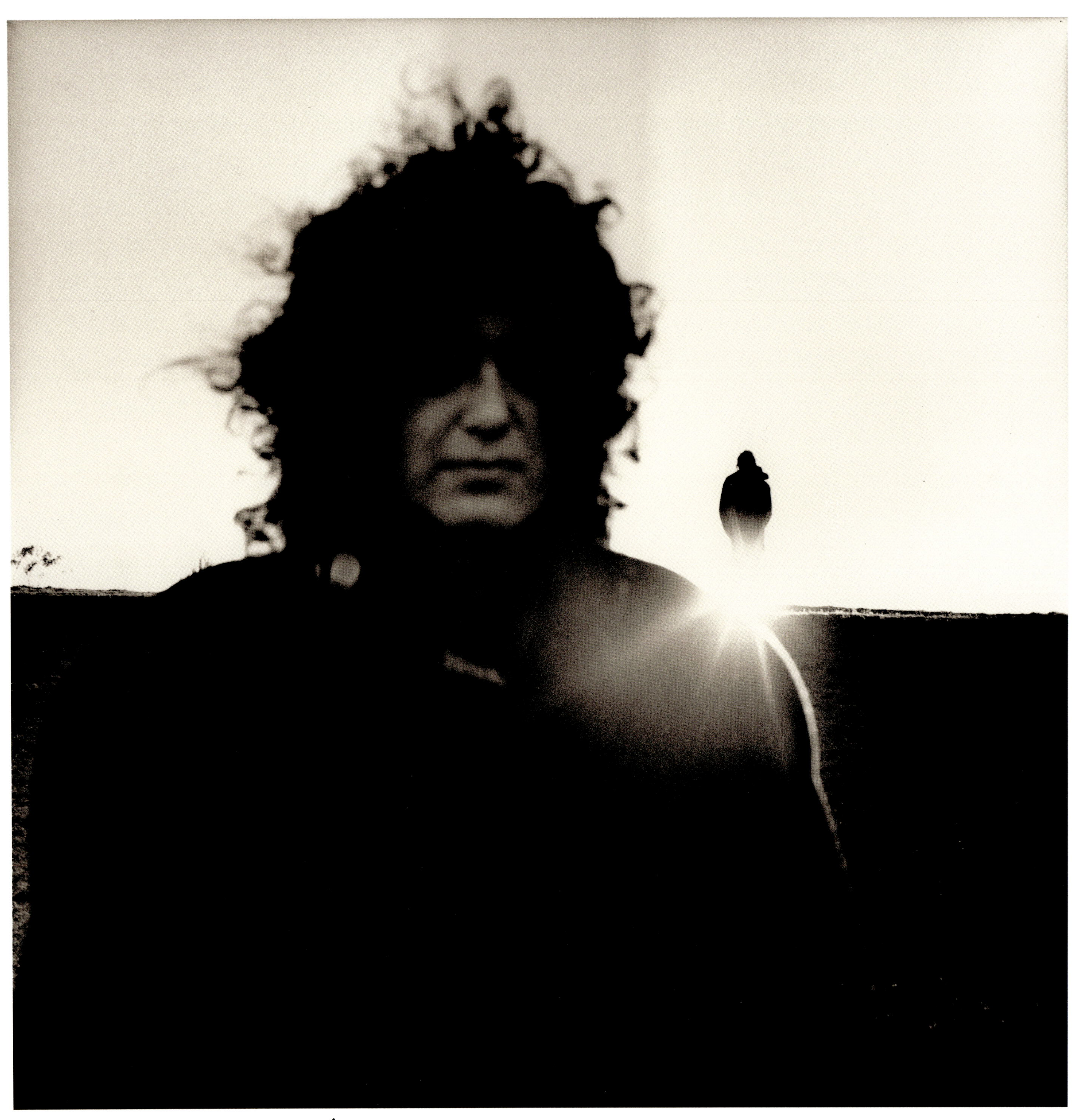

jimmy page & robert plant

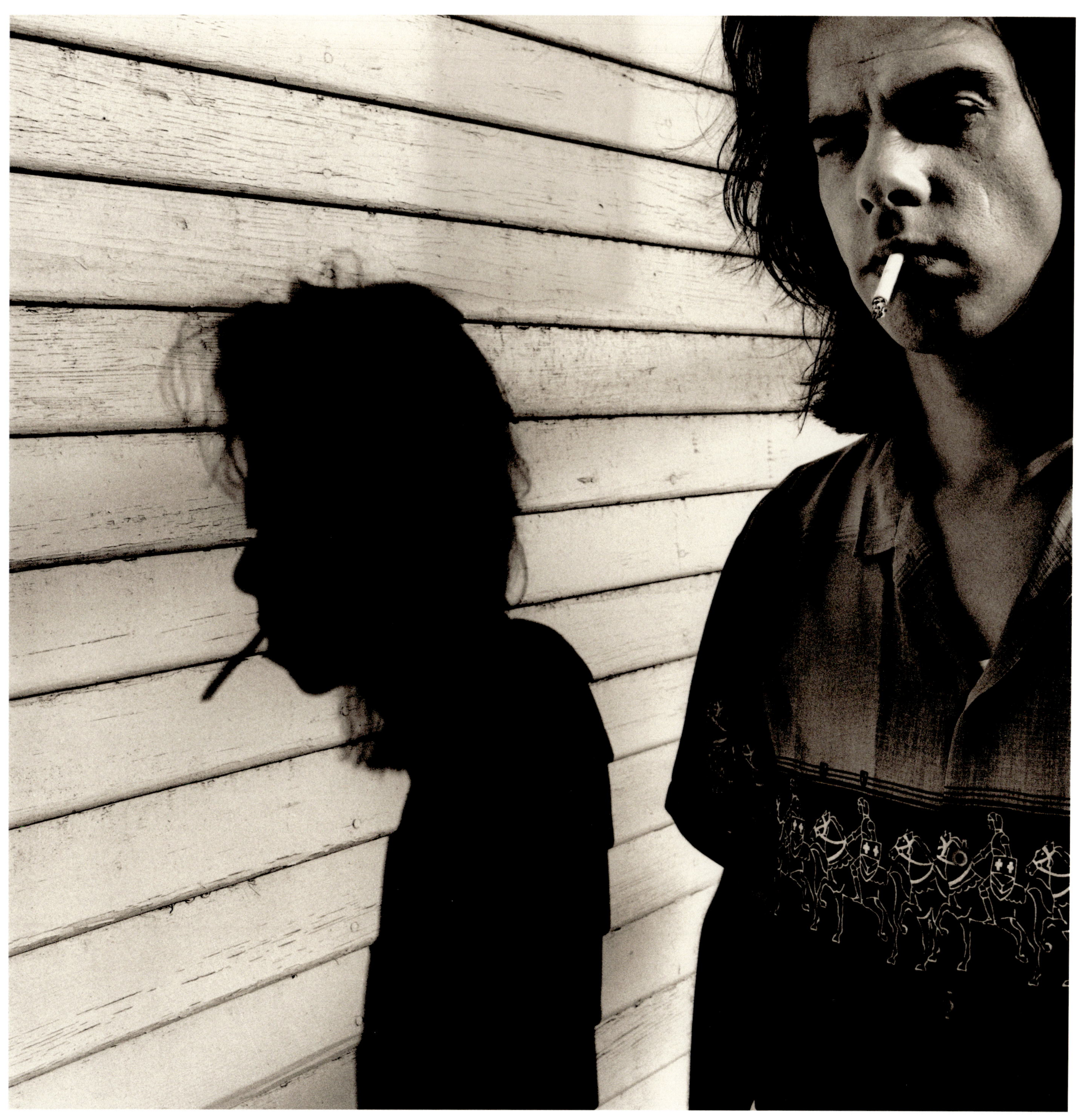
nick cave
41

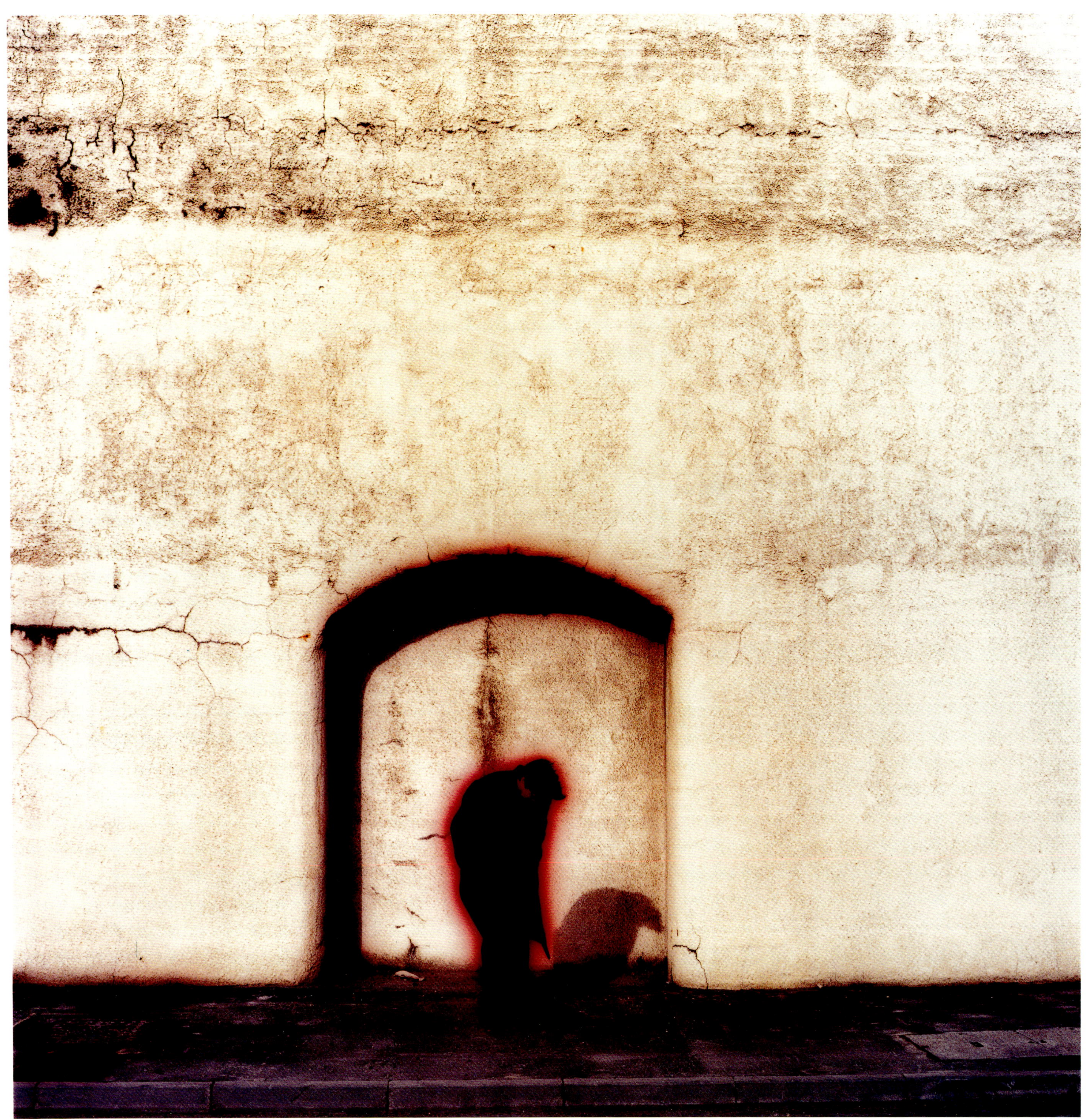

bryan ferry

42

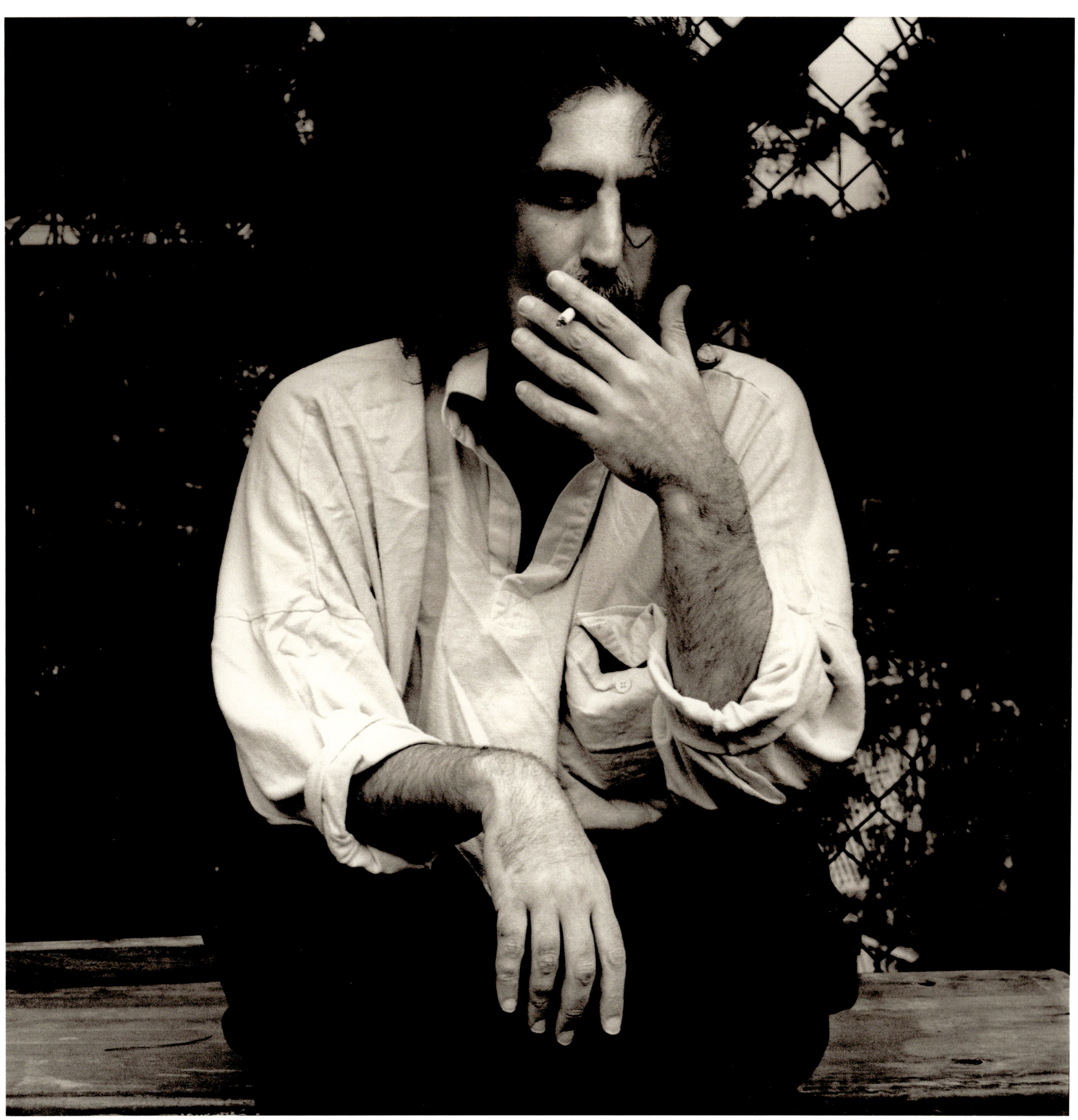

frank zappa

43

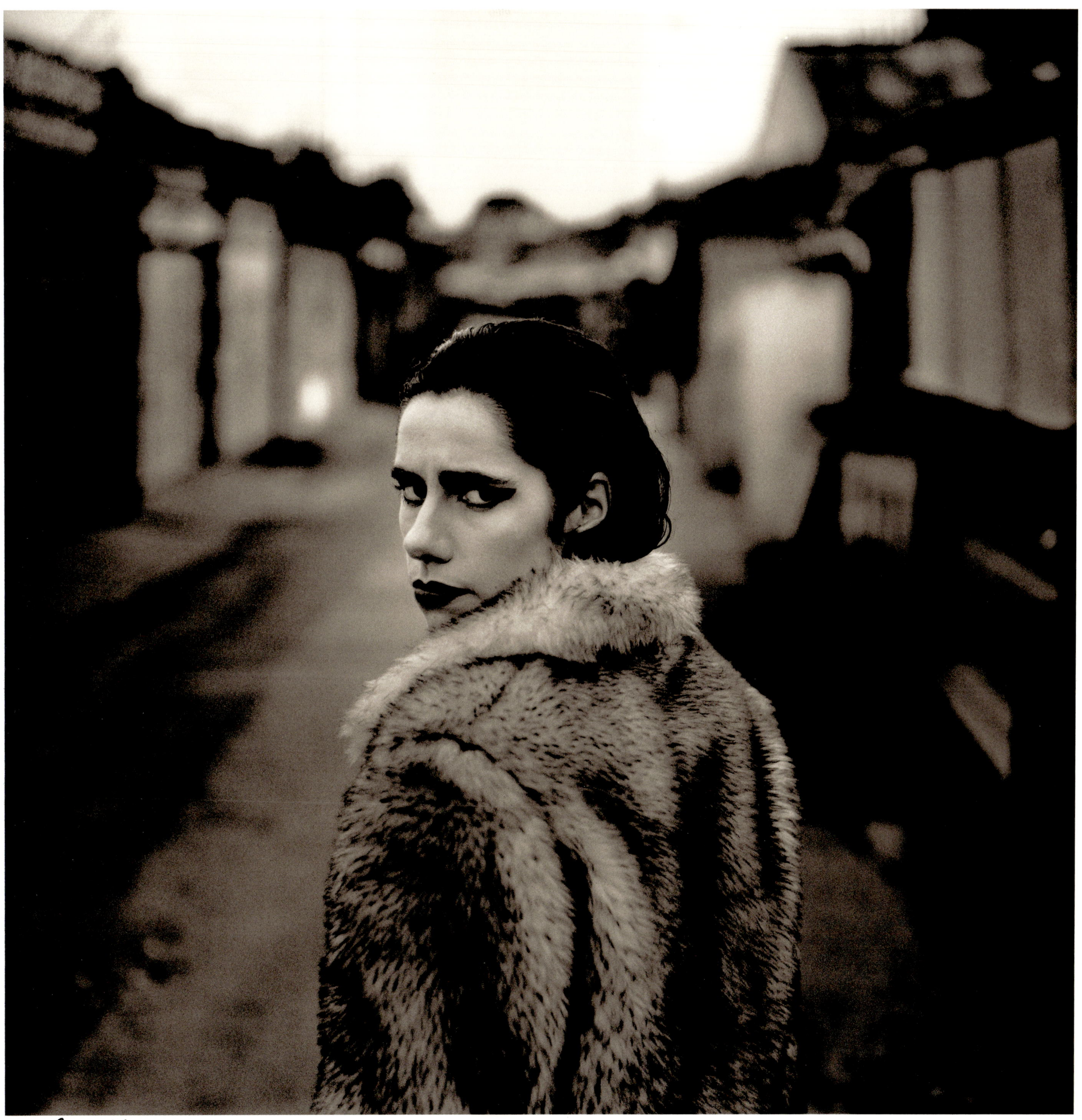

polly harvey

44

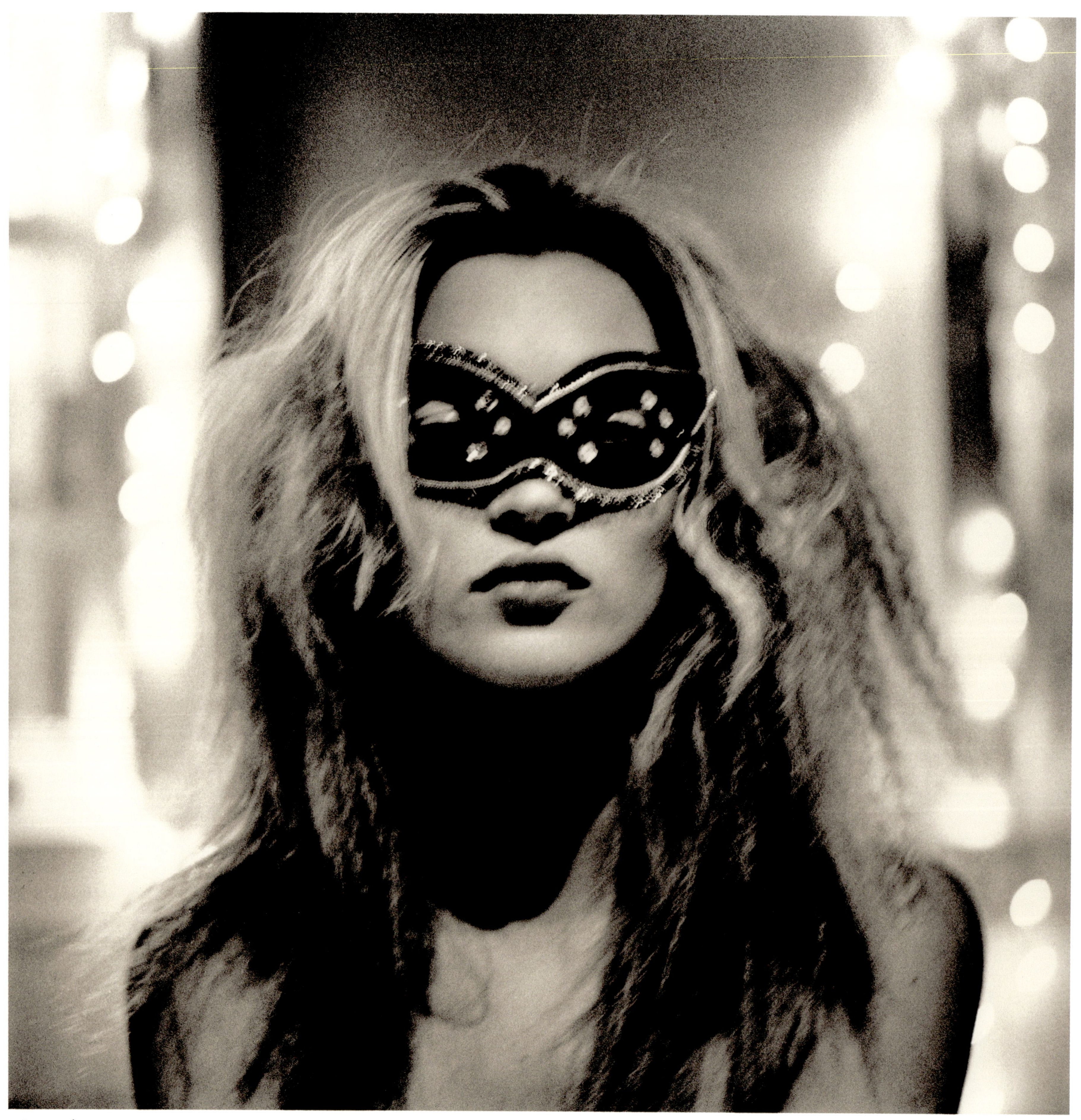

kate moss

45

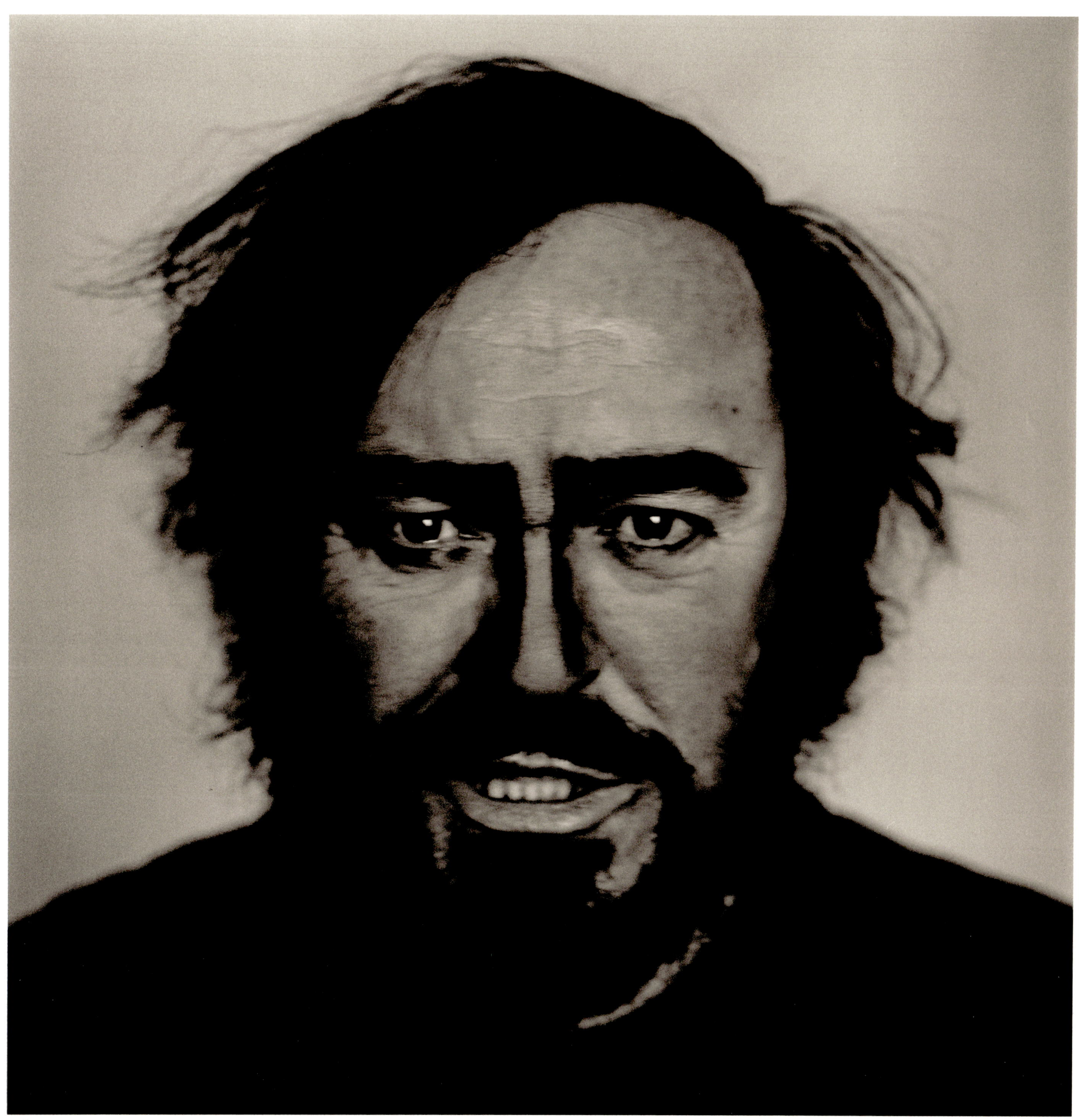

luciano pavarotti

46

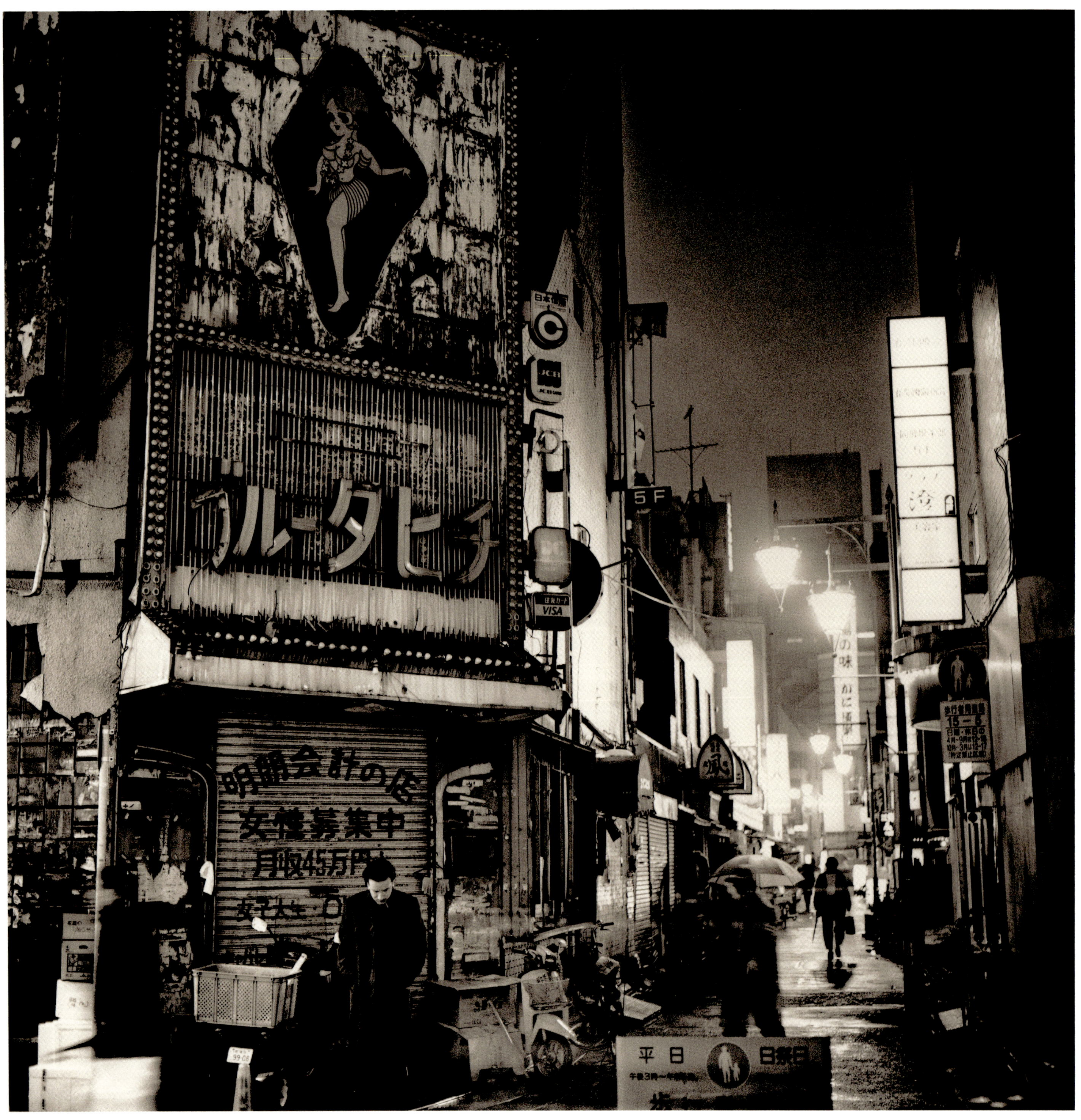

bono

47

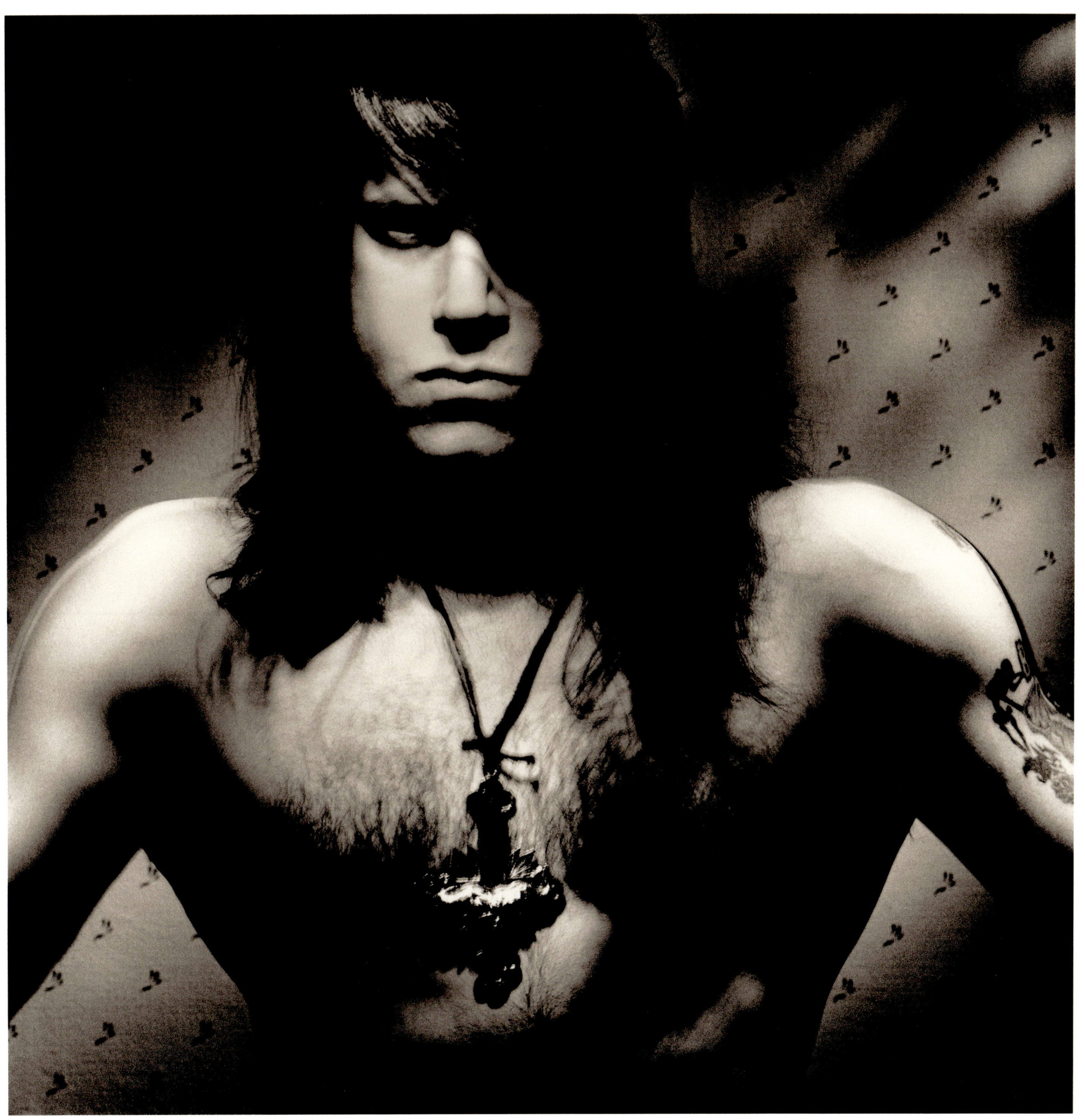

glenn danzig

48

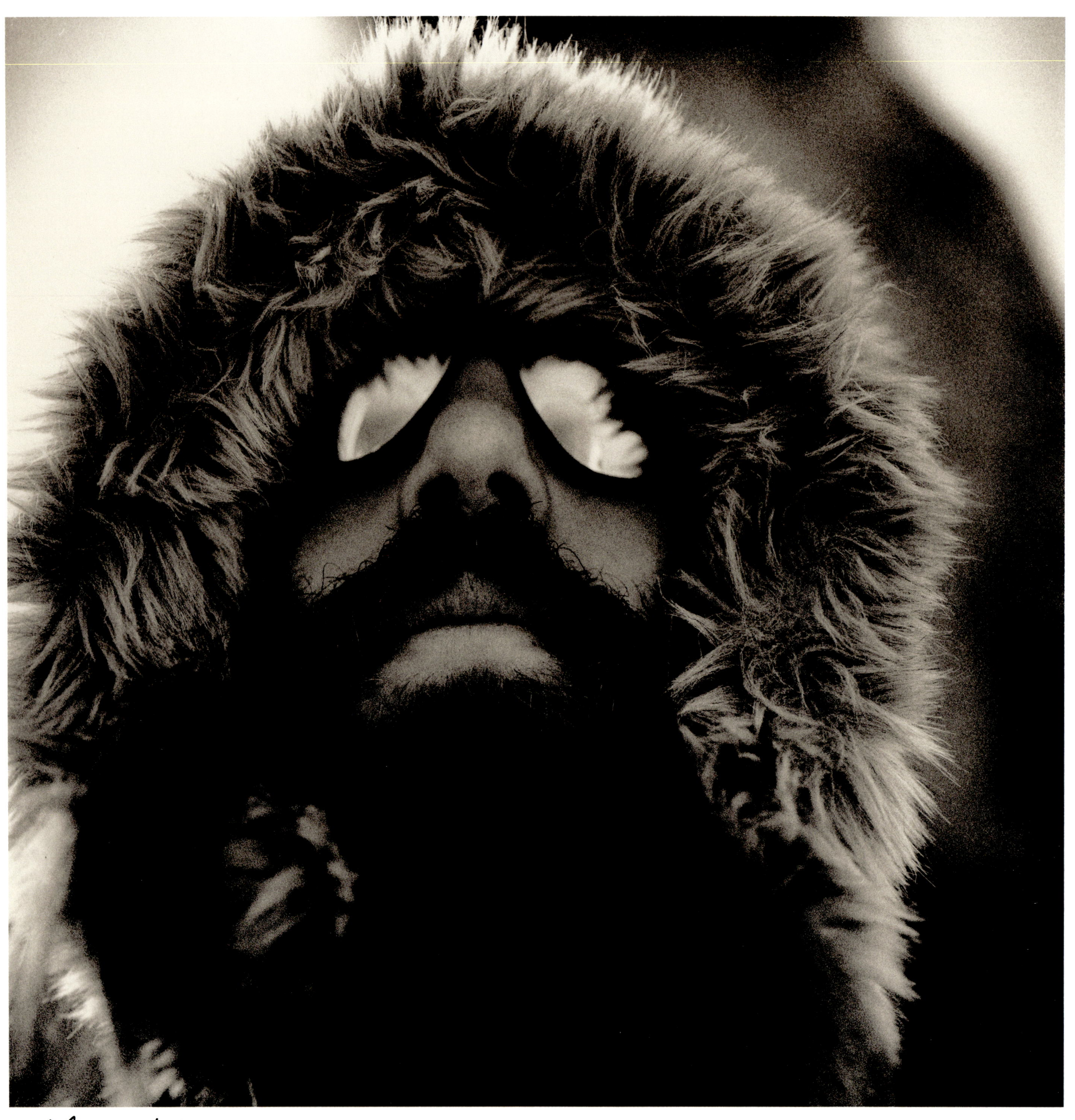

rich rubin

49

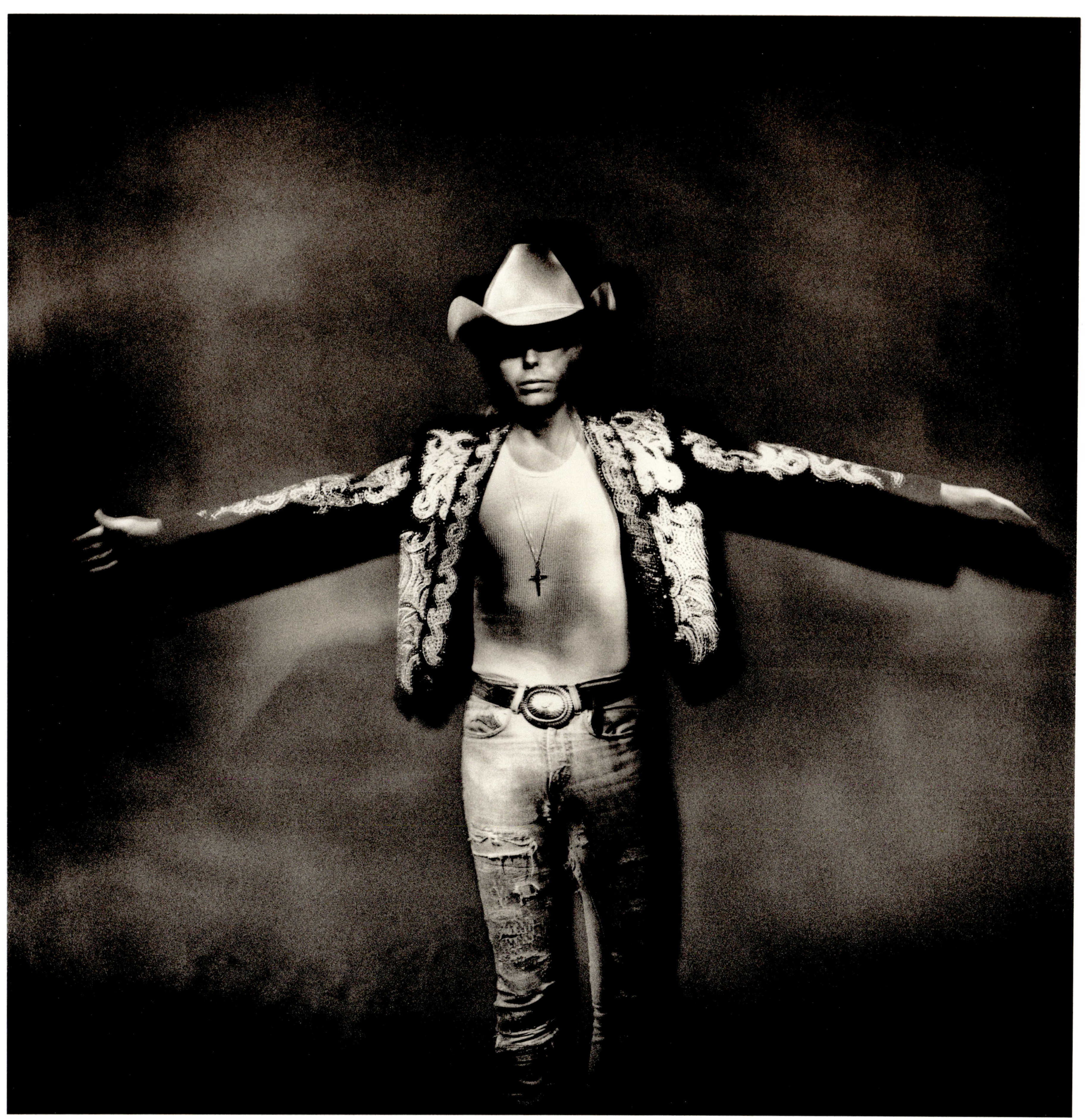

dwight yoakam

50

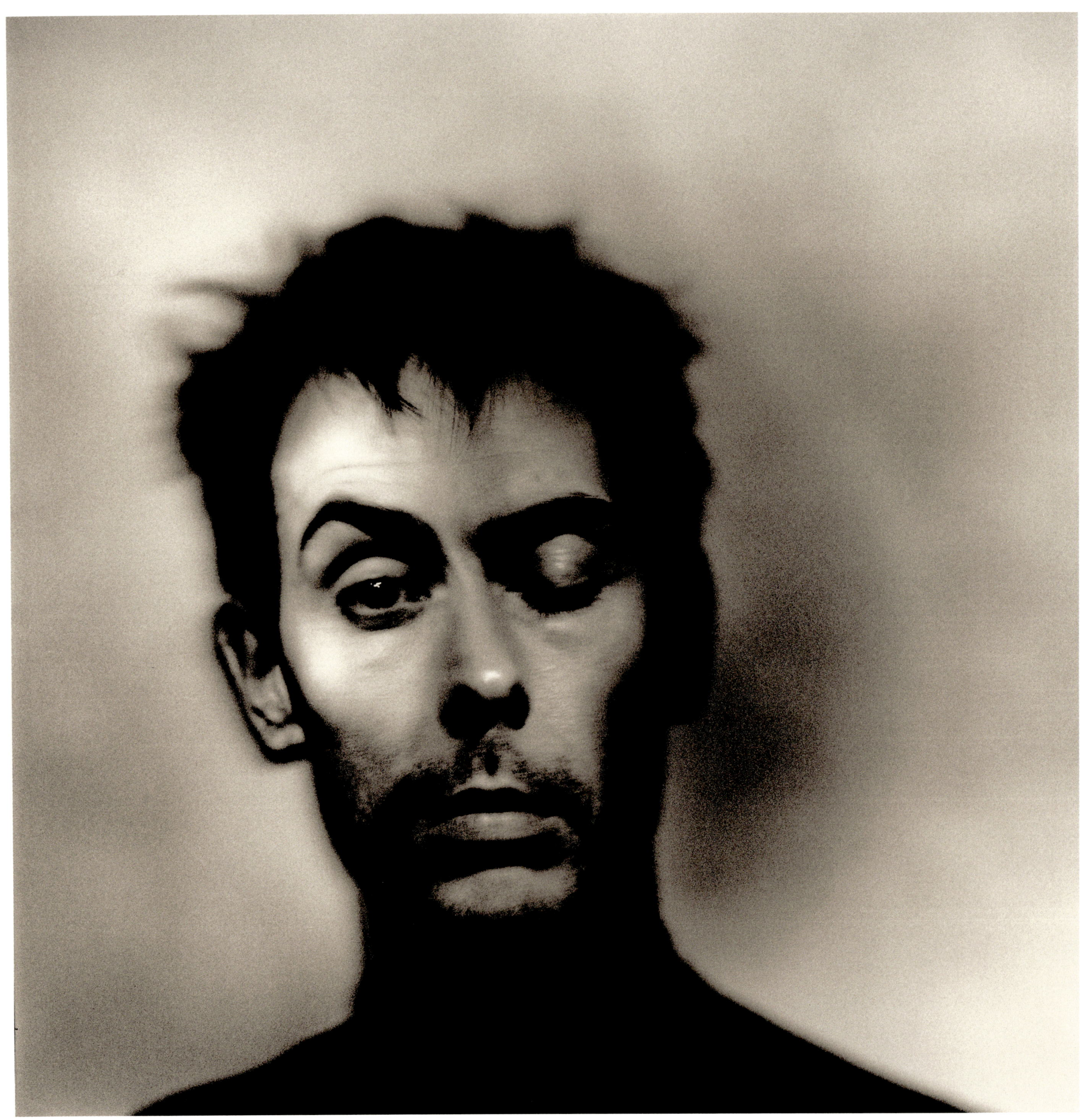

peter murphy

51

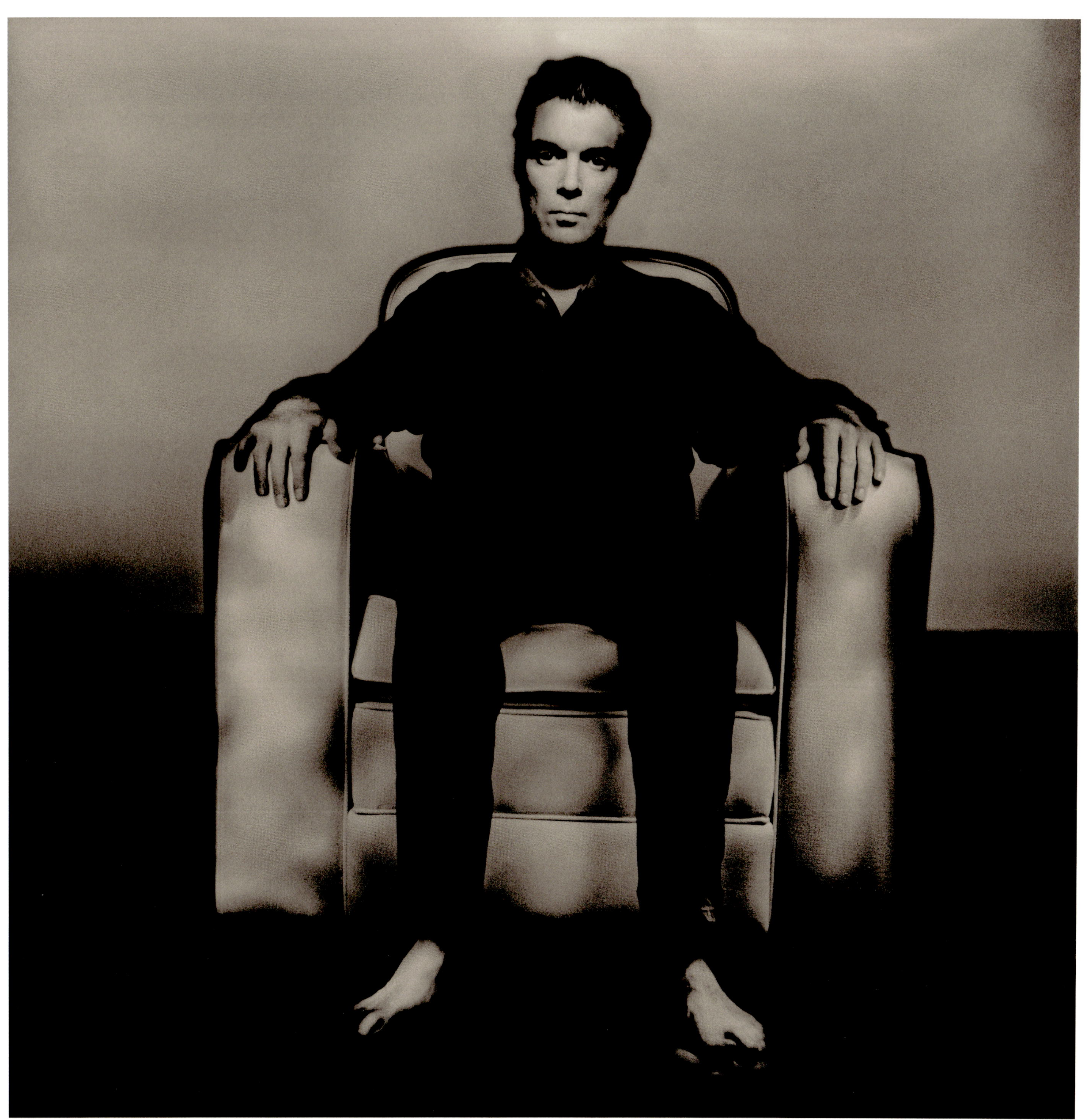

david byrne

52

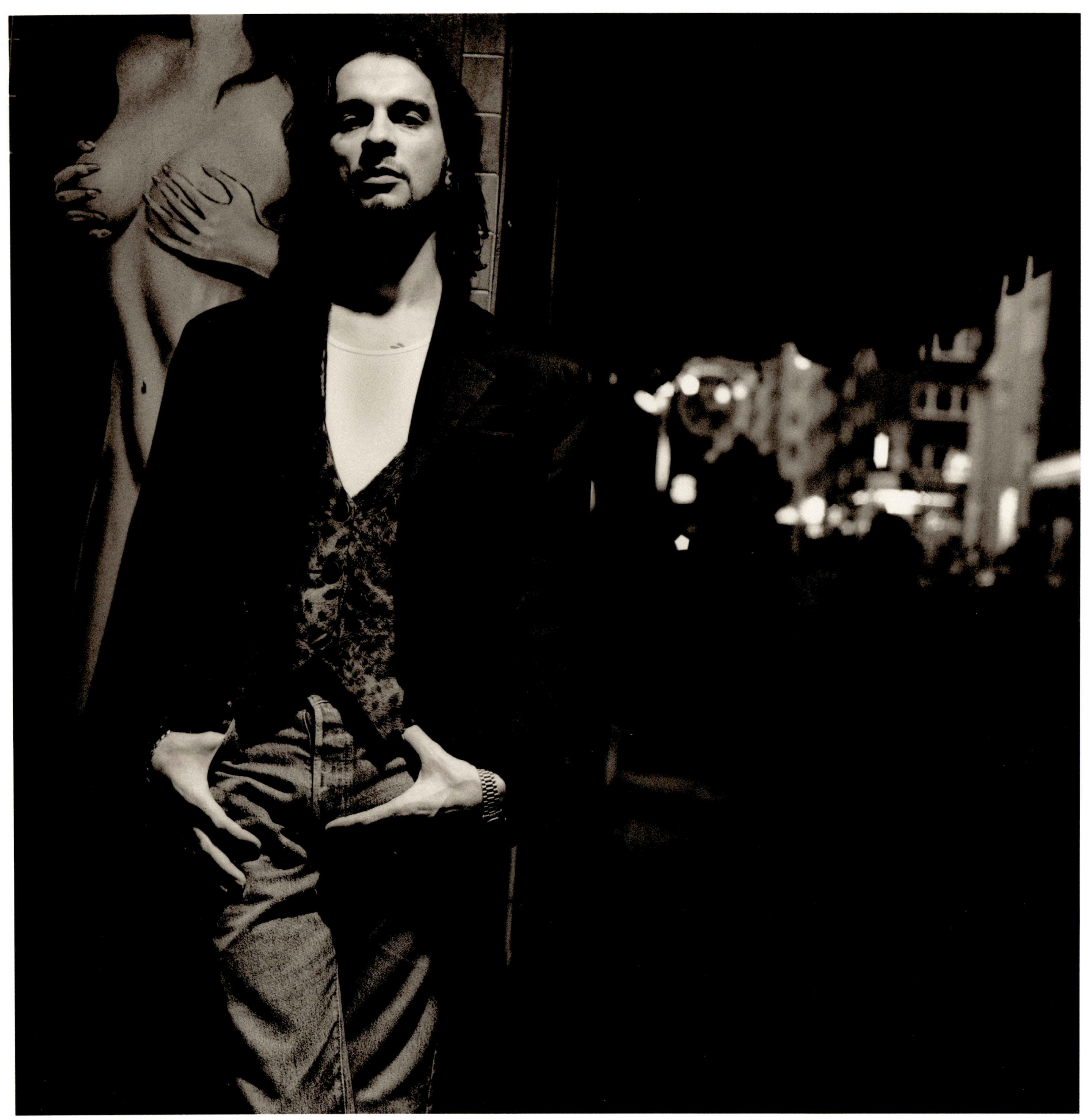

dave gahan
53

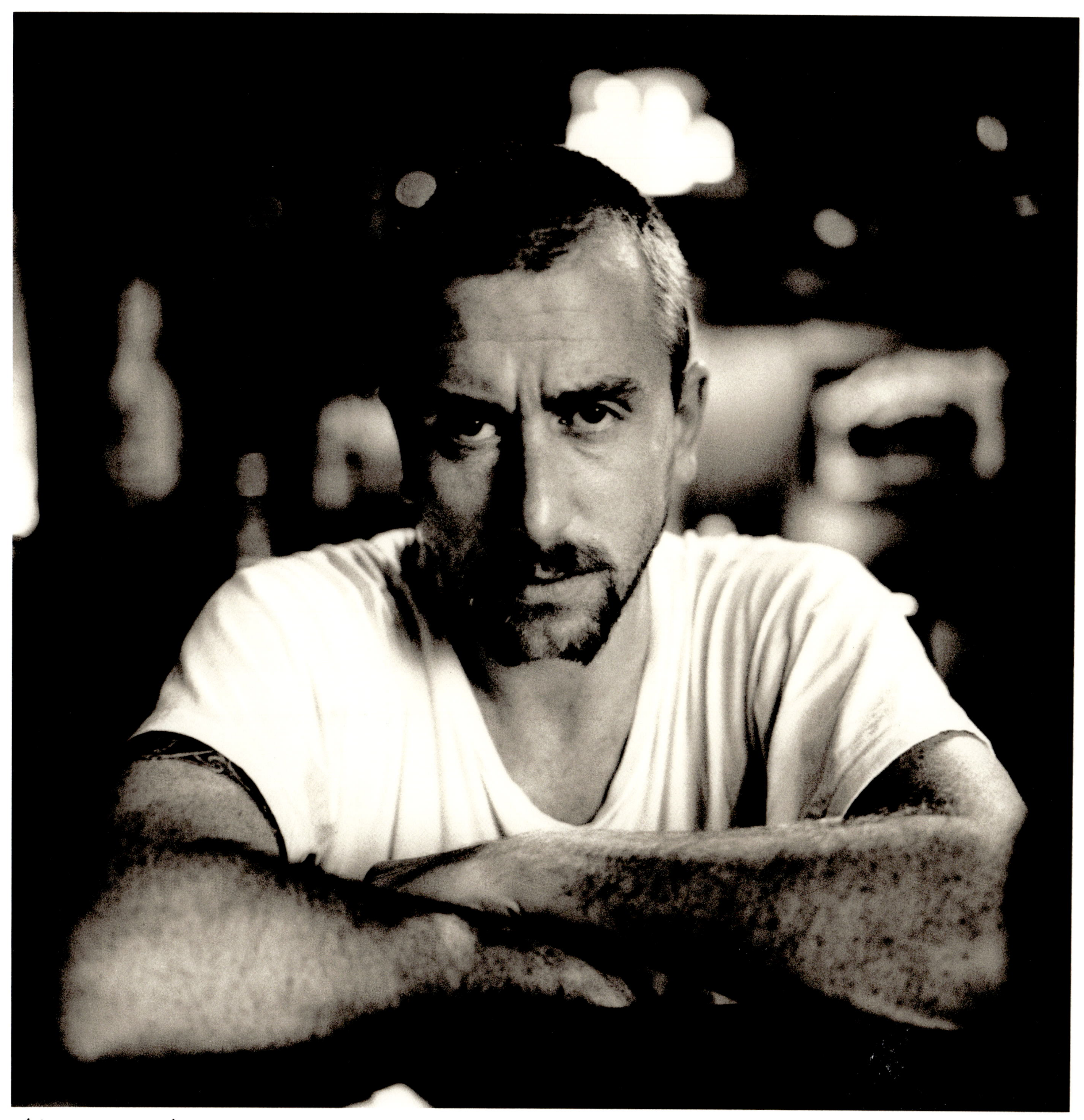

tim roth
54

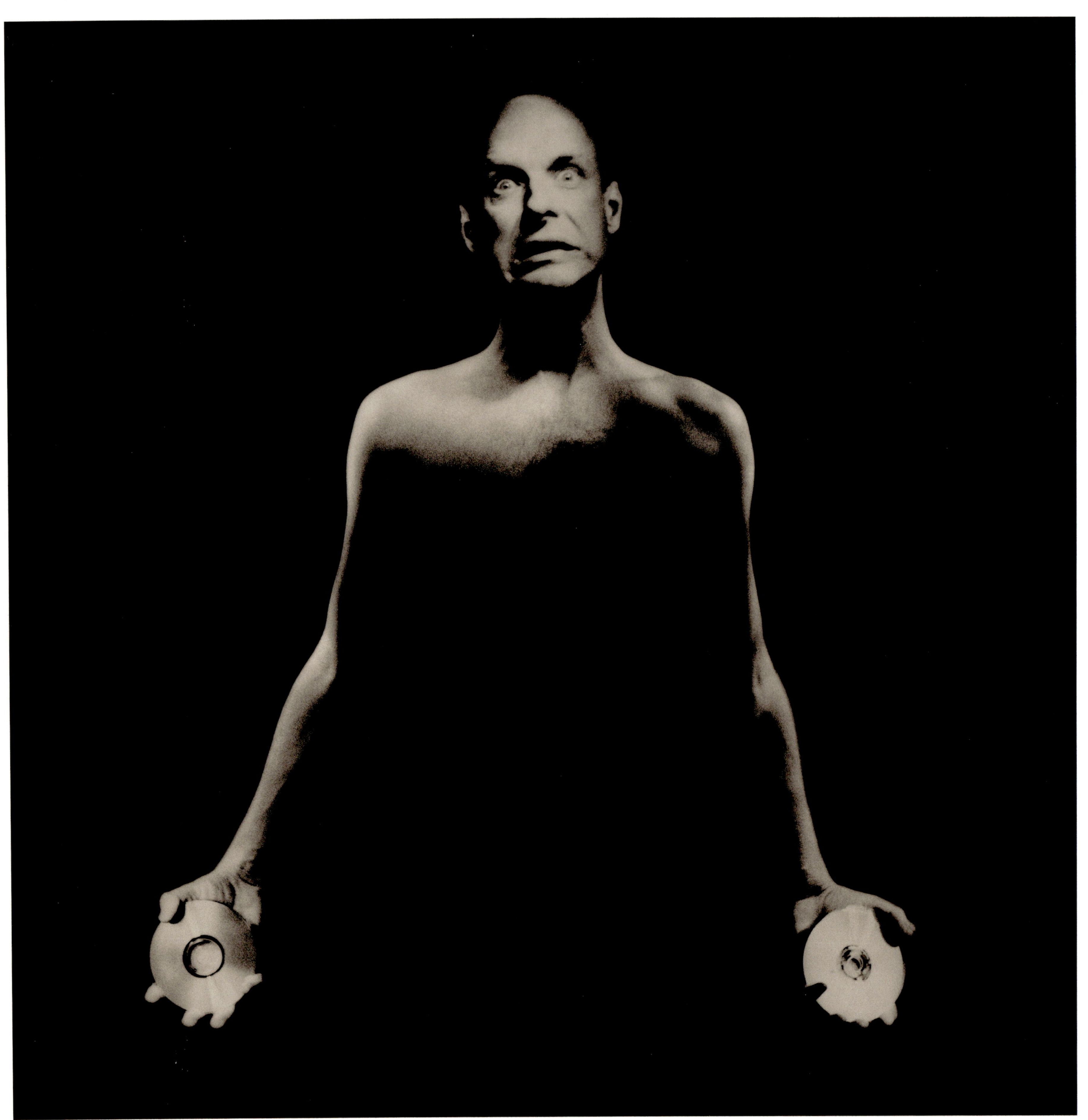

brian eno
55

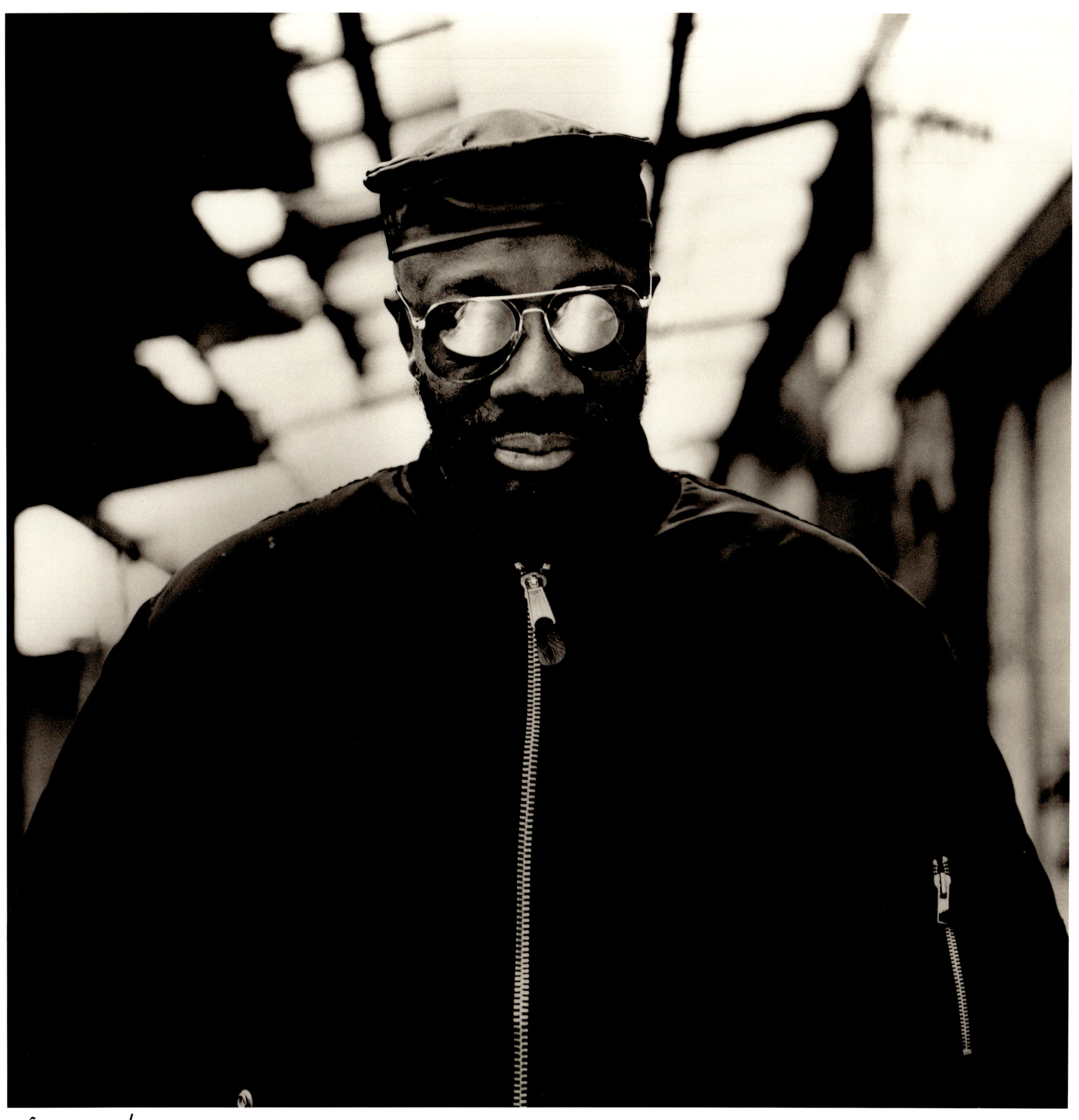

isaac hayes
56

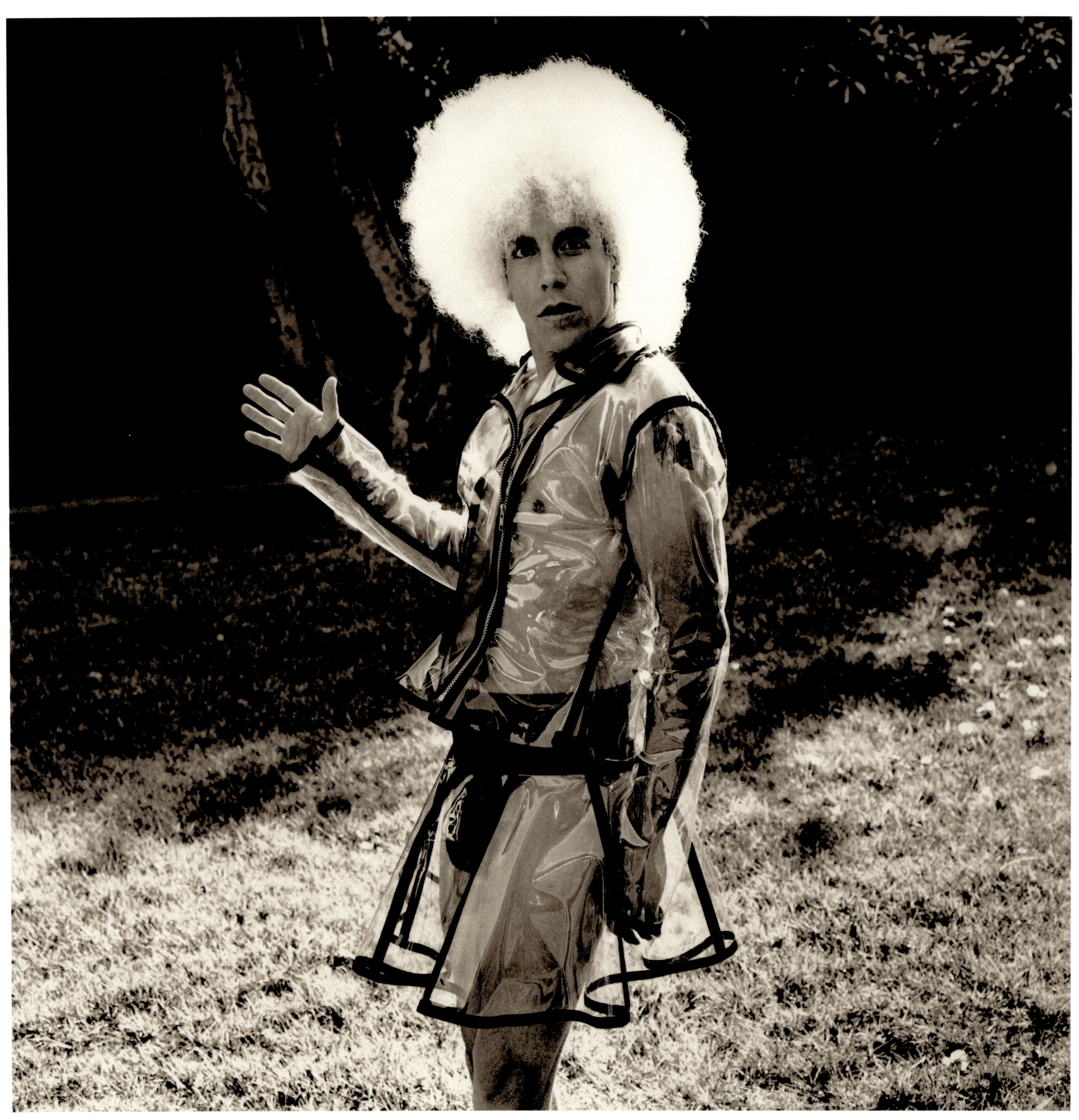
anthony kiedis
57

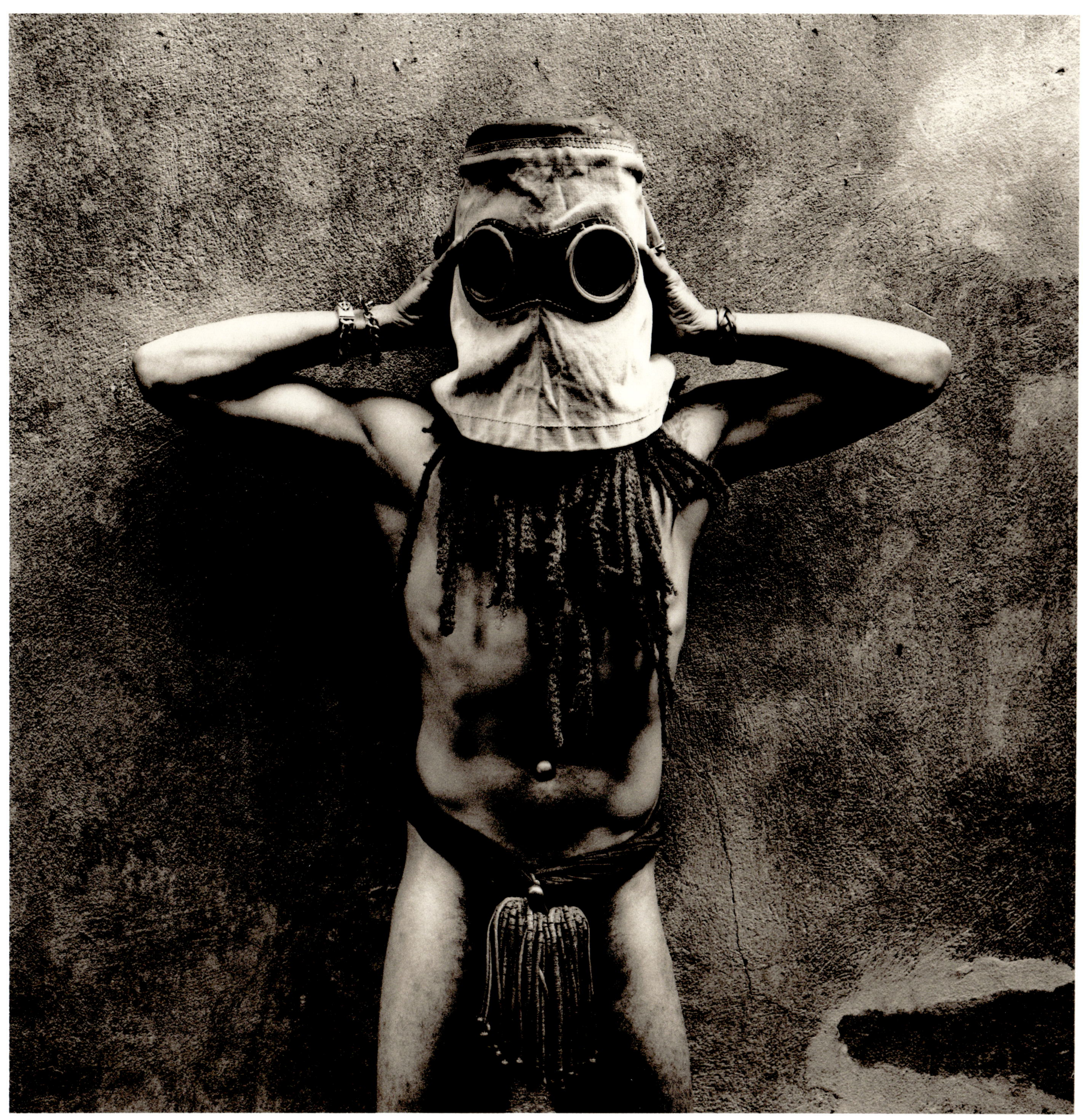

lenny kravitz   58

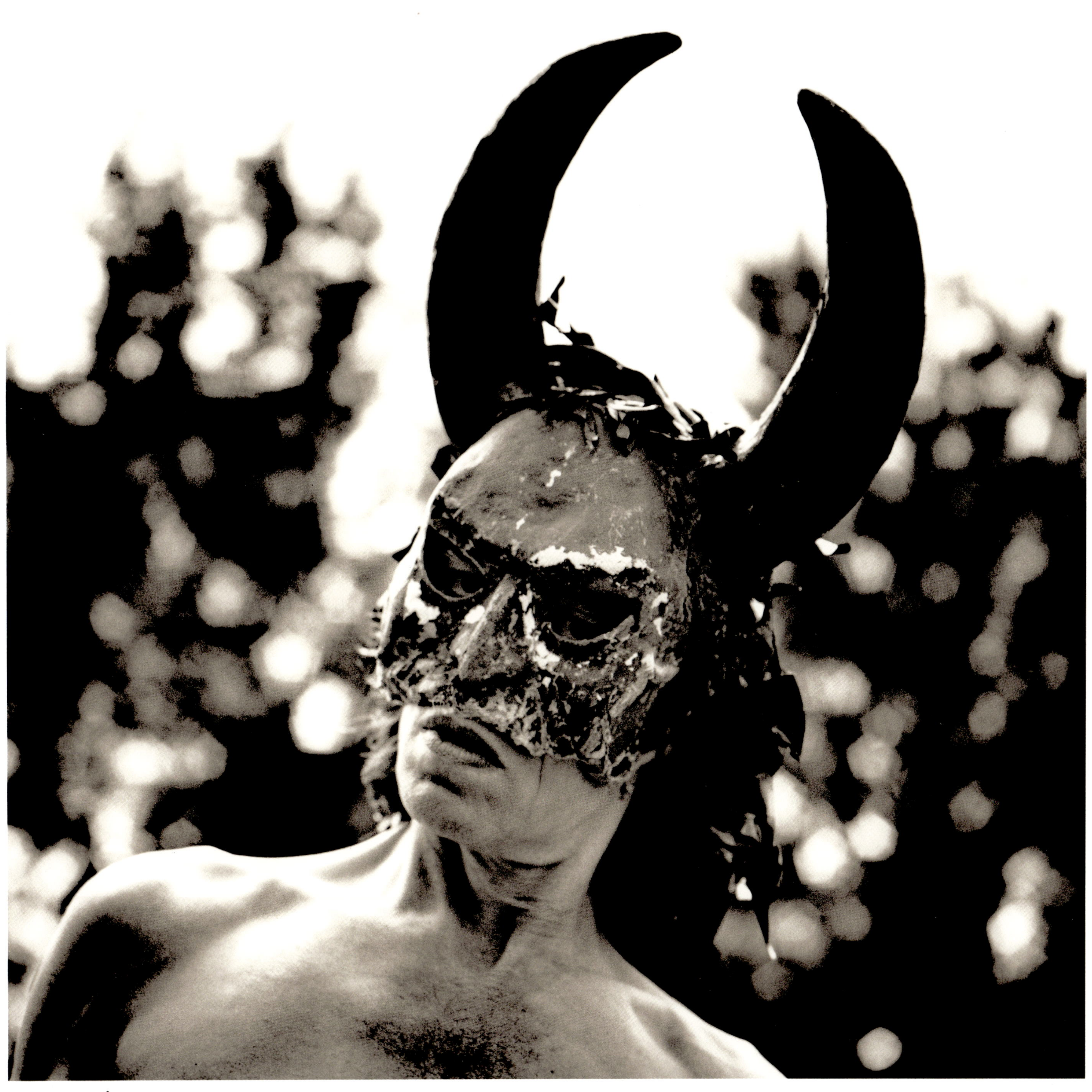

mick jagger

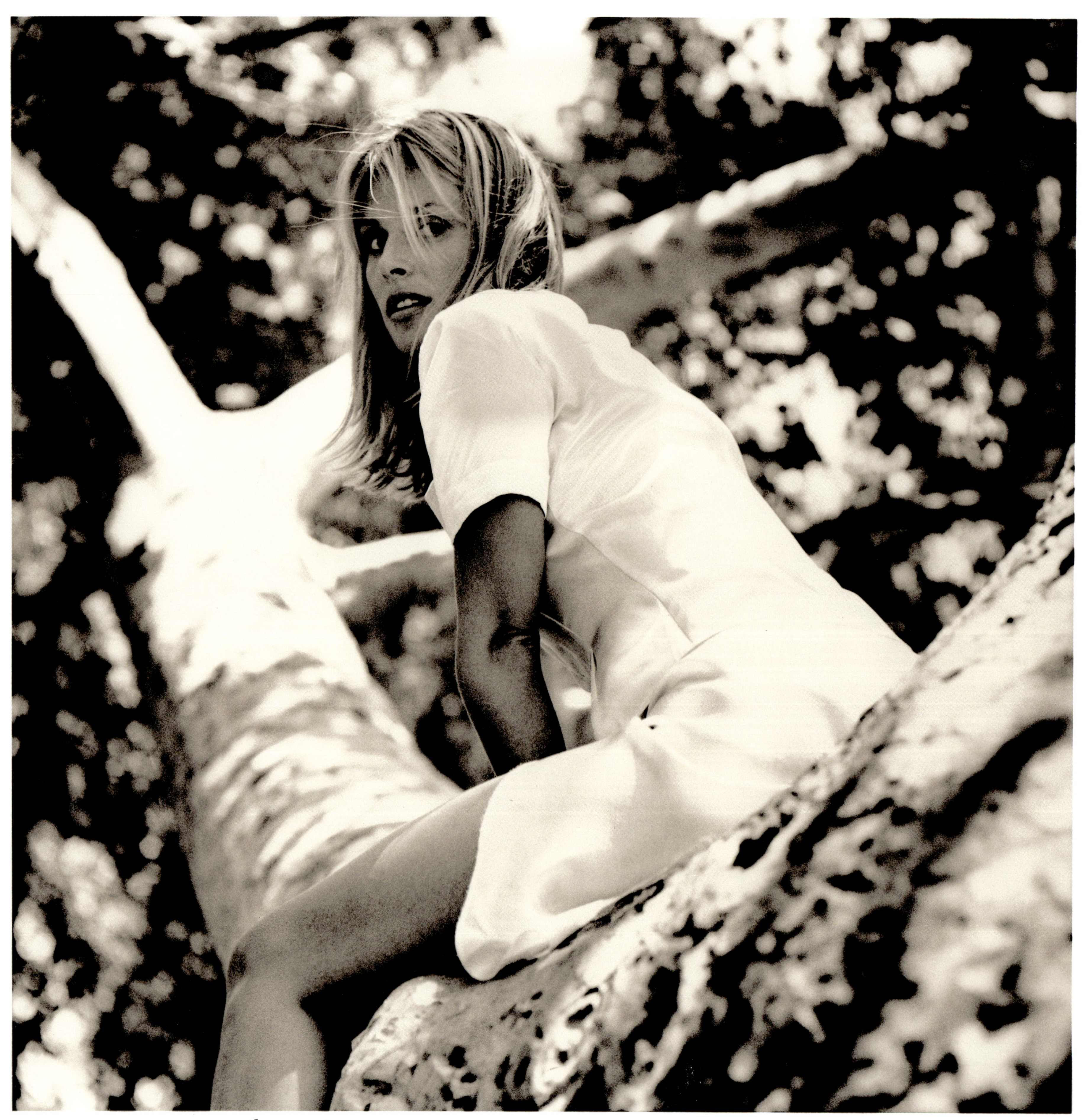

60

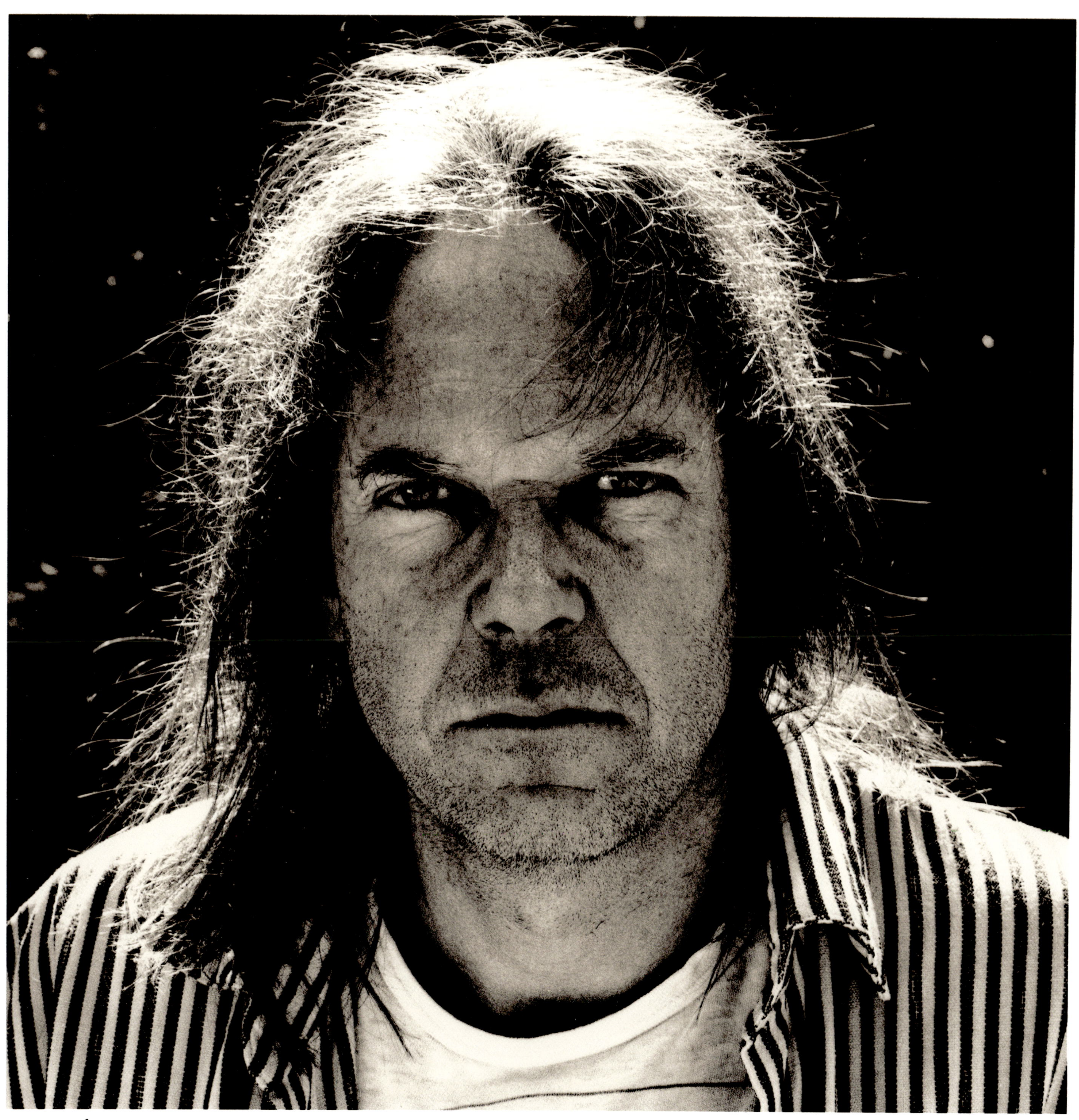

neil young

61

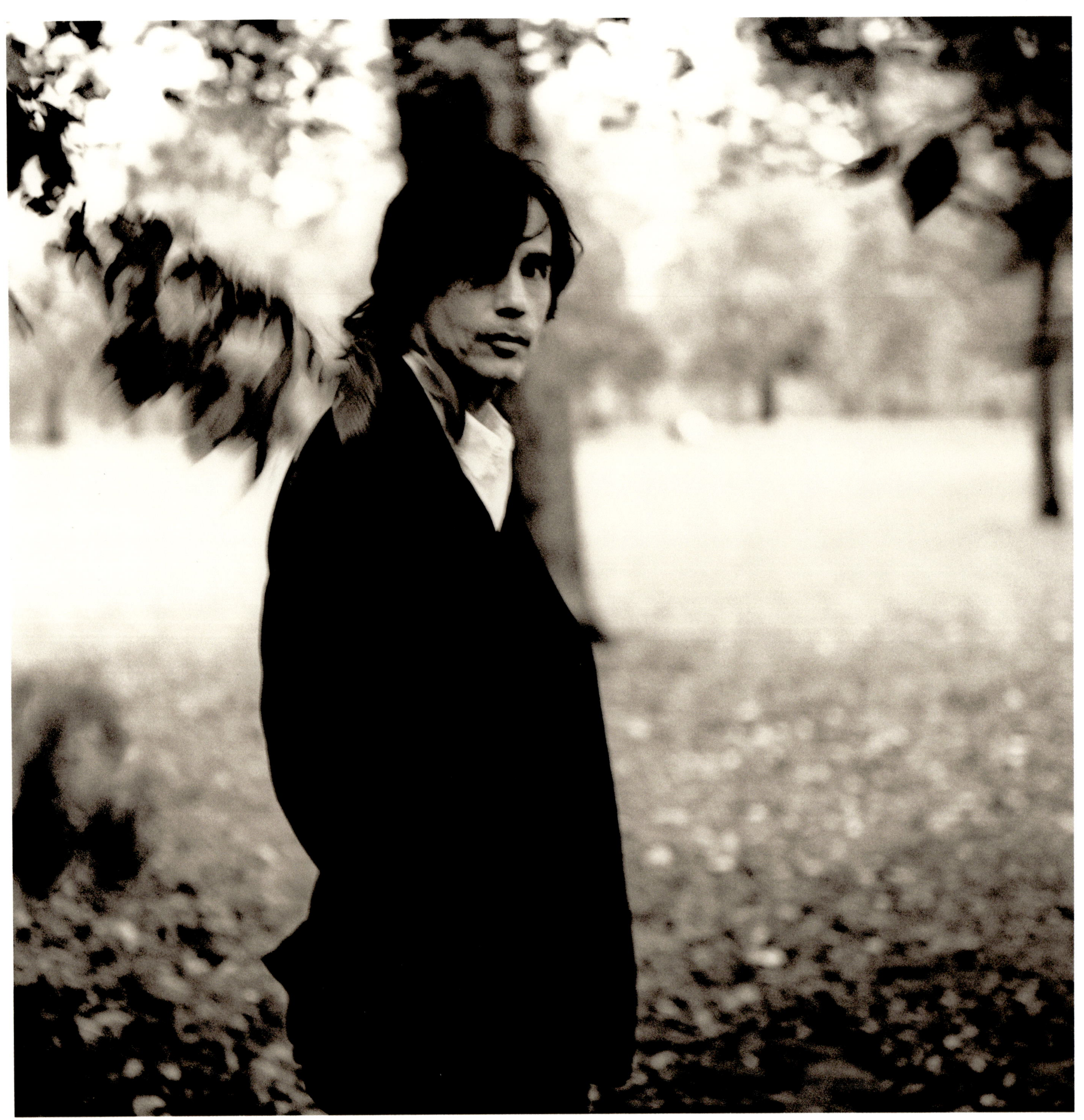

jackson browne

62

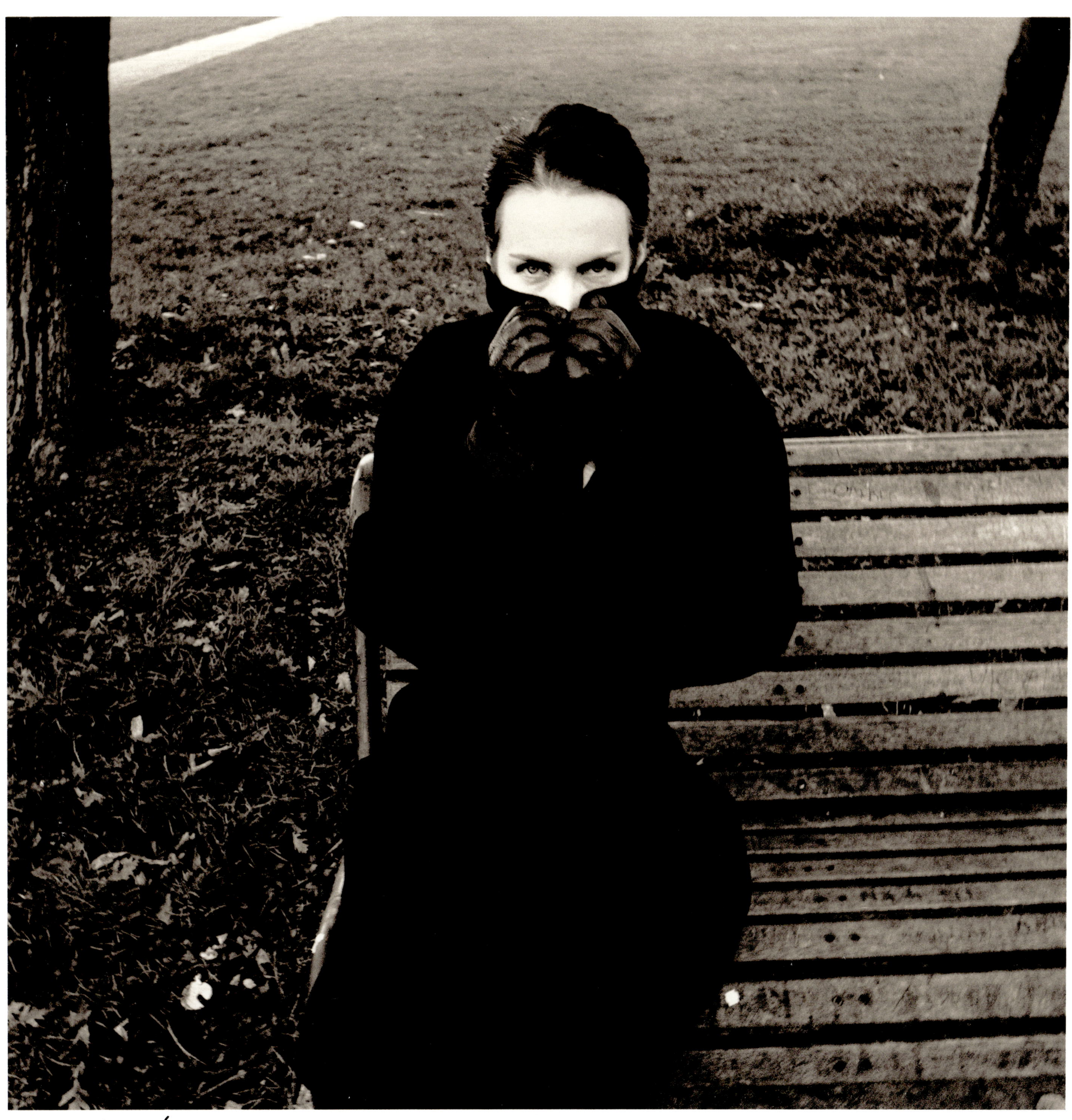

annie lennox

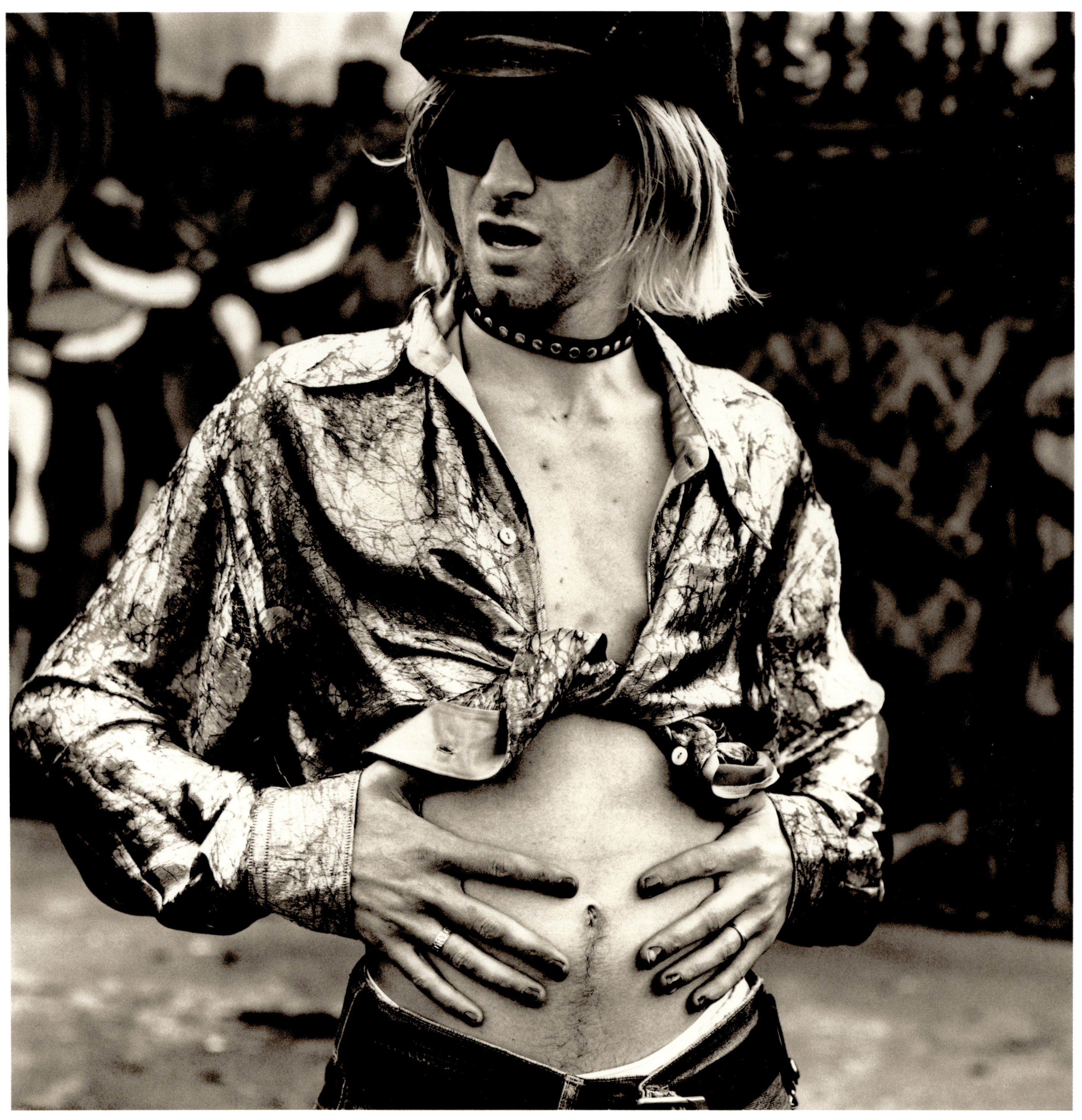

kurt cobain
64

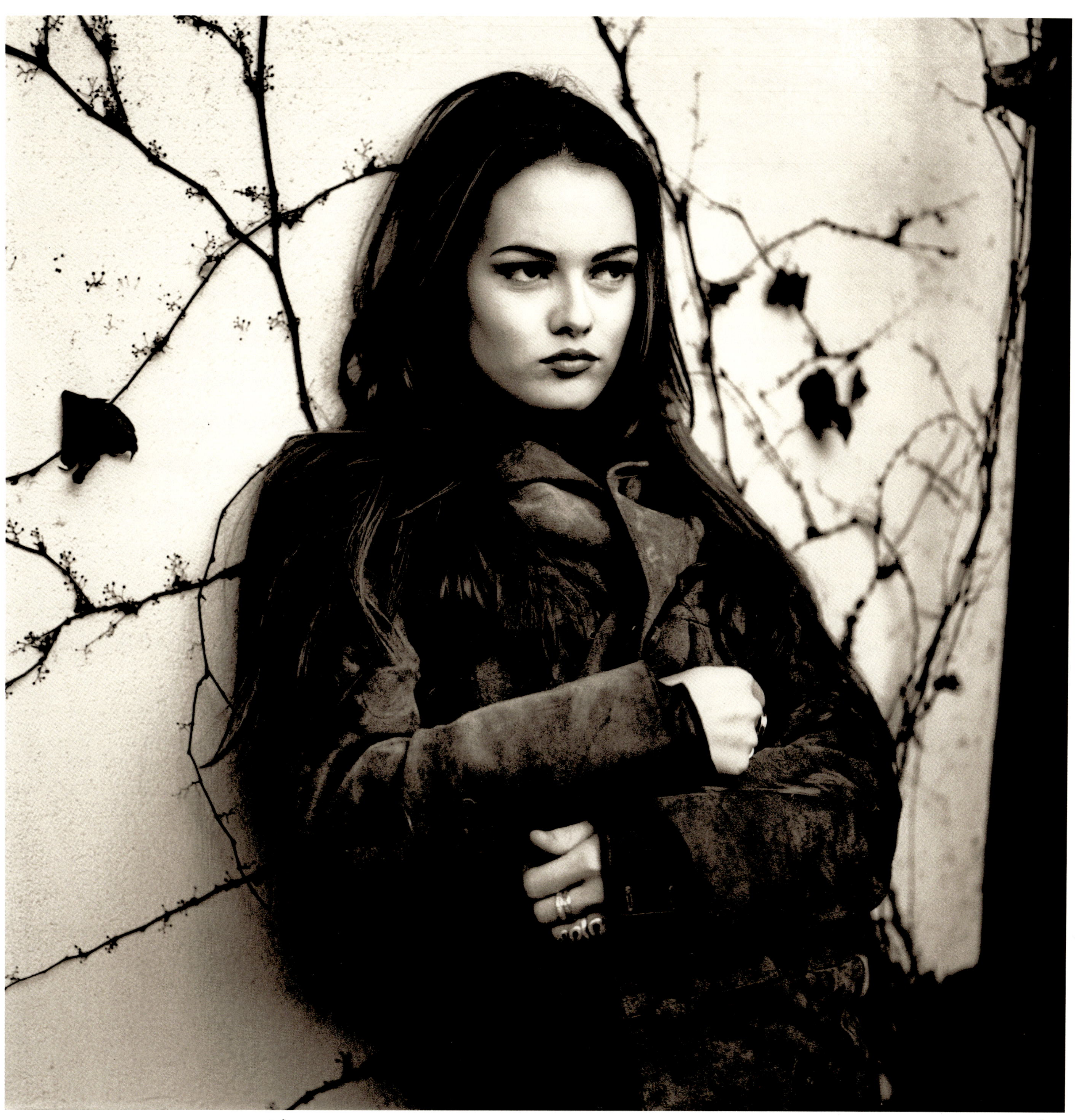

vanessa paradis

65

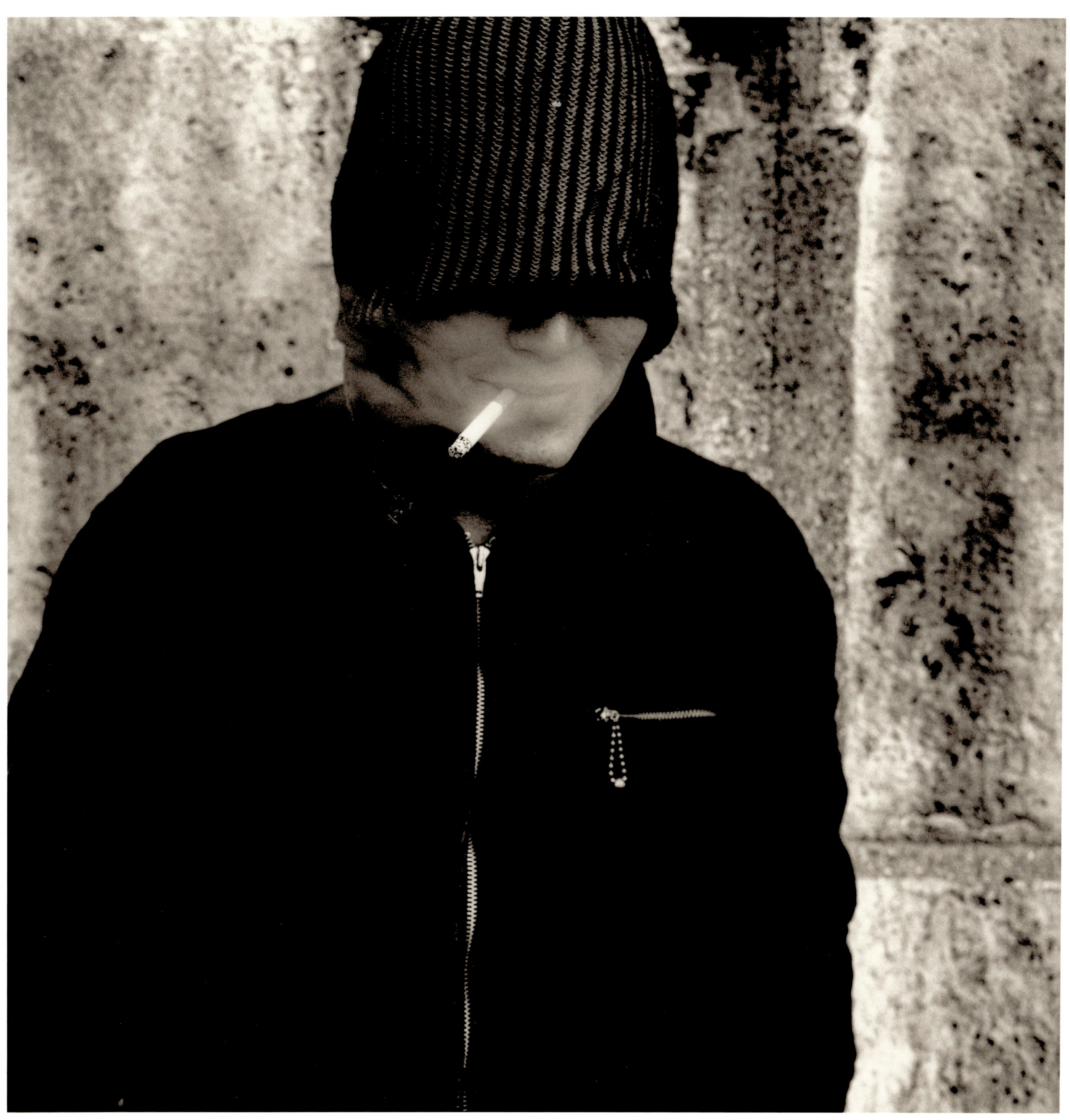

johnny depp

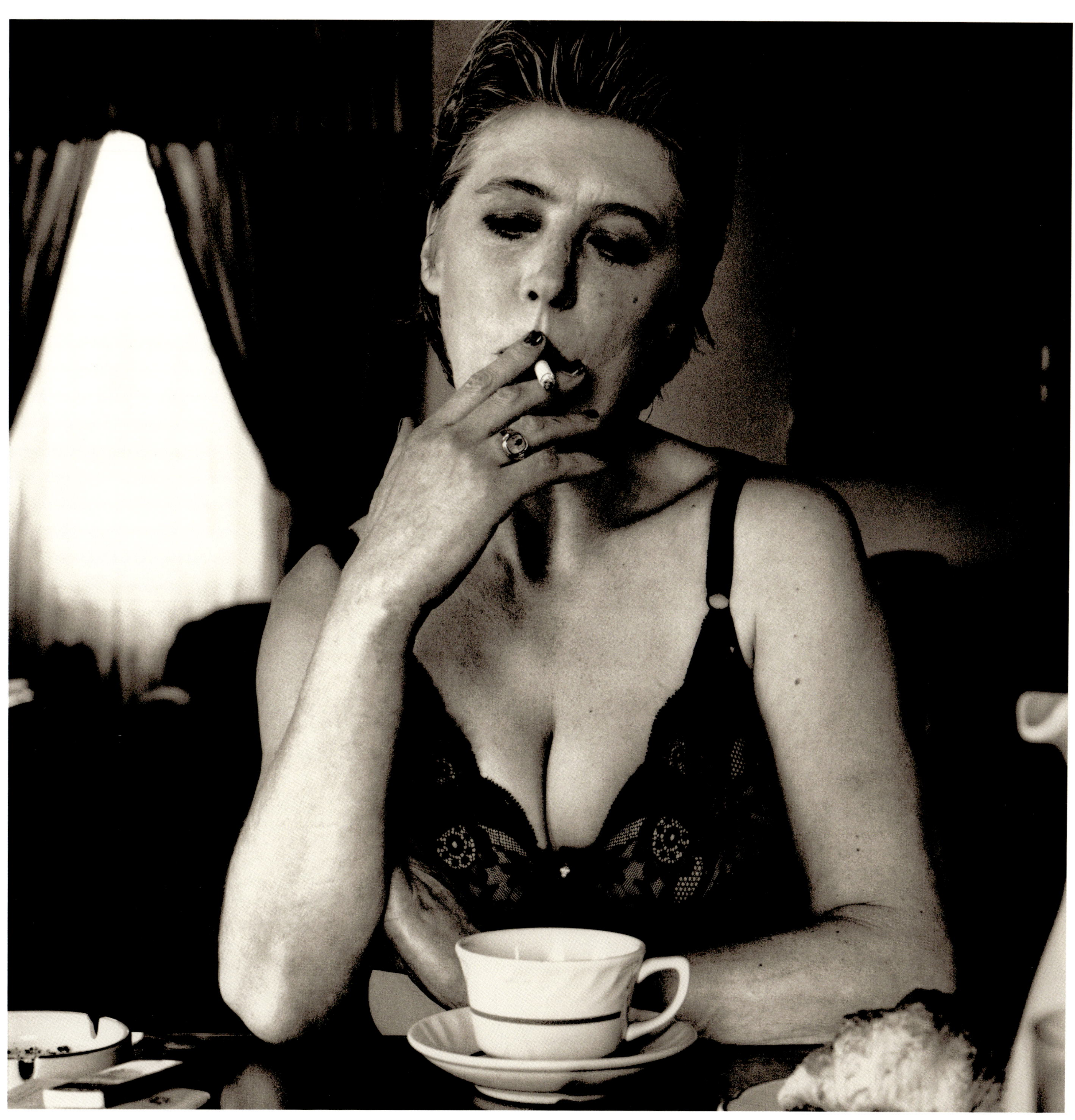

67

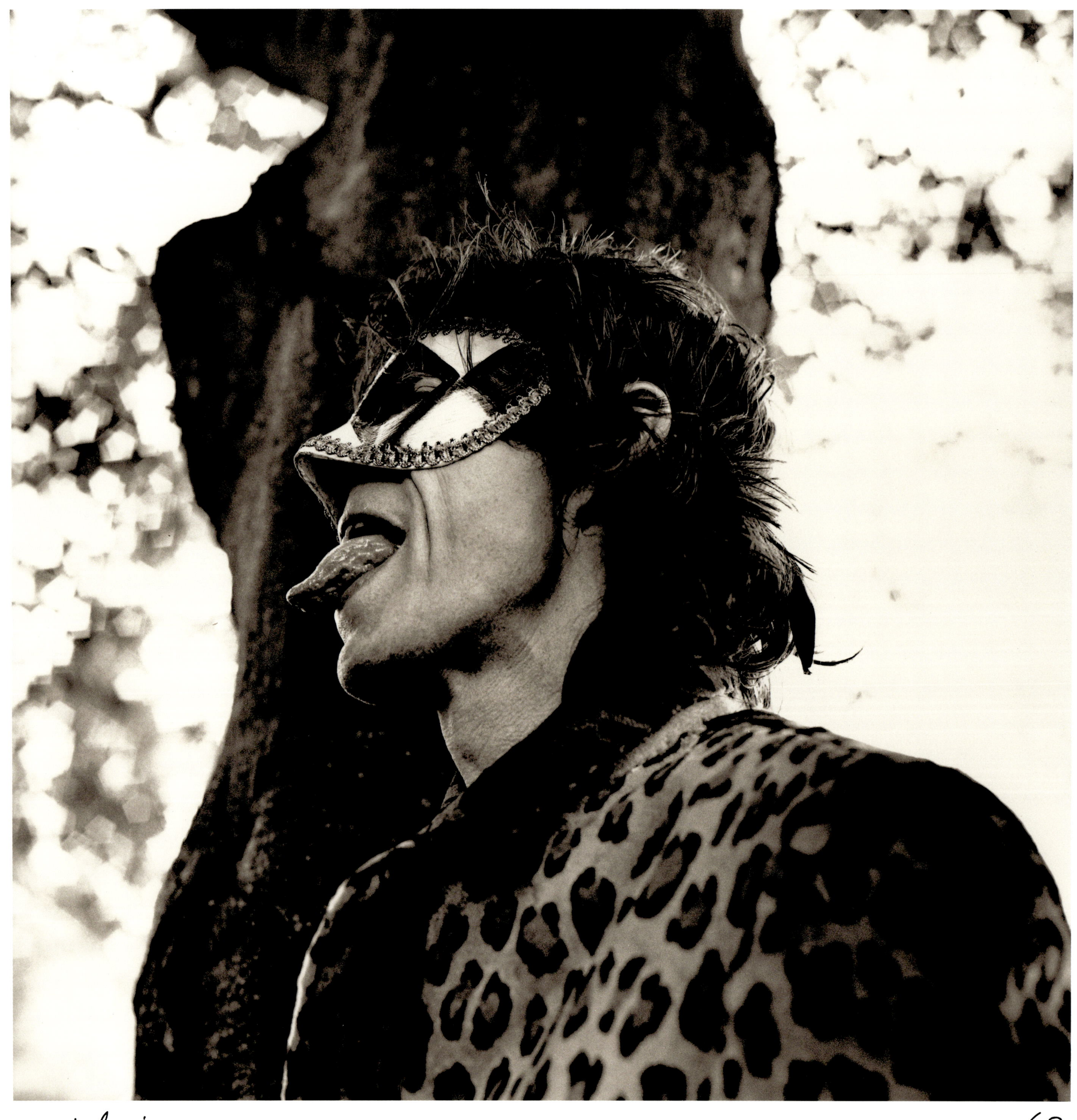

mick jagger

68

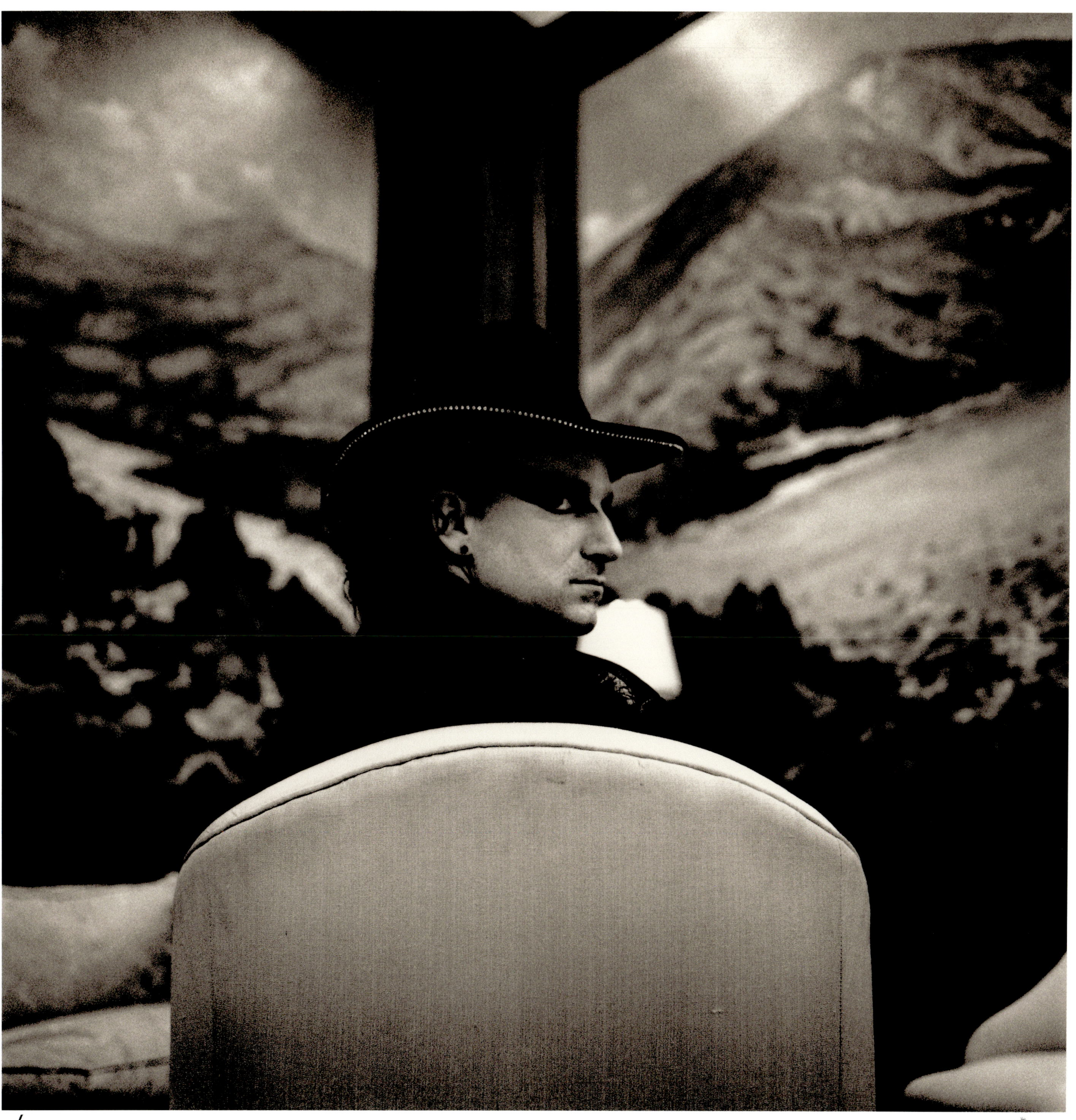

bono

69

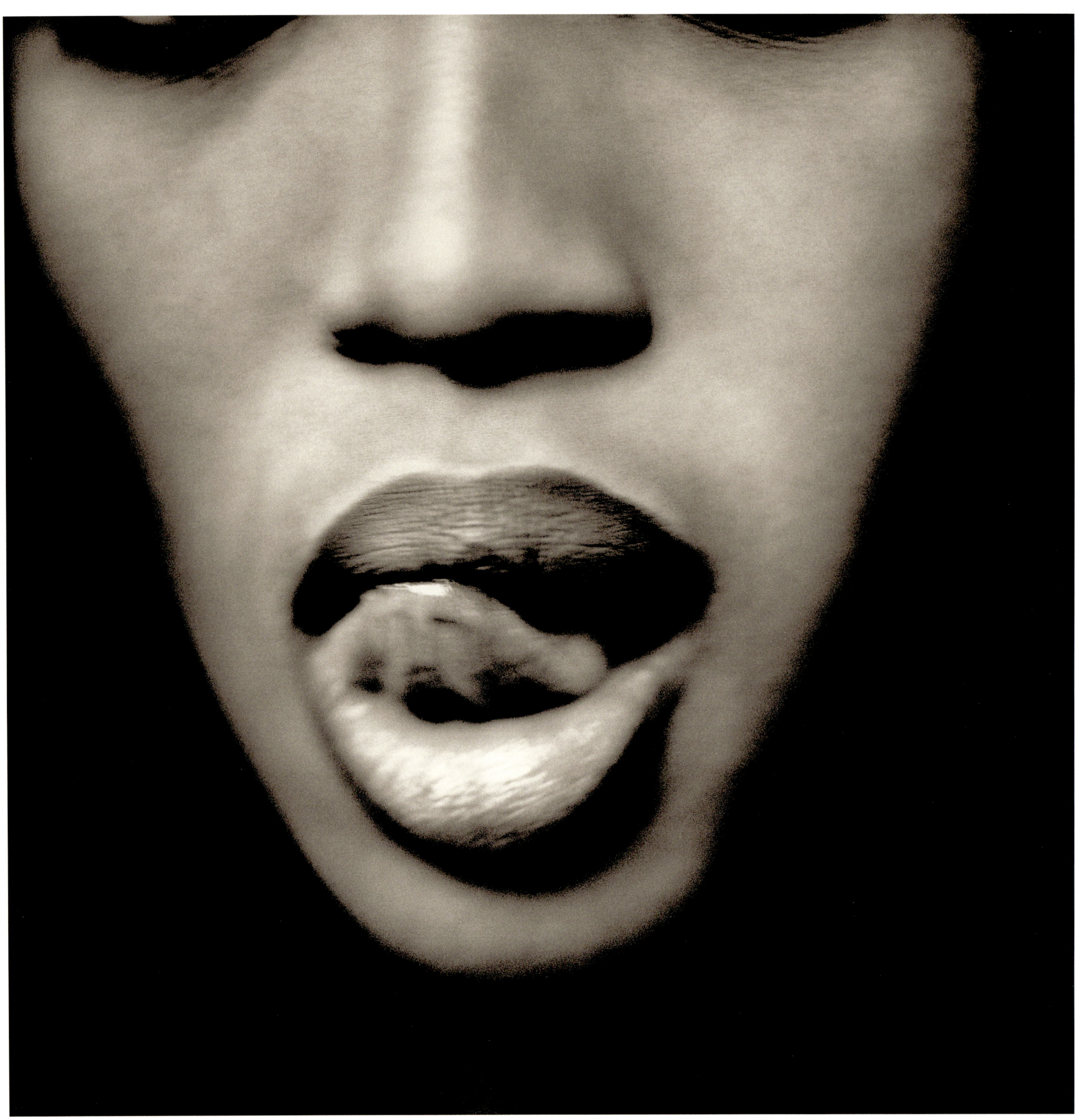

naomi campbell

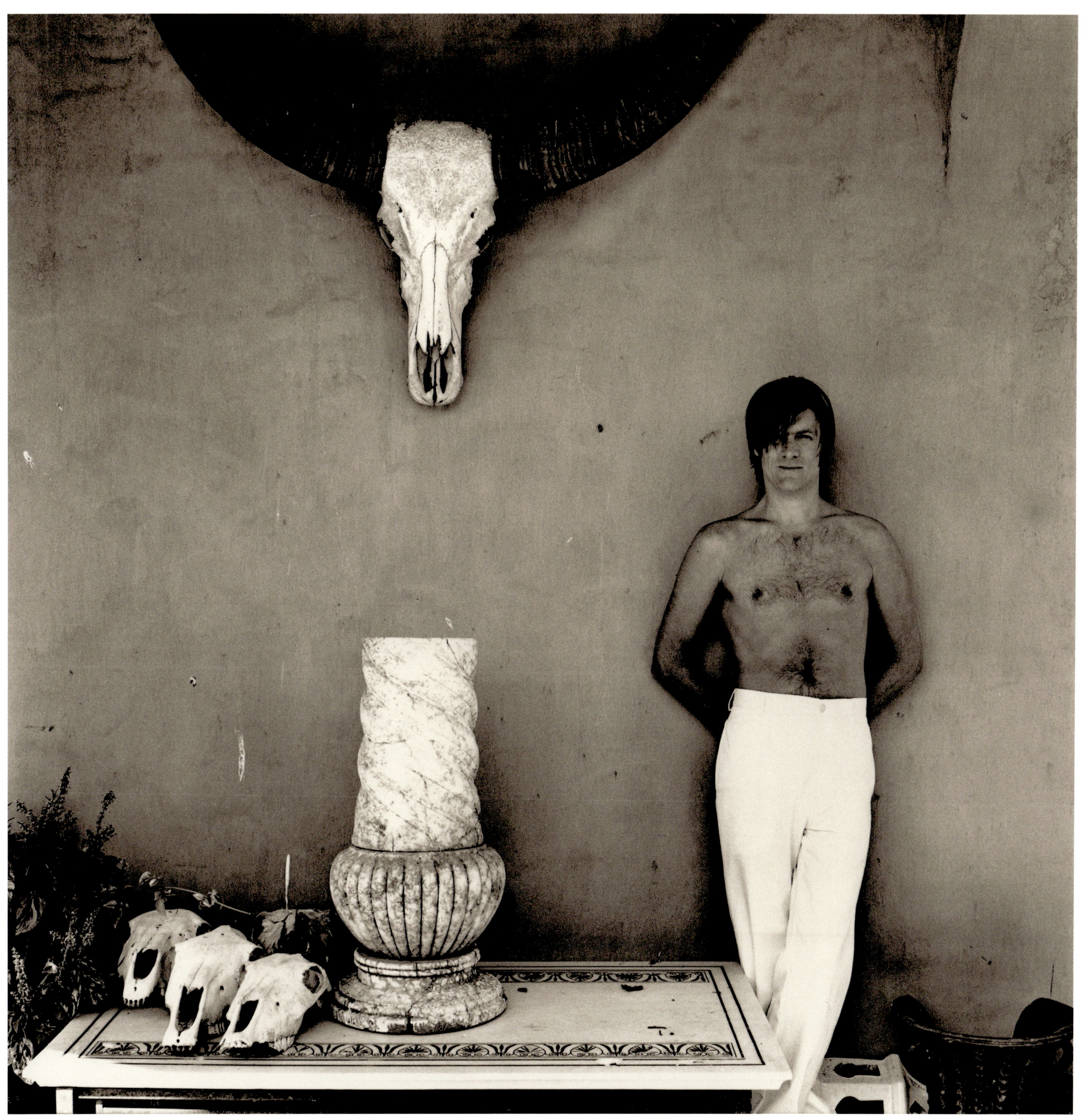

bryan adams

71

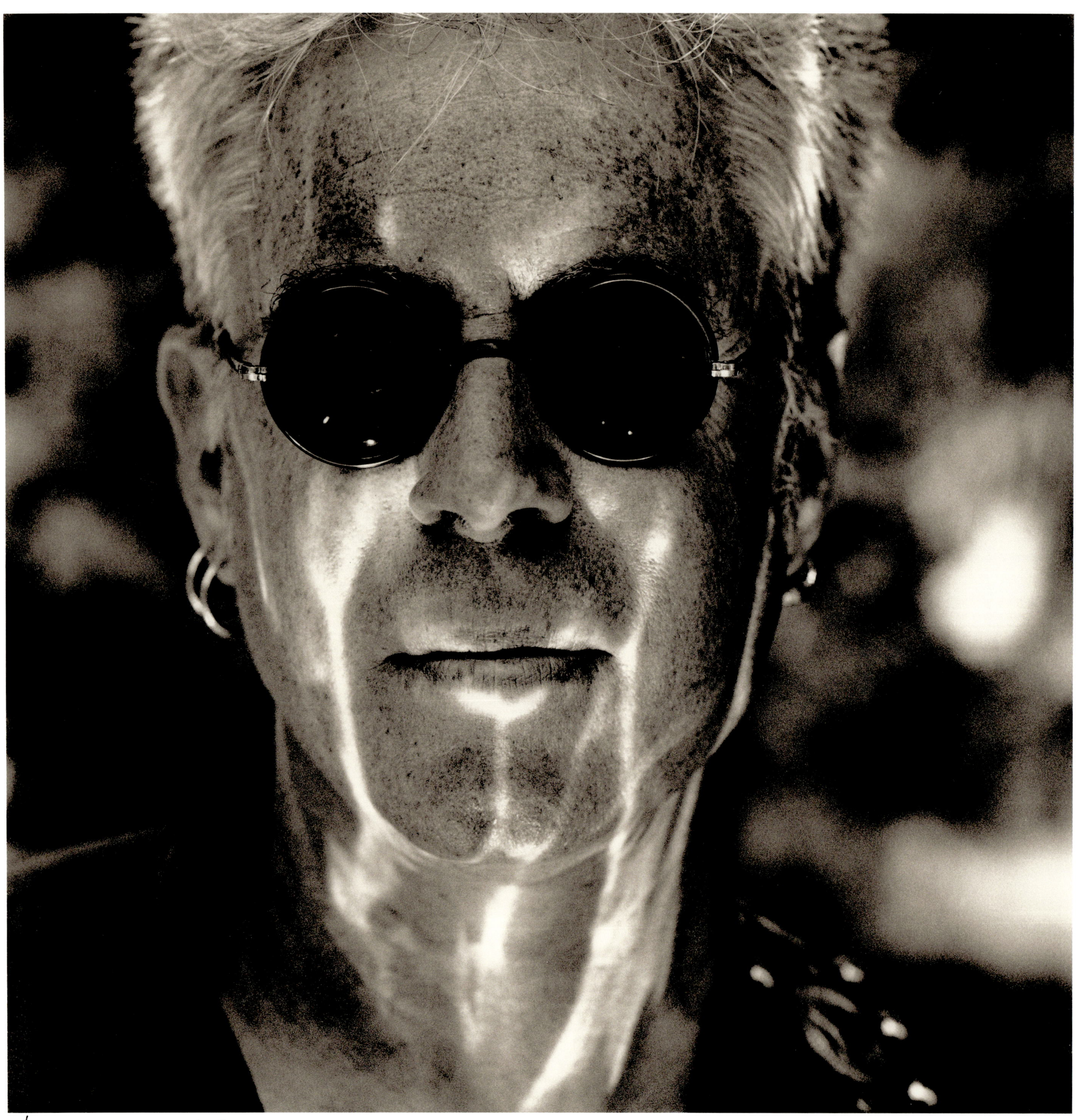

bruce cockburn

72

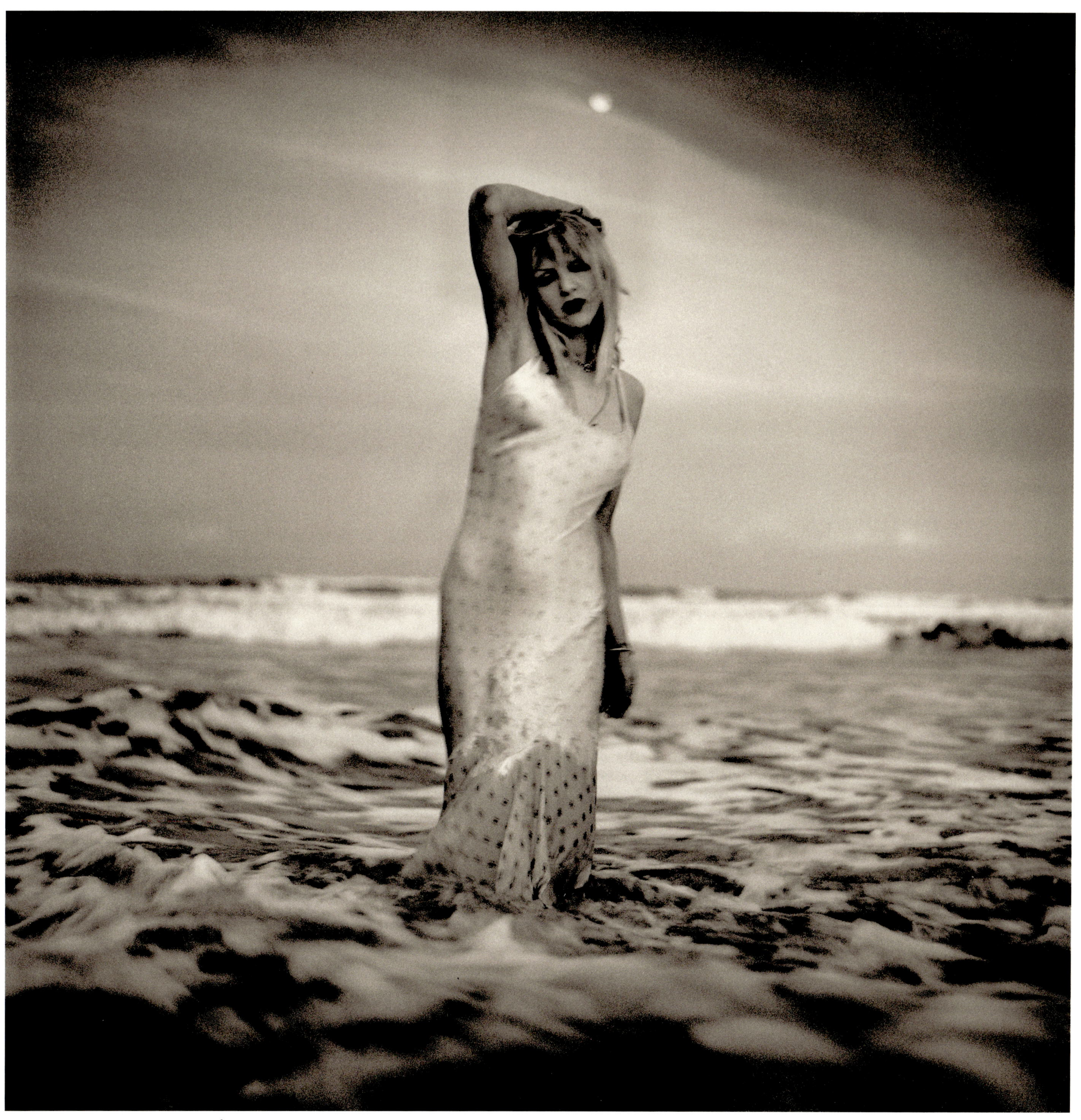

courtney love

73

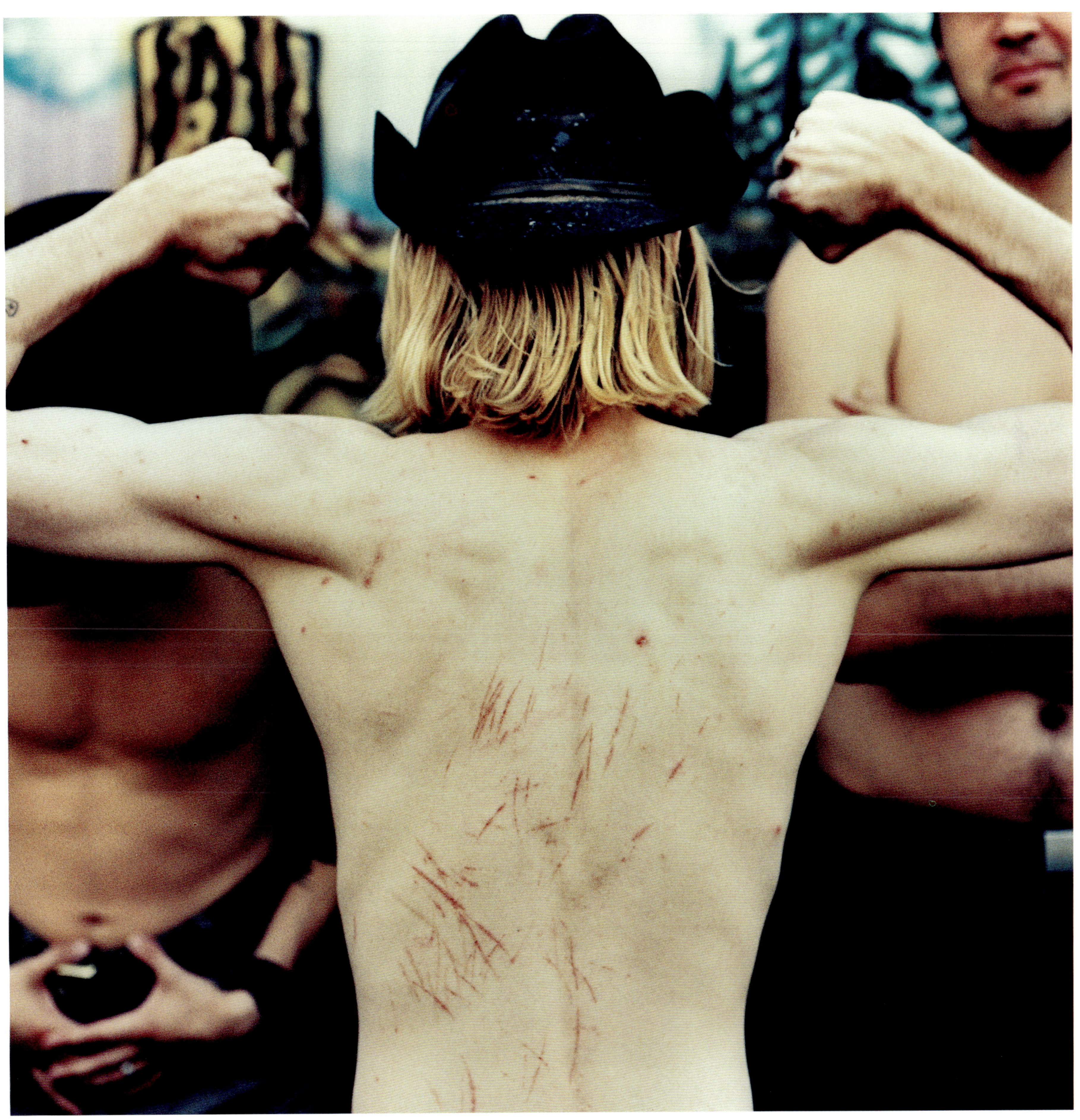

kurt's back

74

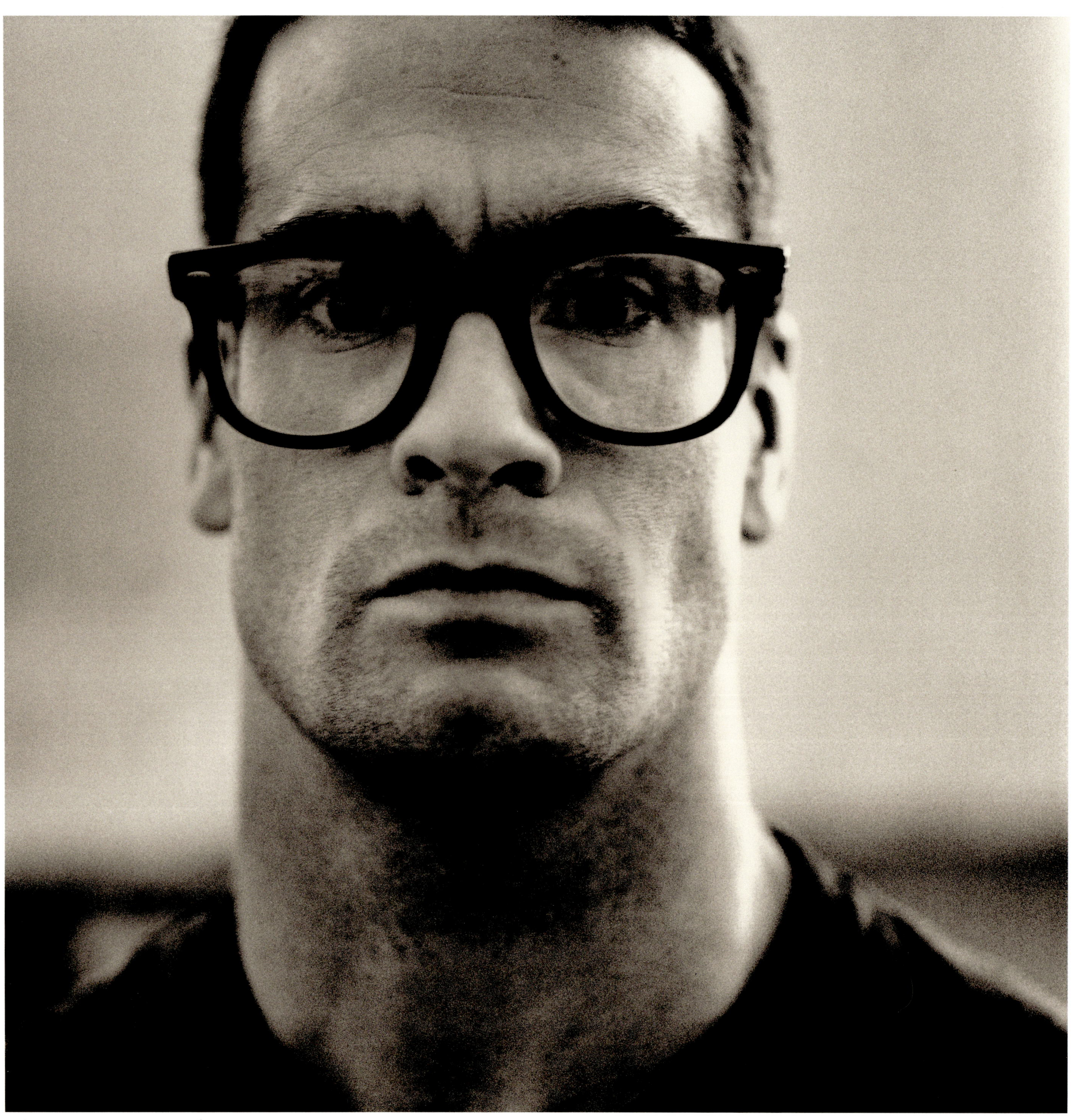

henry rollins

75

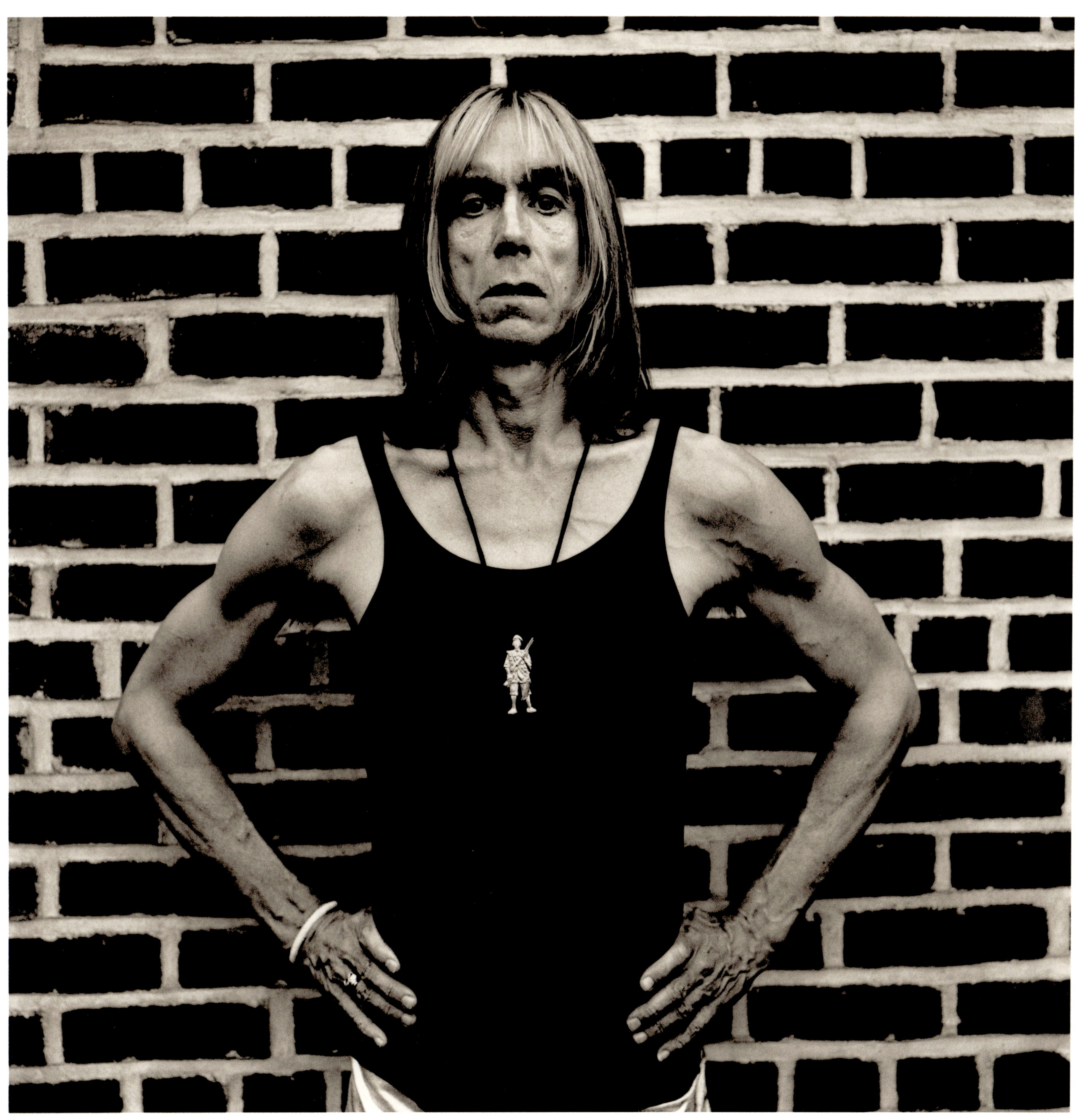

iggy pop
76

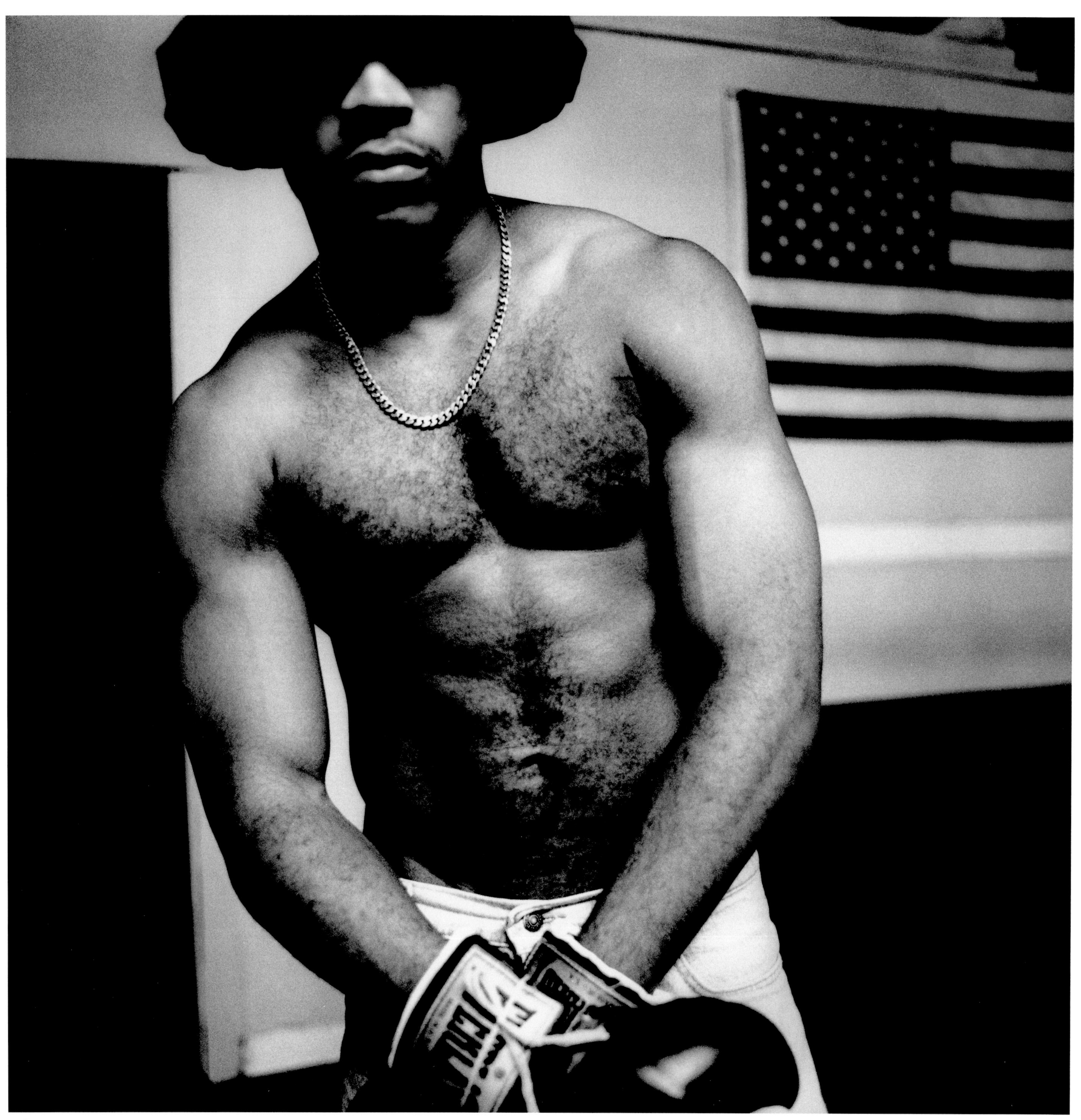

llcoolj

77

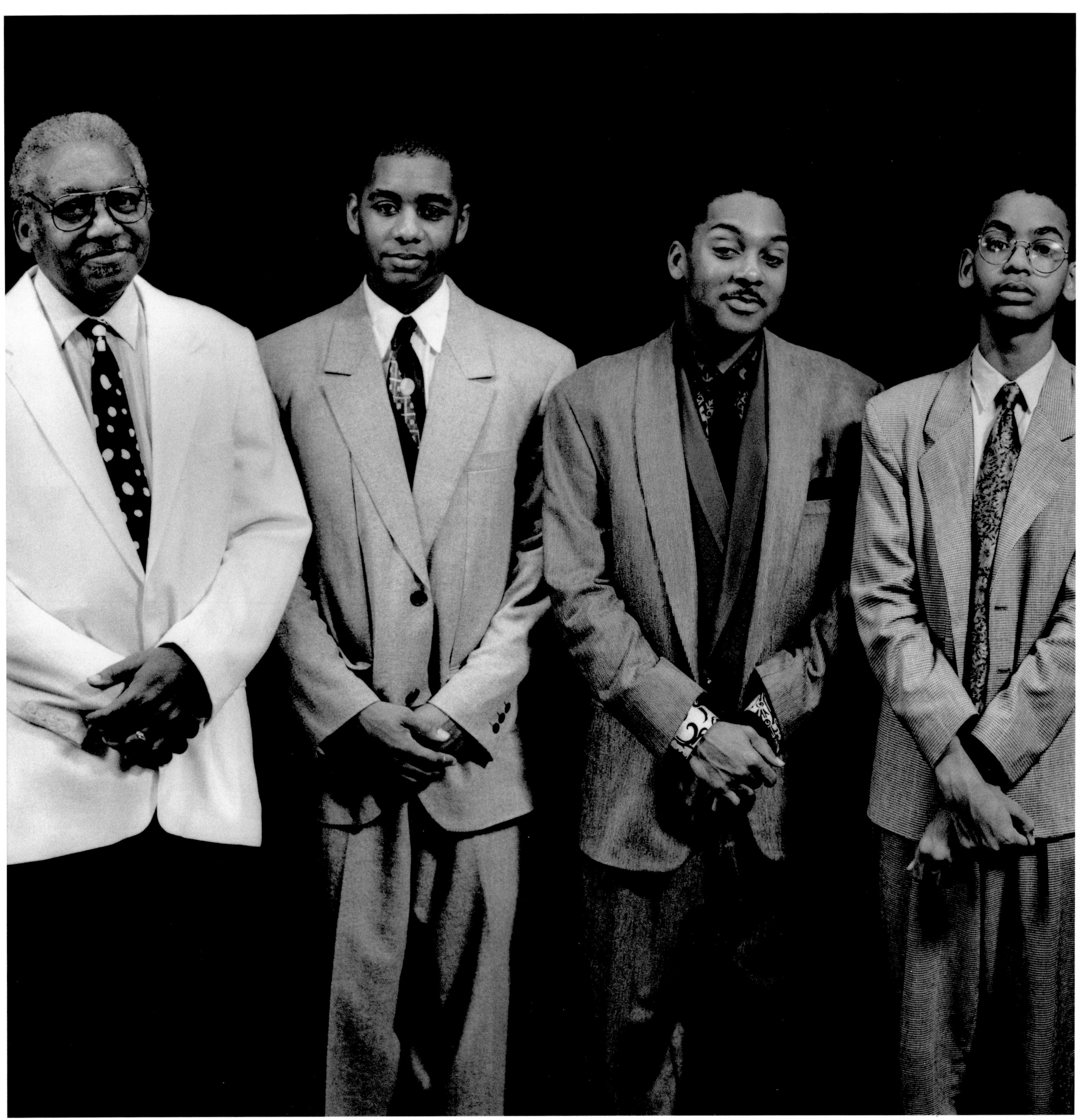

the marsalis family

78

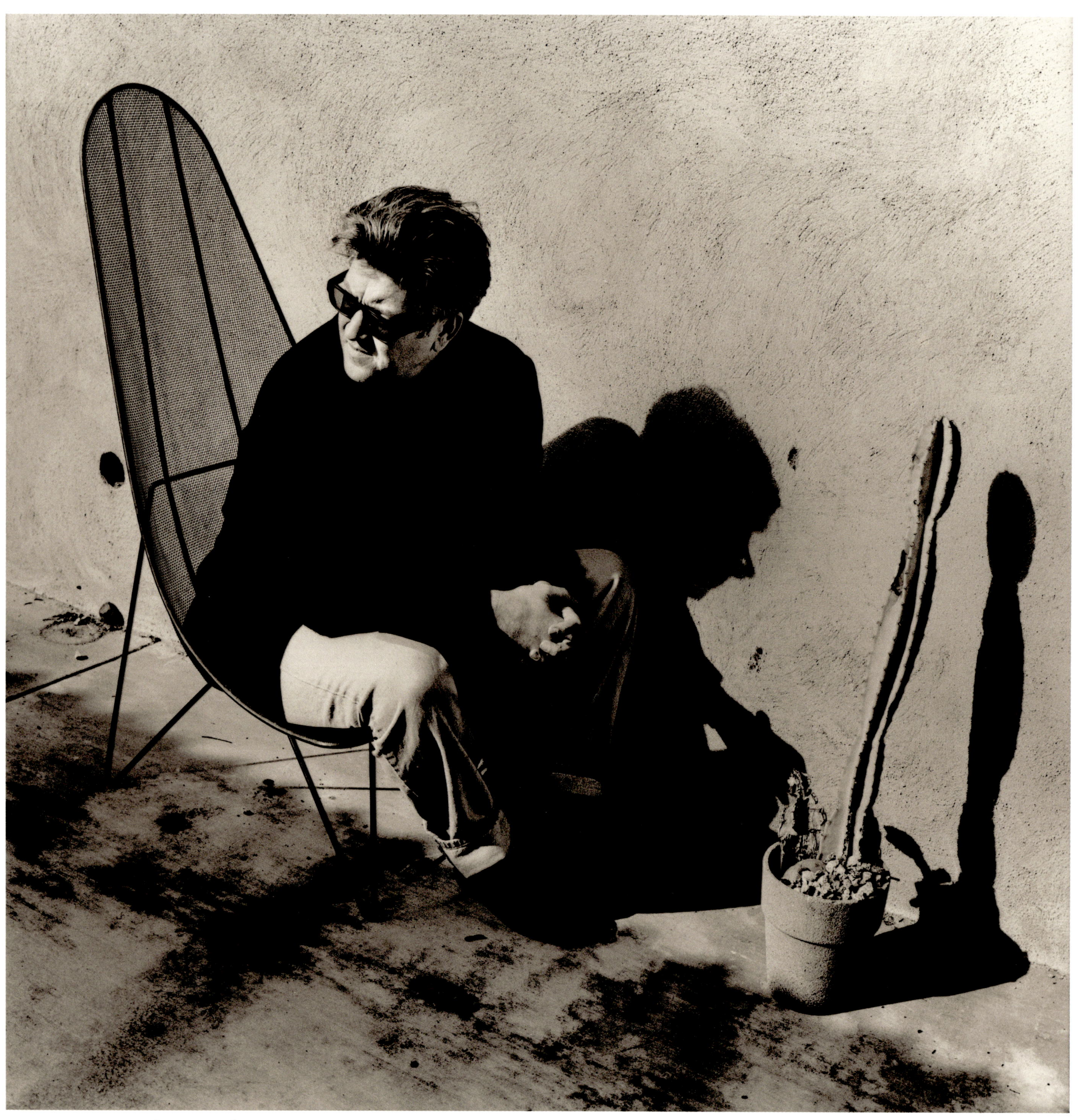
david lynch
79

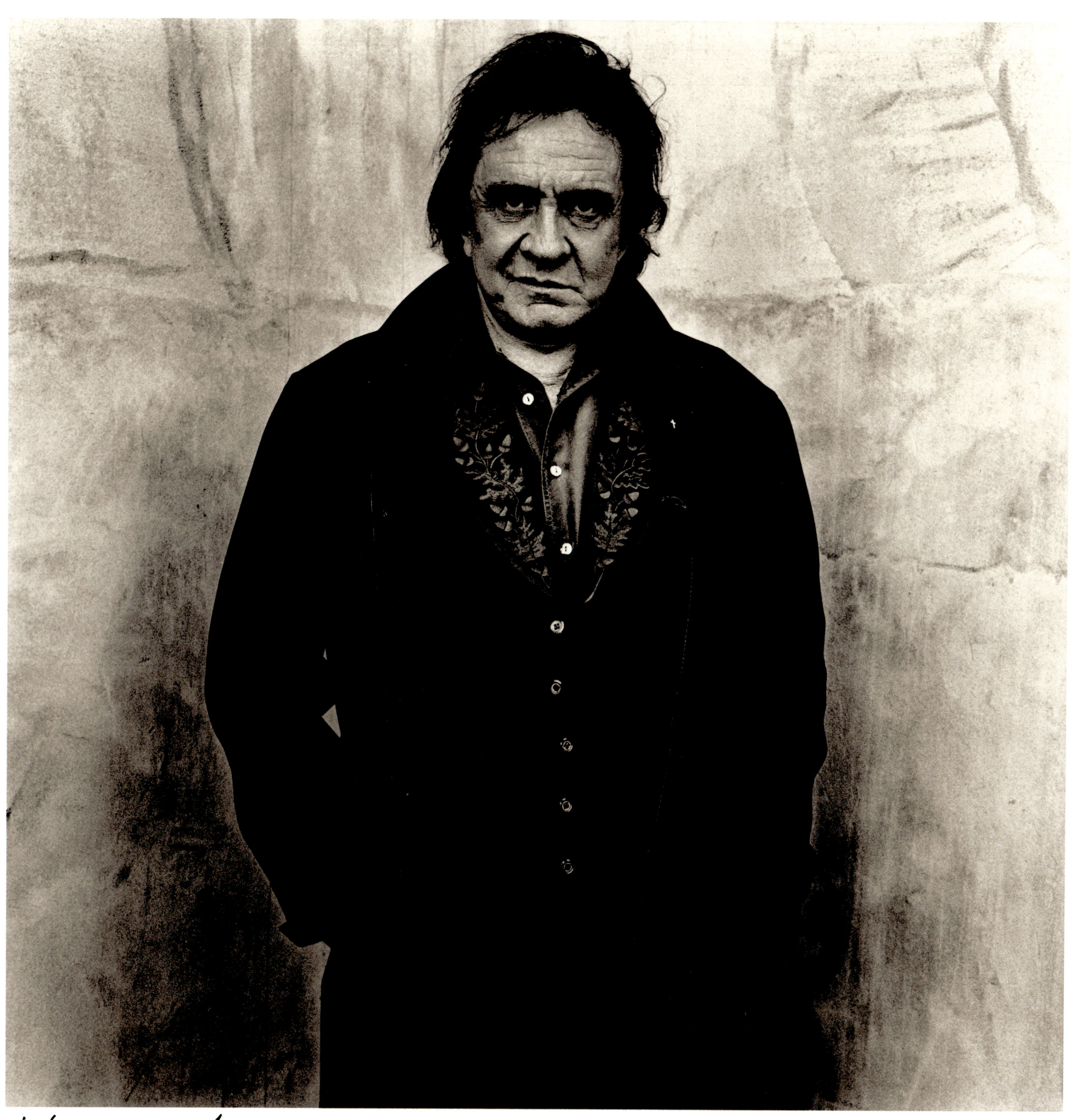

johnny cash
80

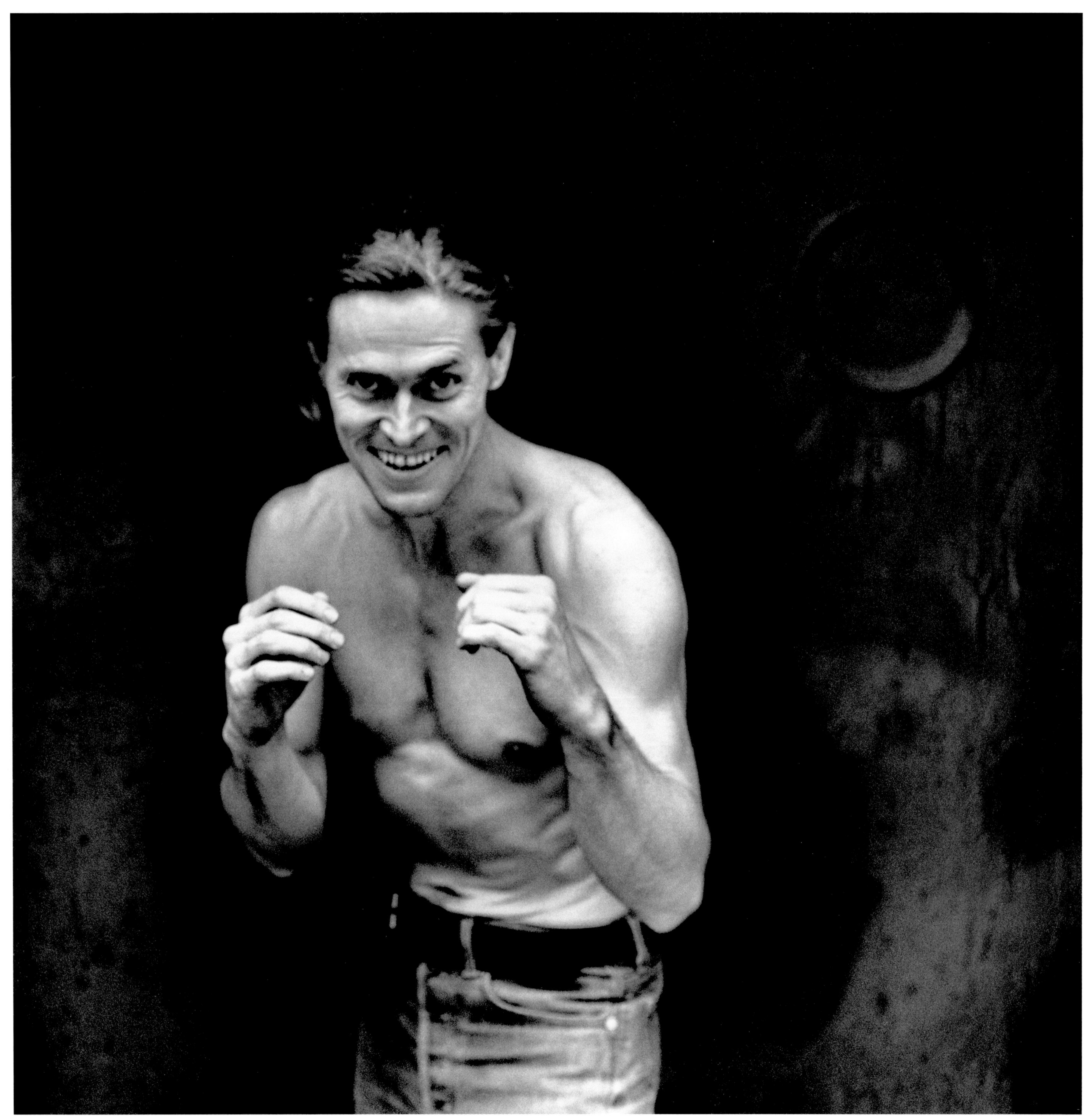

willem dafoe
81

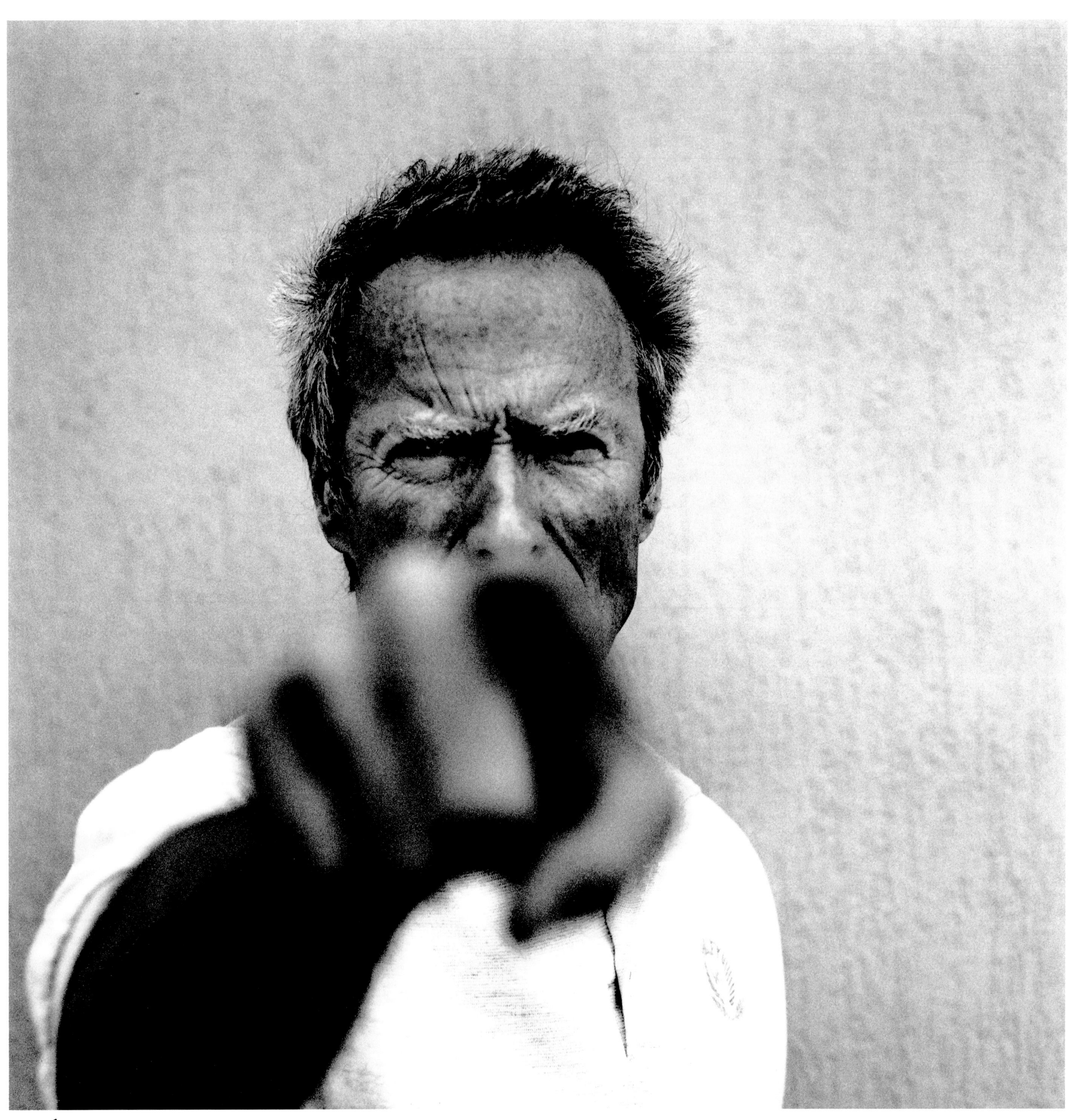

clint eastwood

82

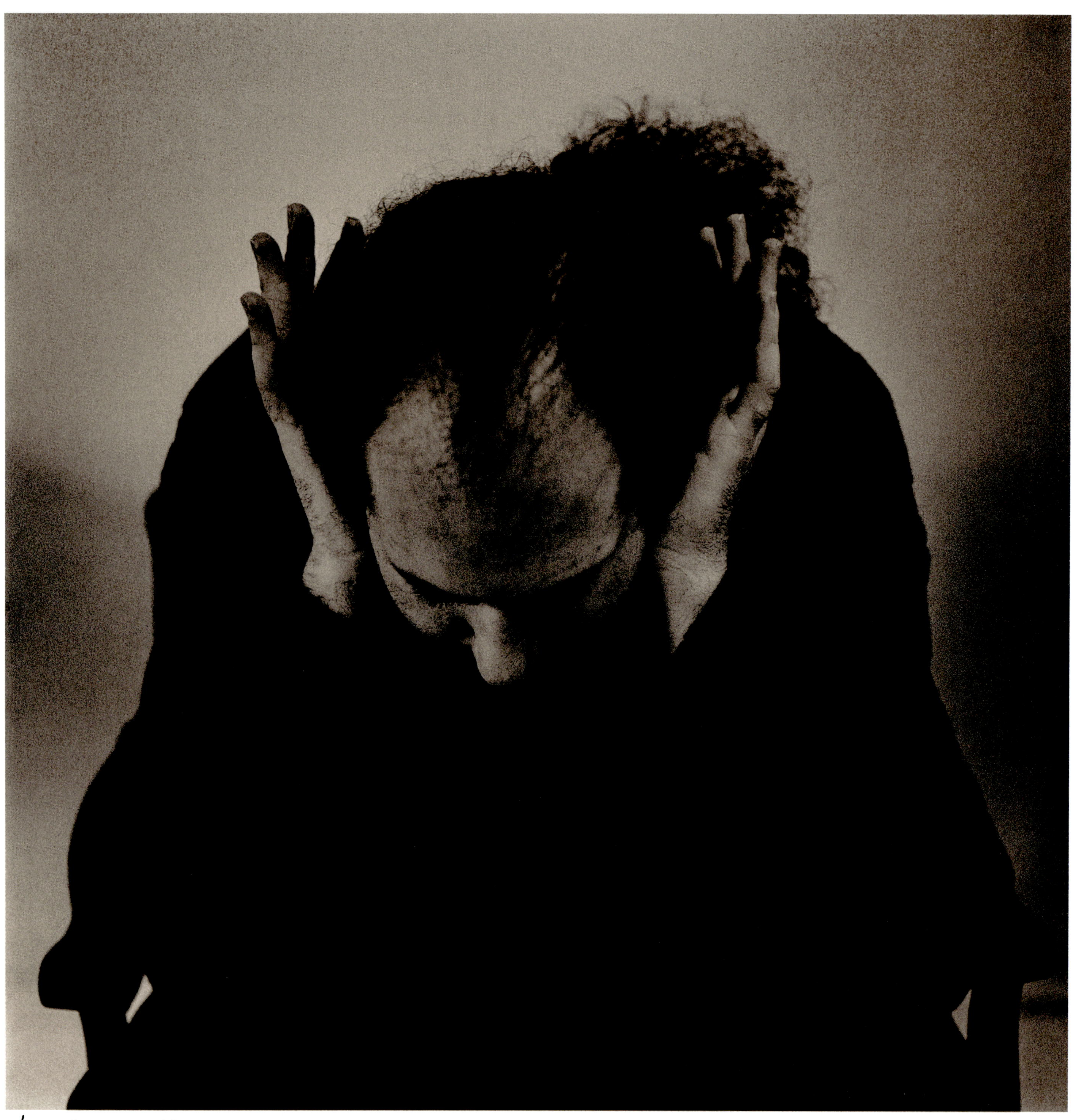

hal willner

83

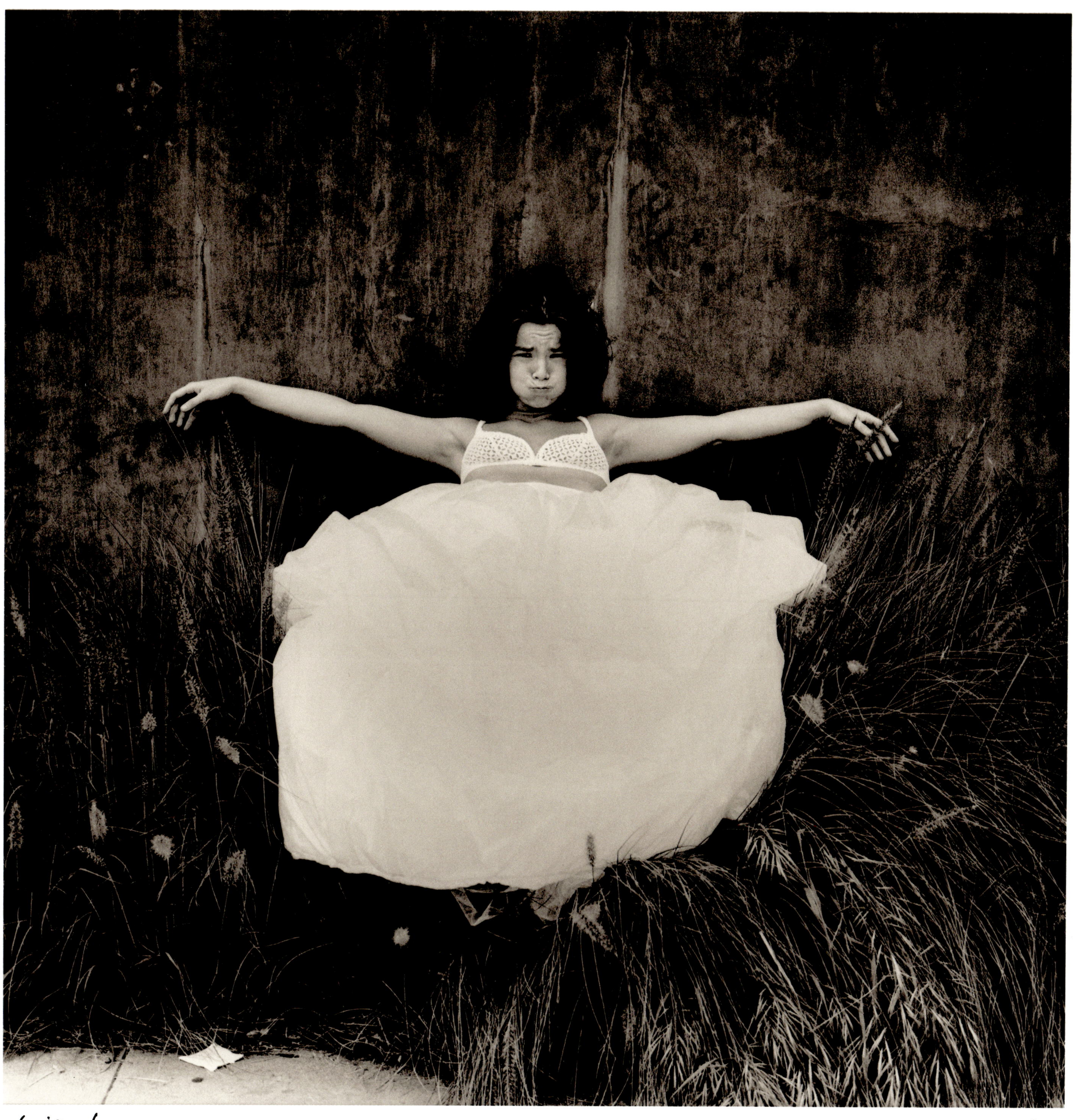

björk

84

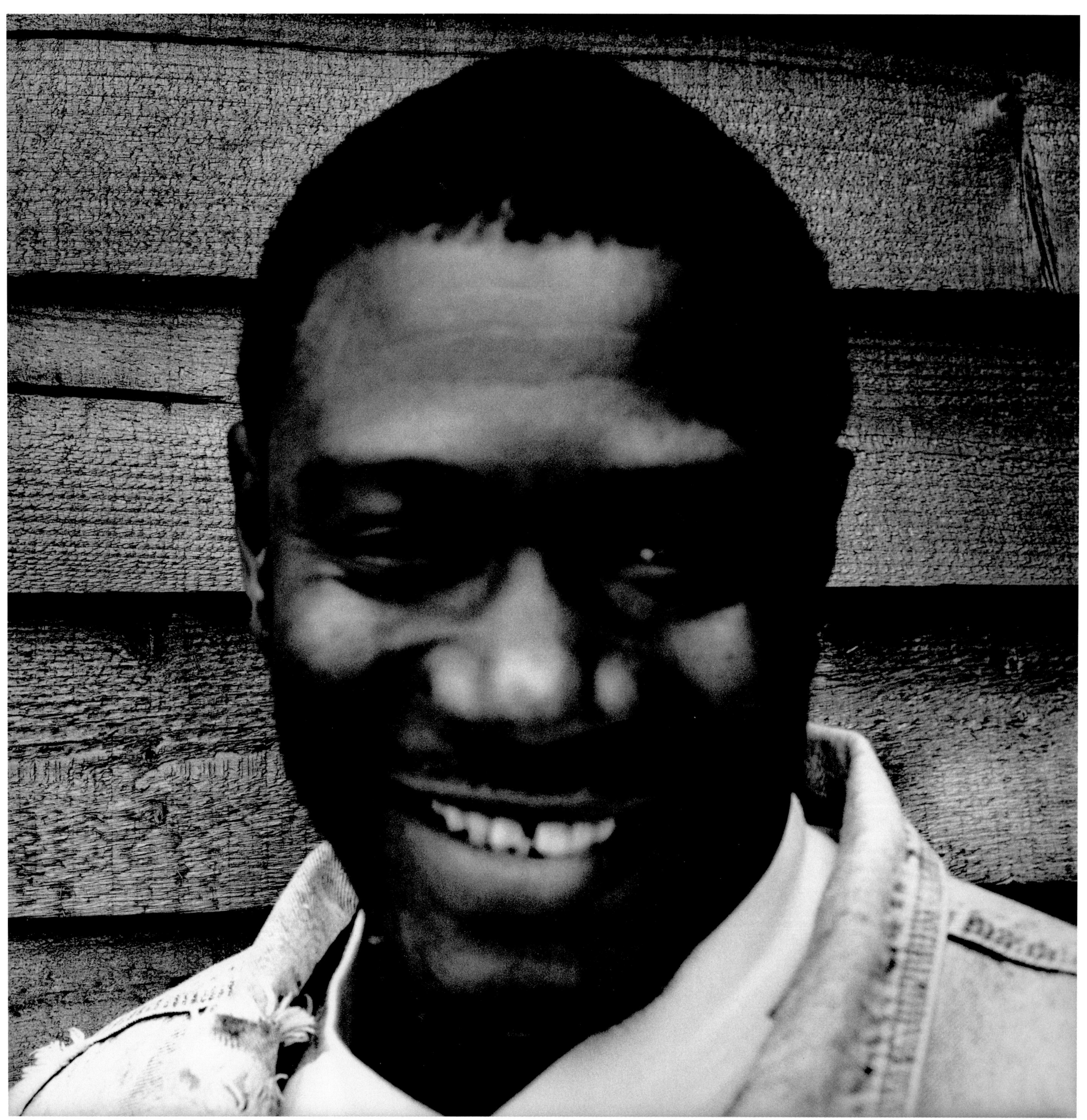

horace andy

85

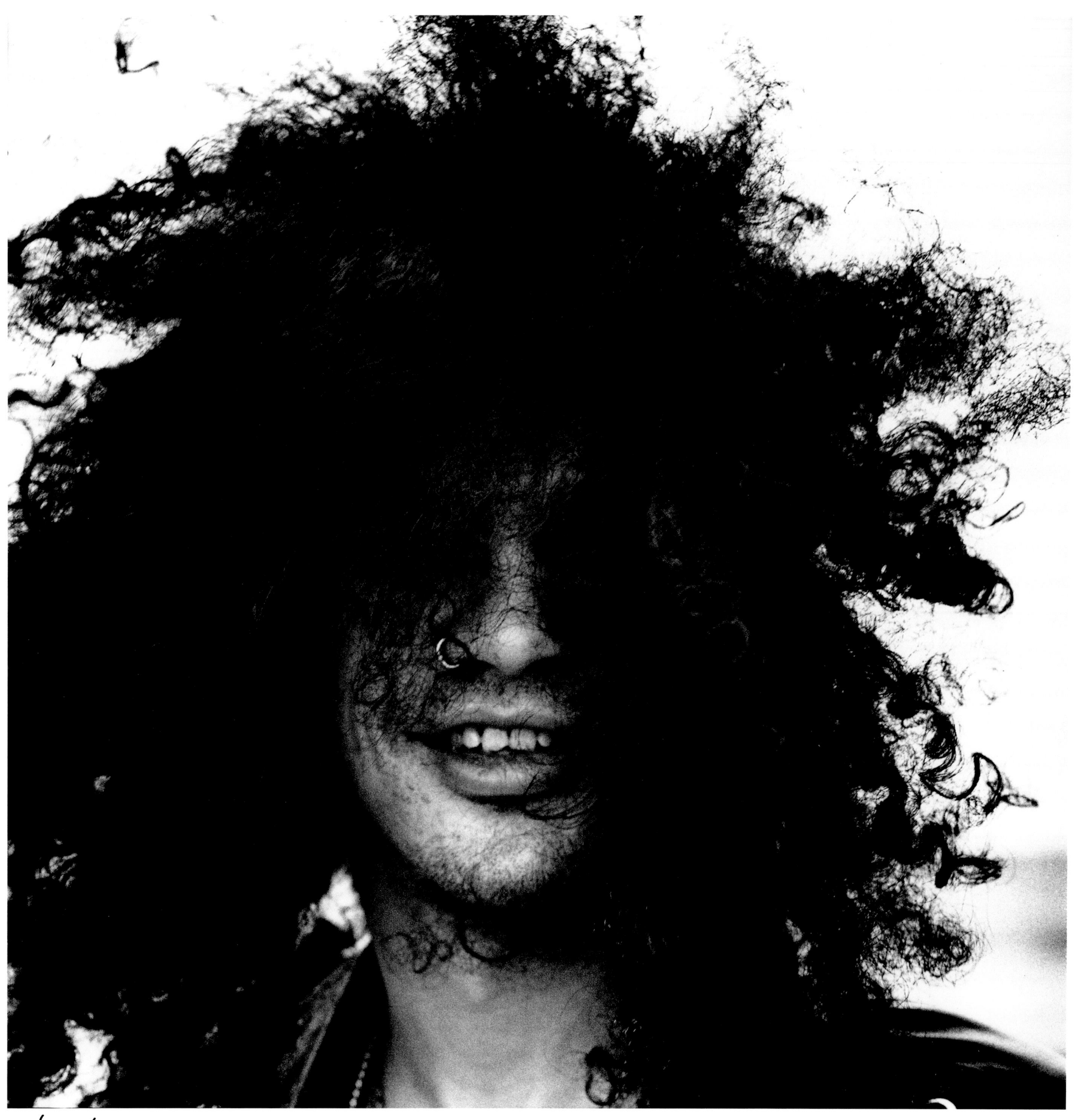

slash
86

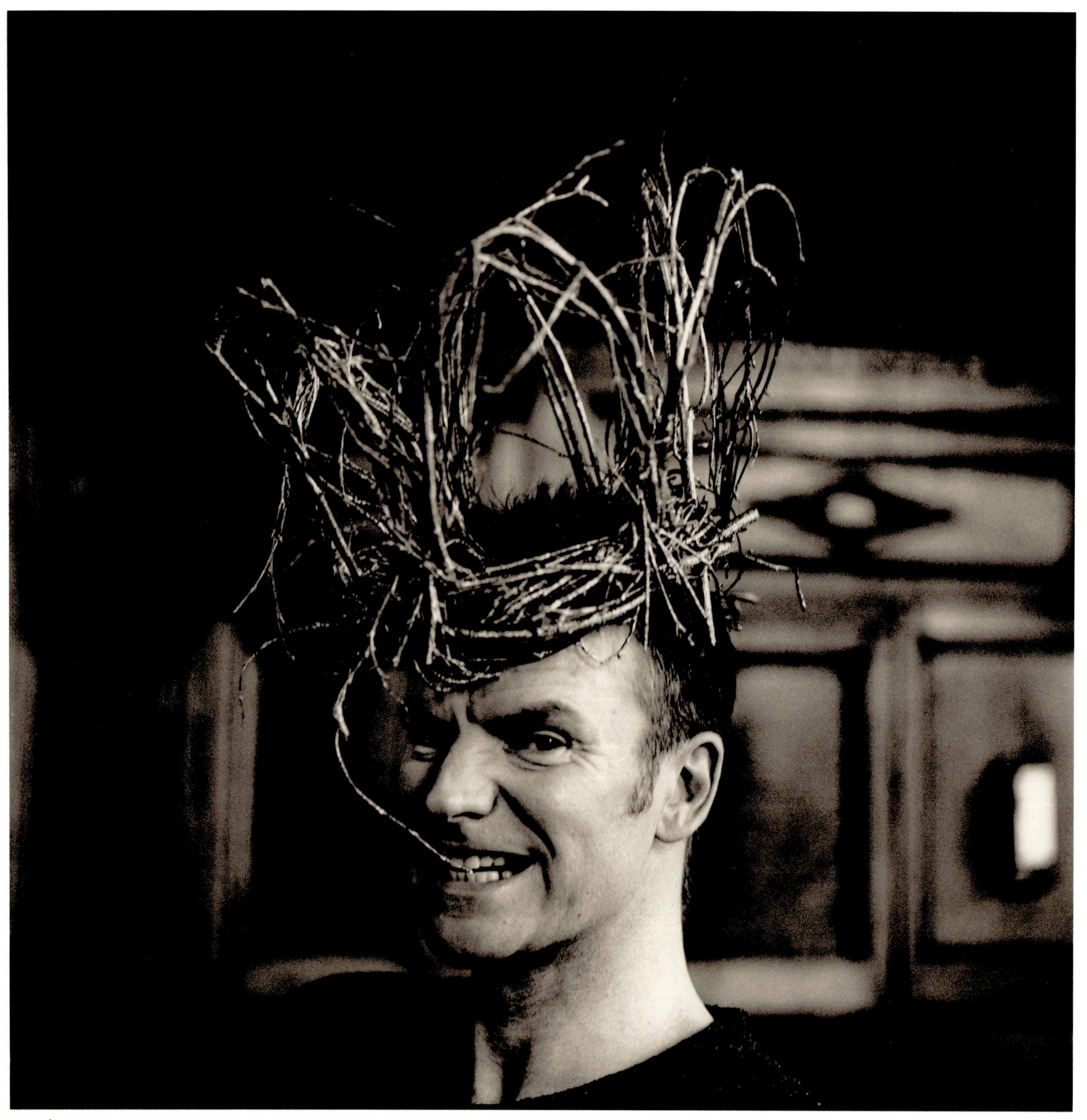
sting
87

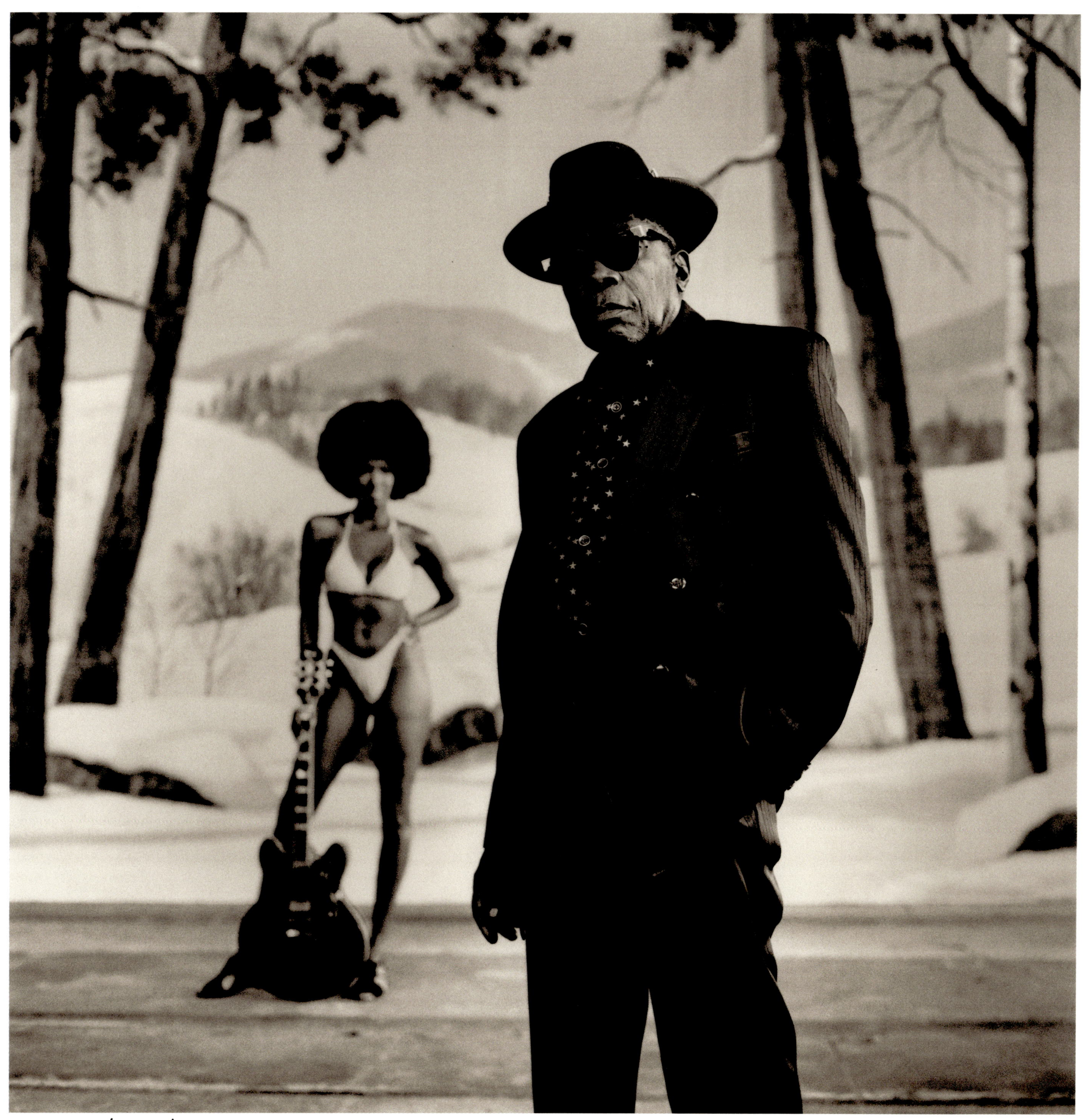

john lee hooker

88

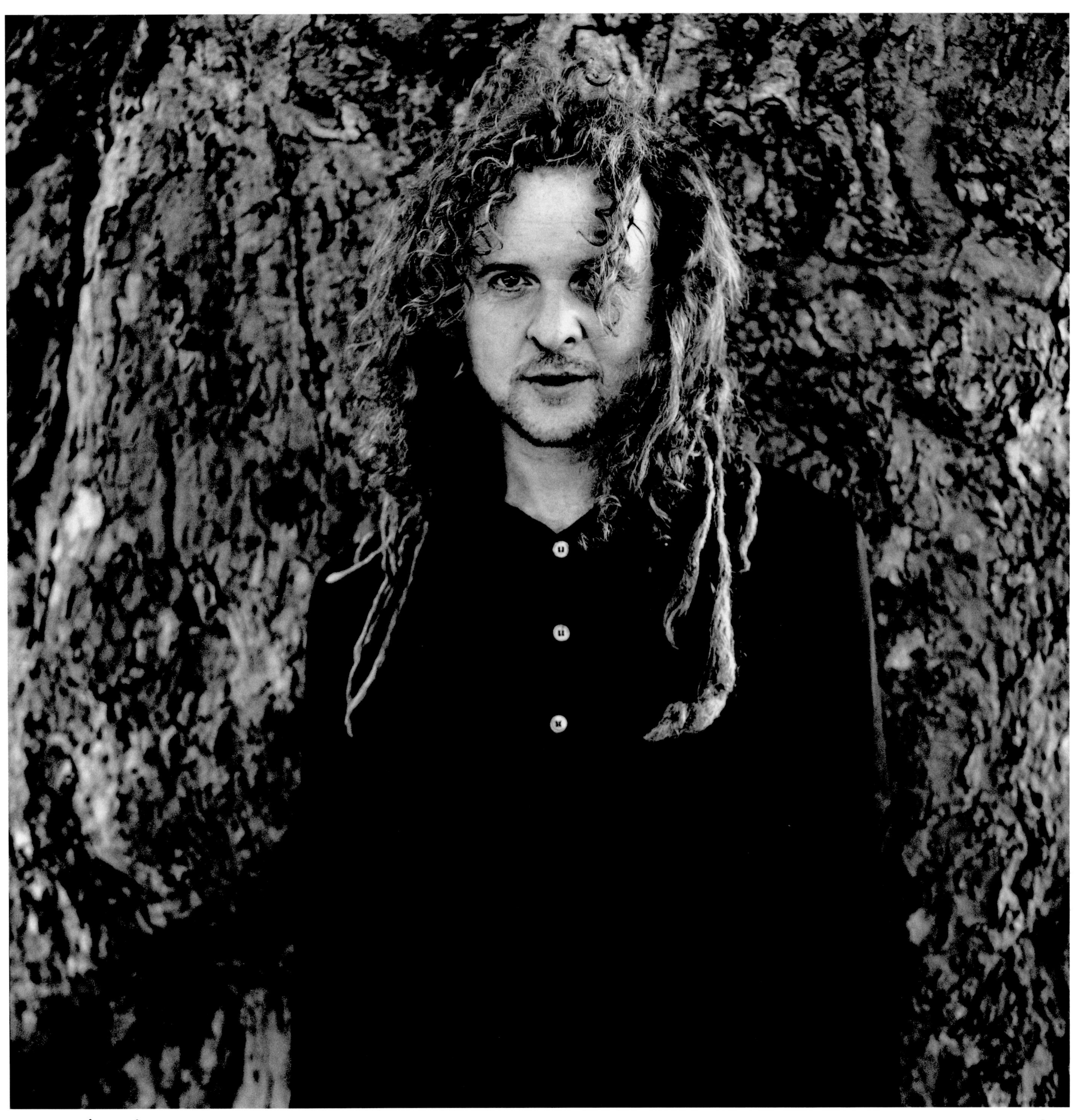

mick hucknall

89

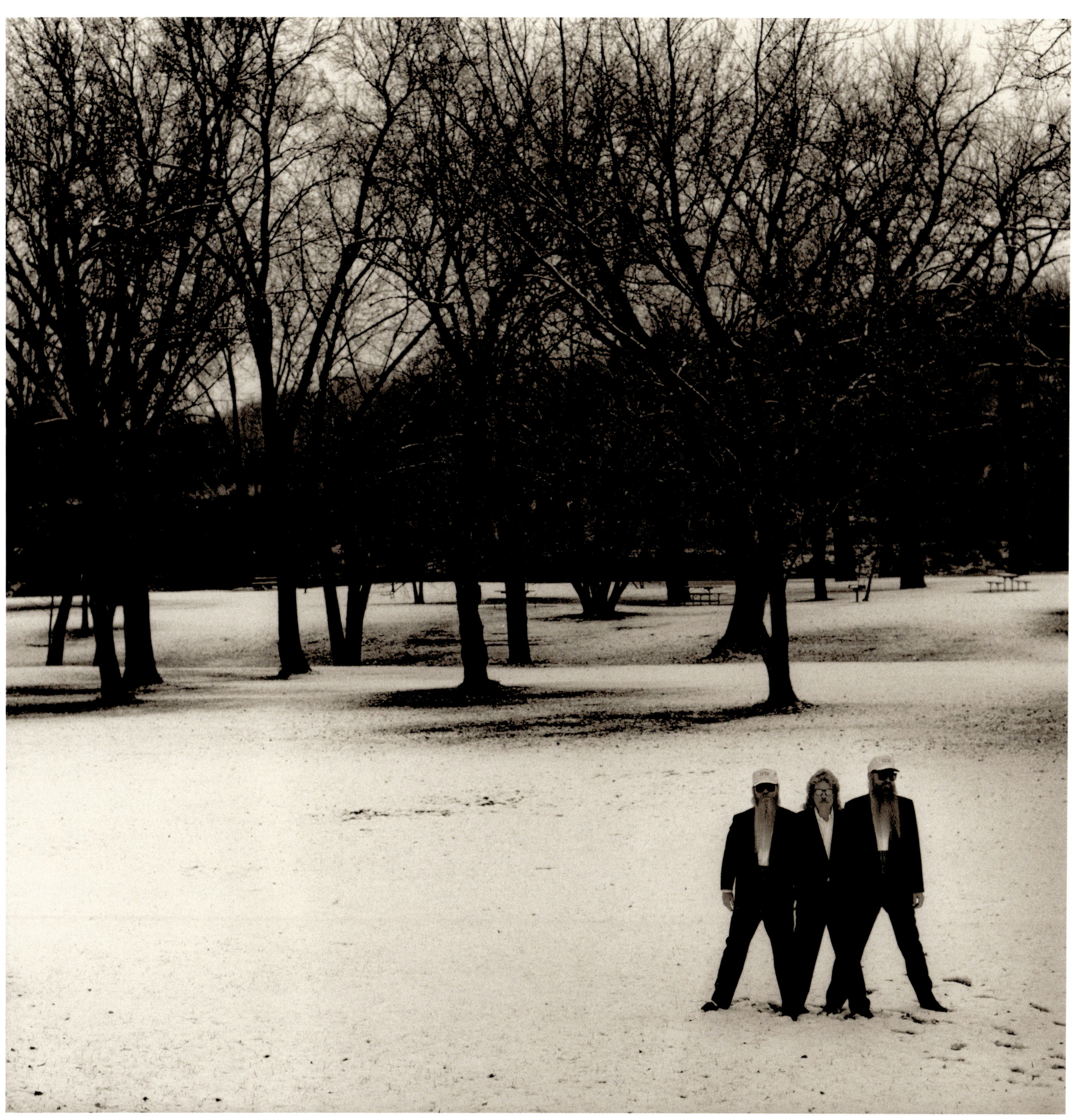

zz top

90

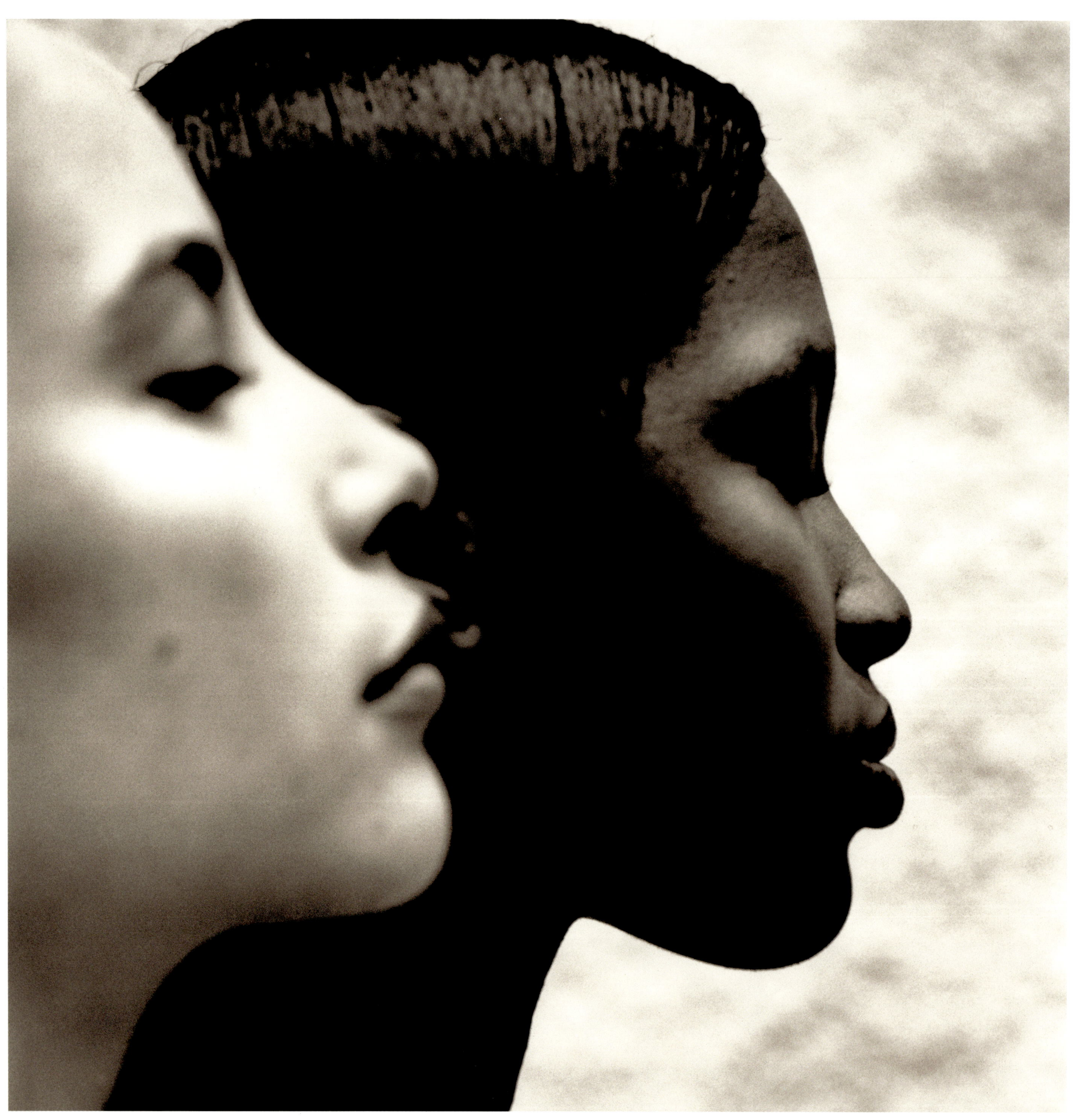

christy & naomi

91

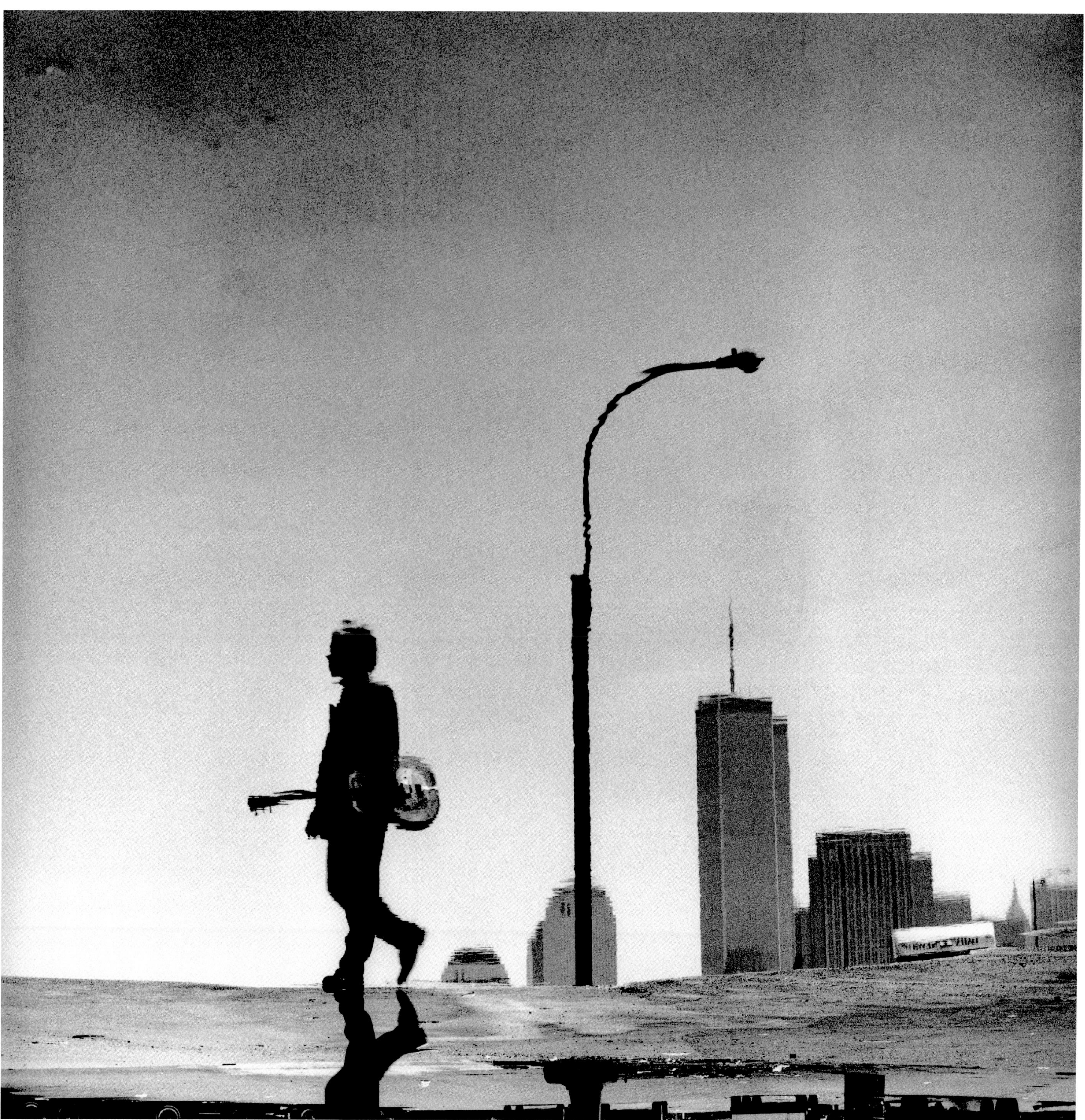

gary lucas

92

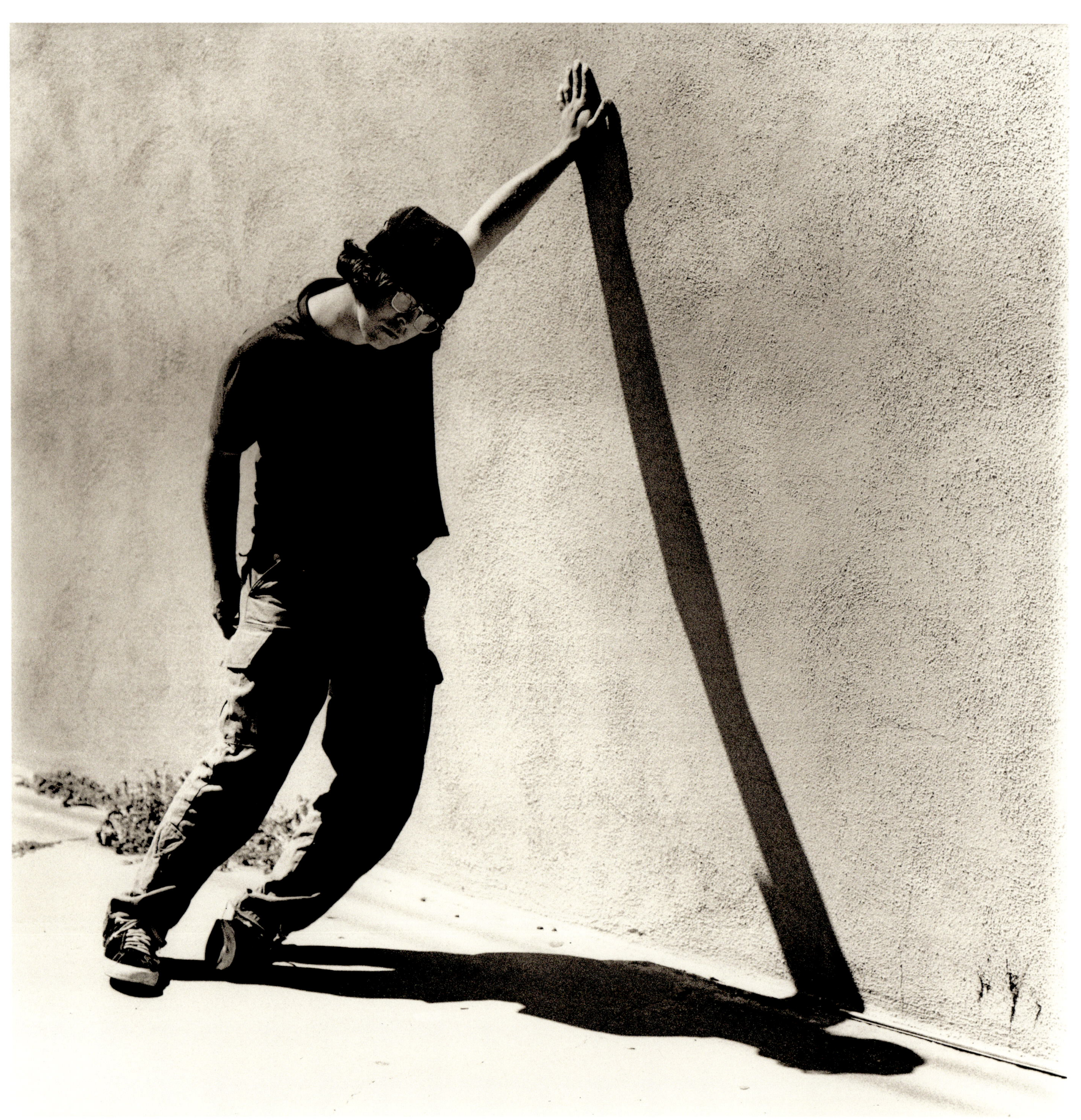
grant lee phillips
93

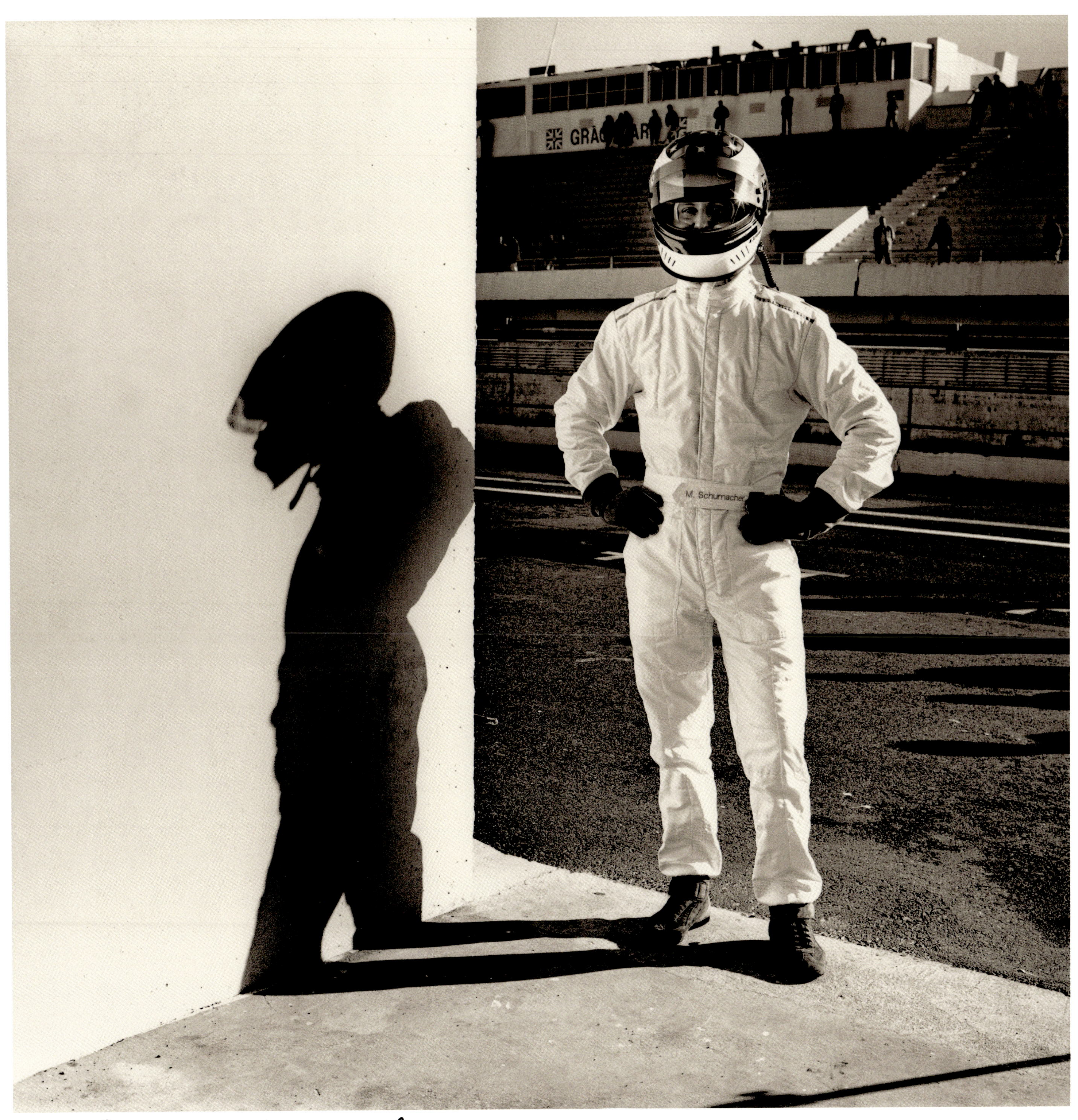

michael schumacher　　　94

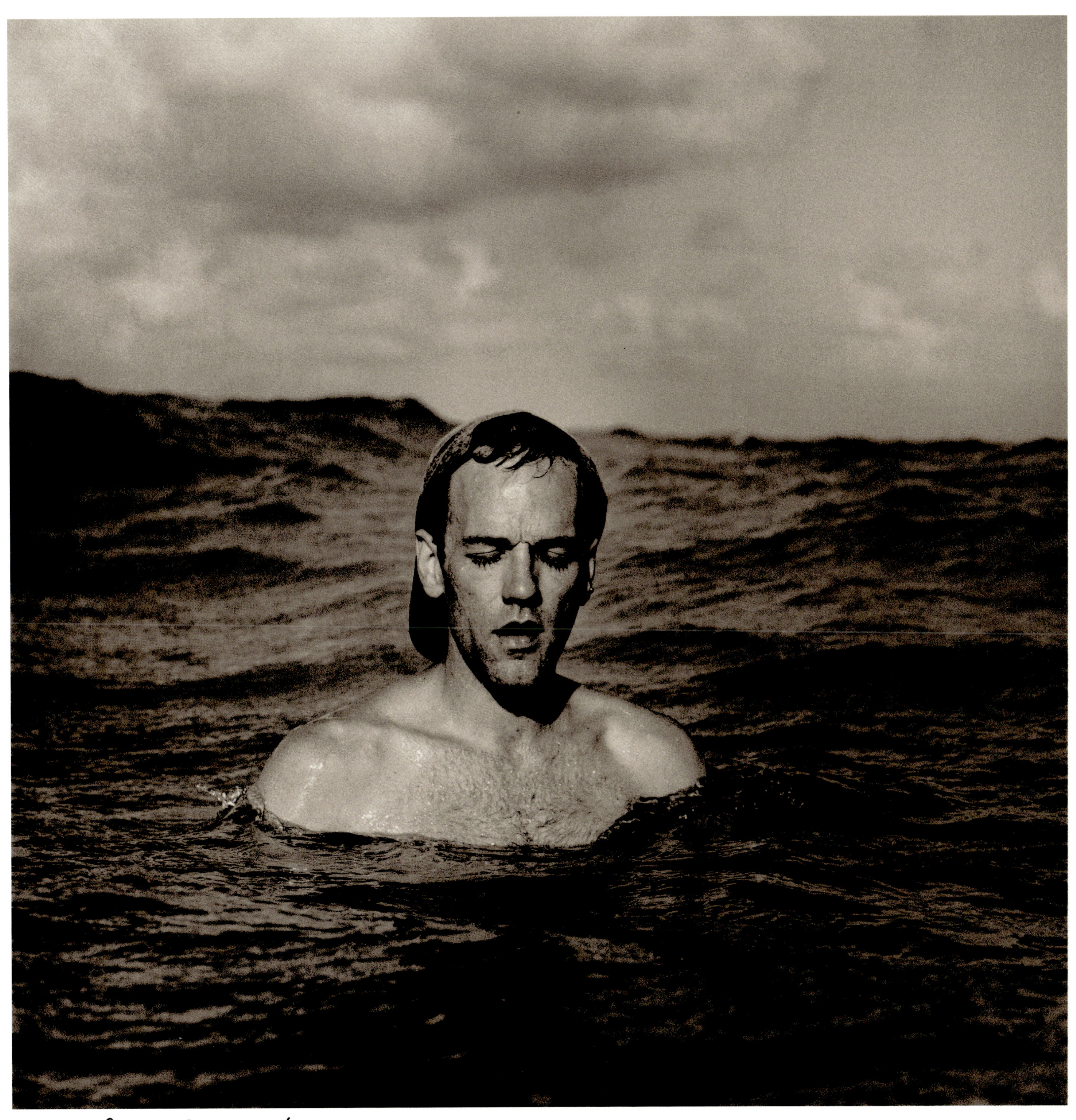
michael stipe
95

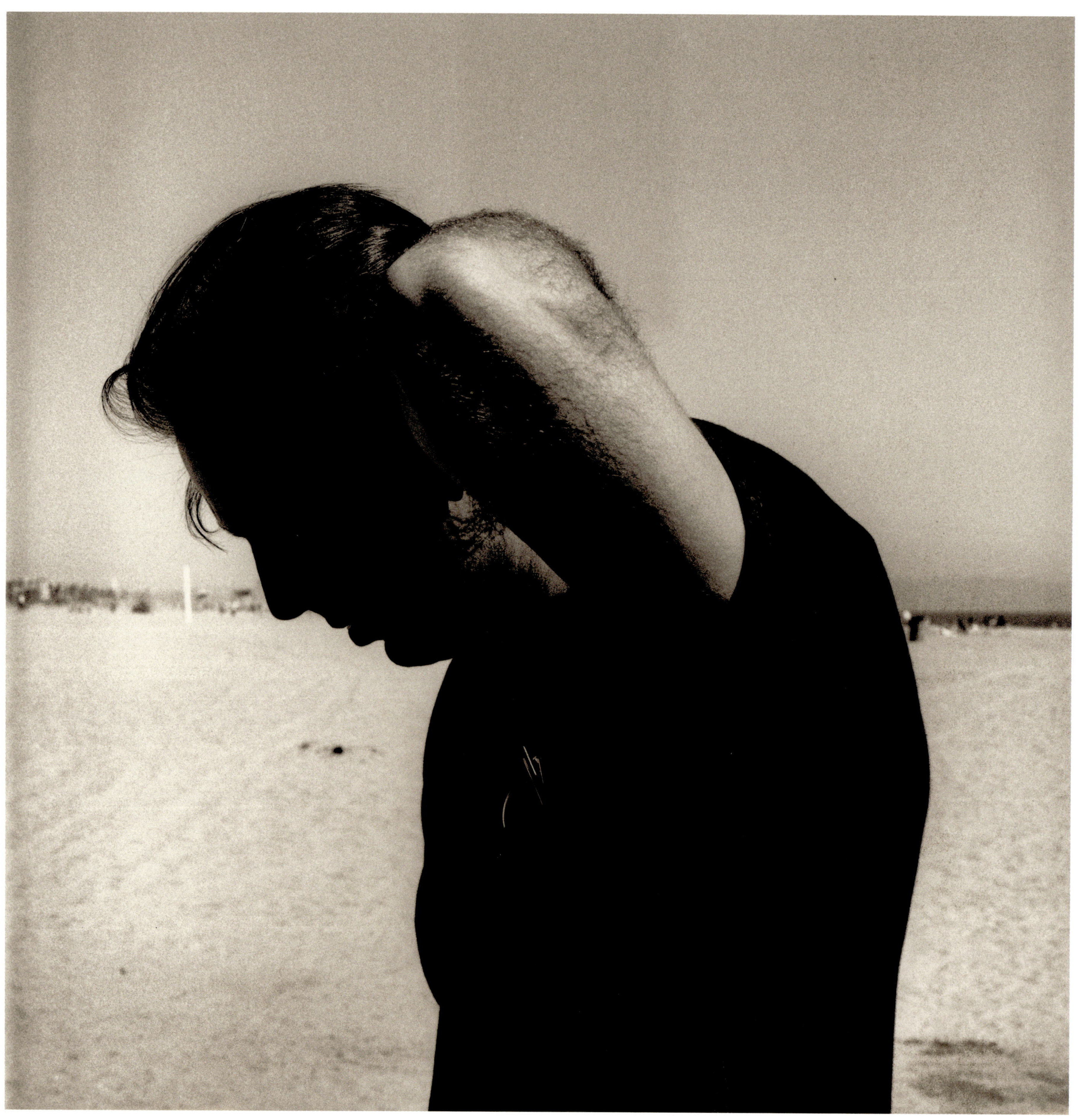
nic cage
96

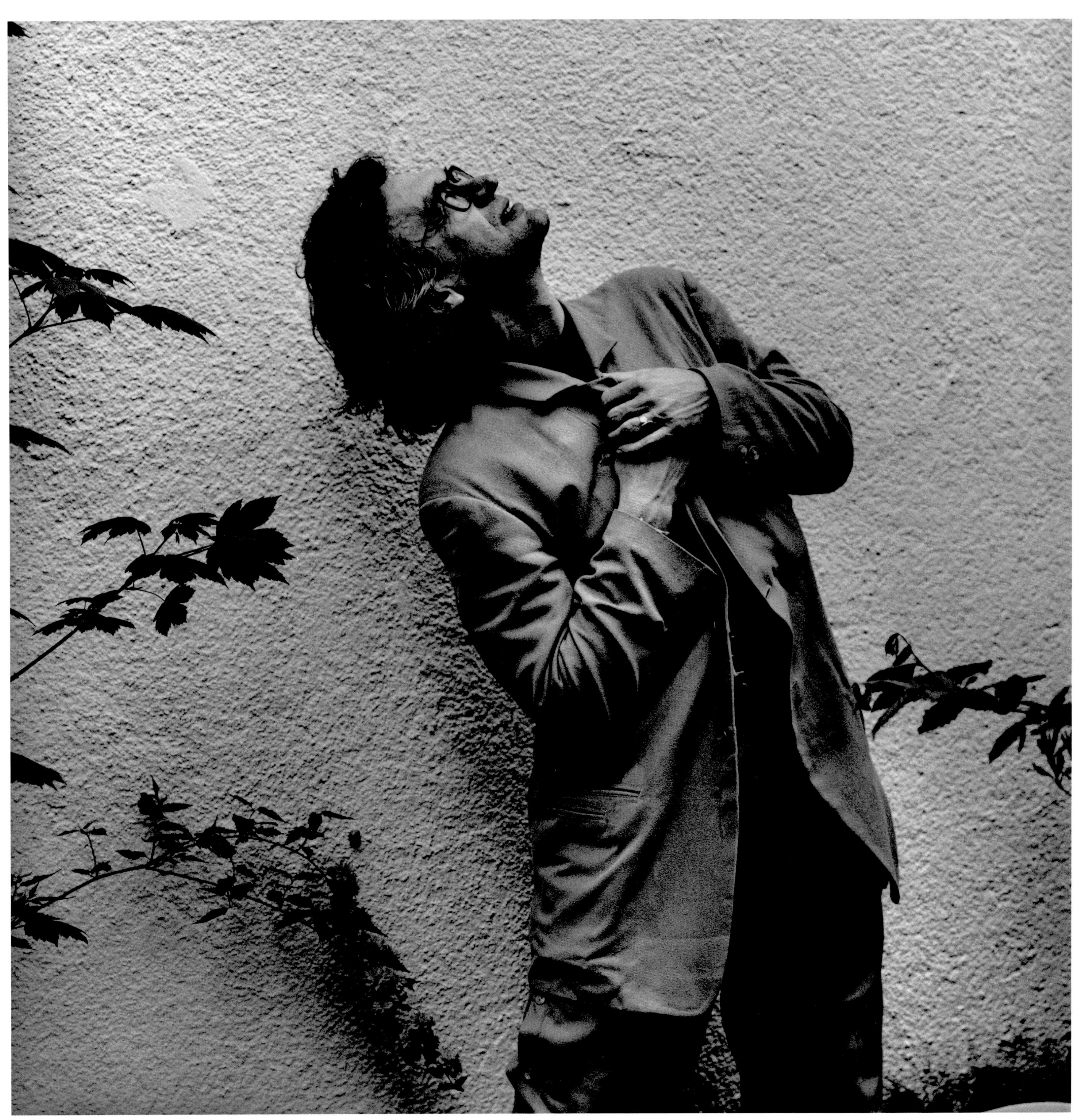

wim wenders   97

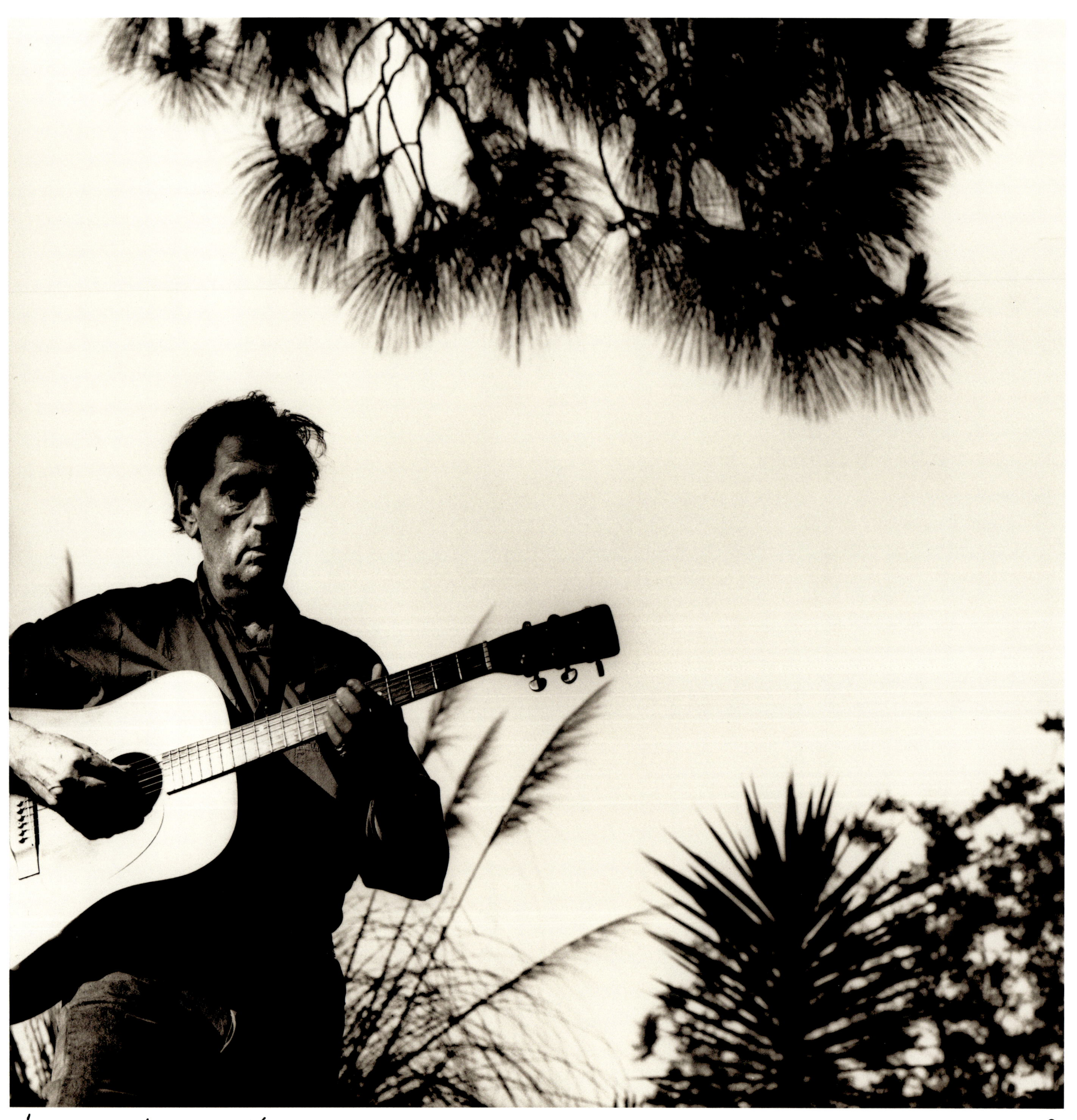

harry dean stanton   98

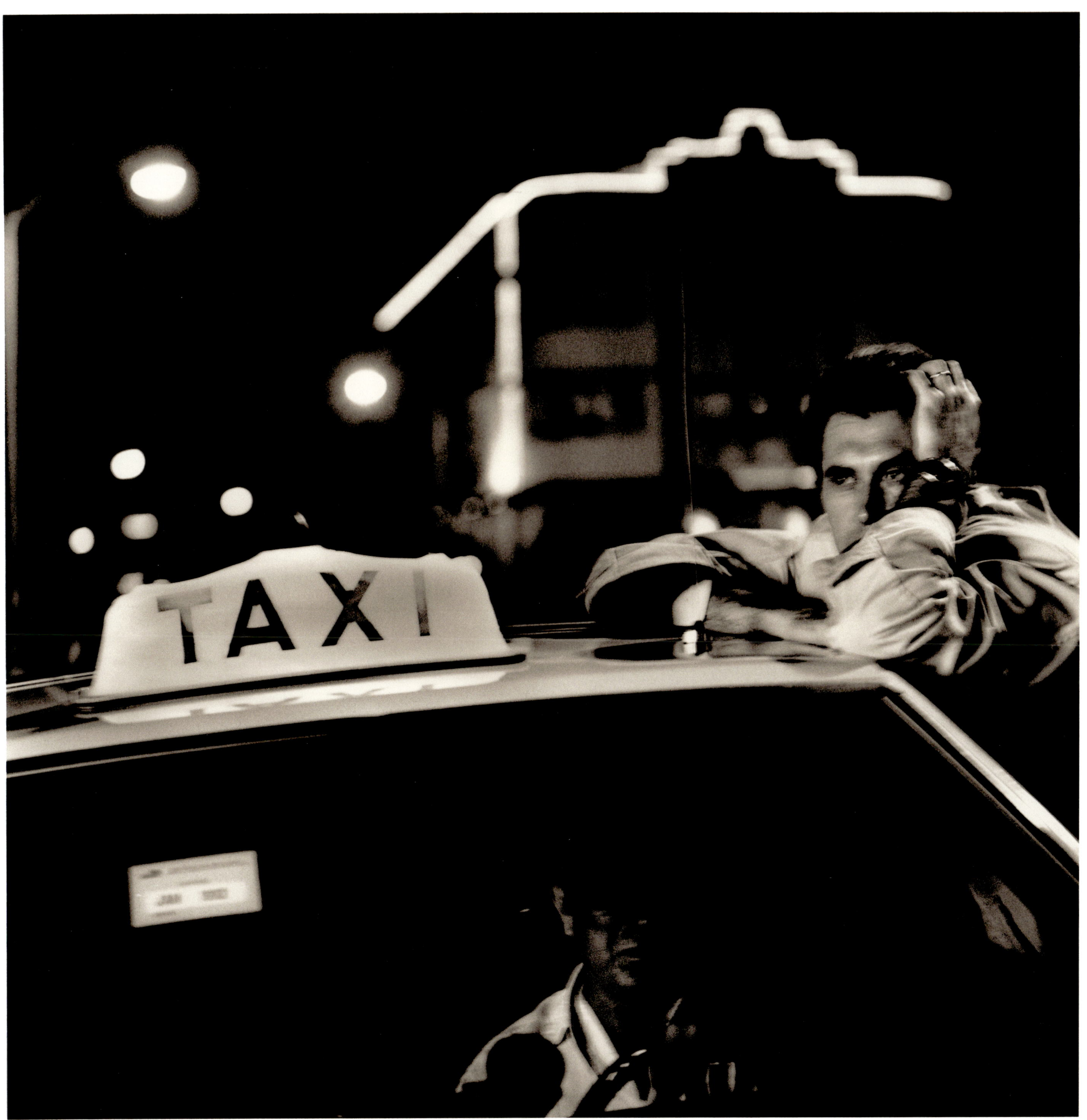

bryan ferry

99

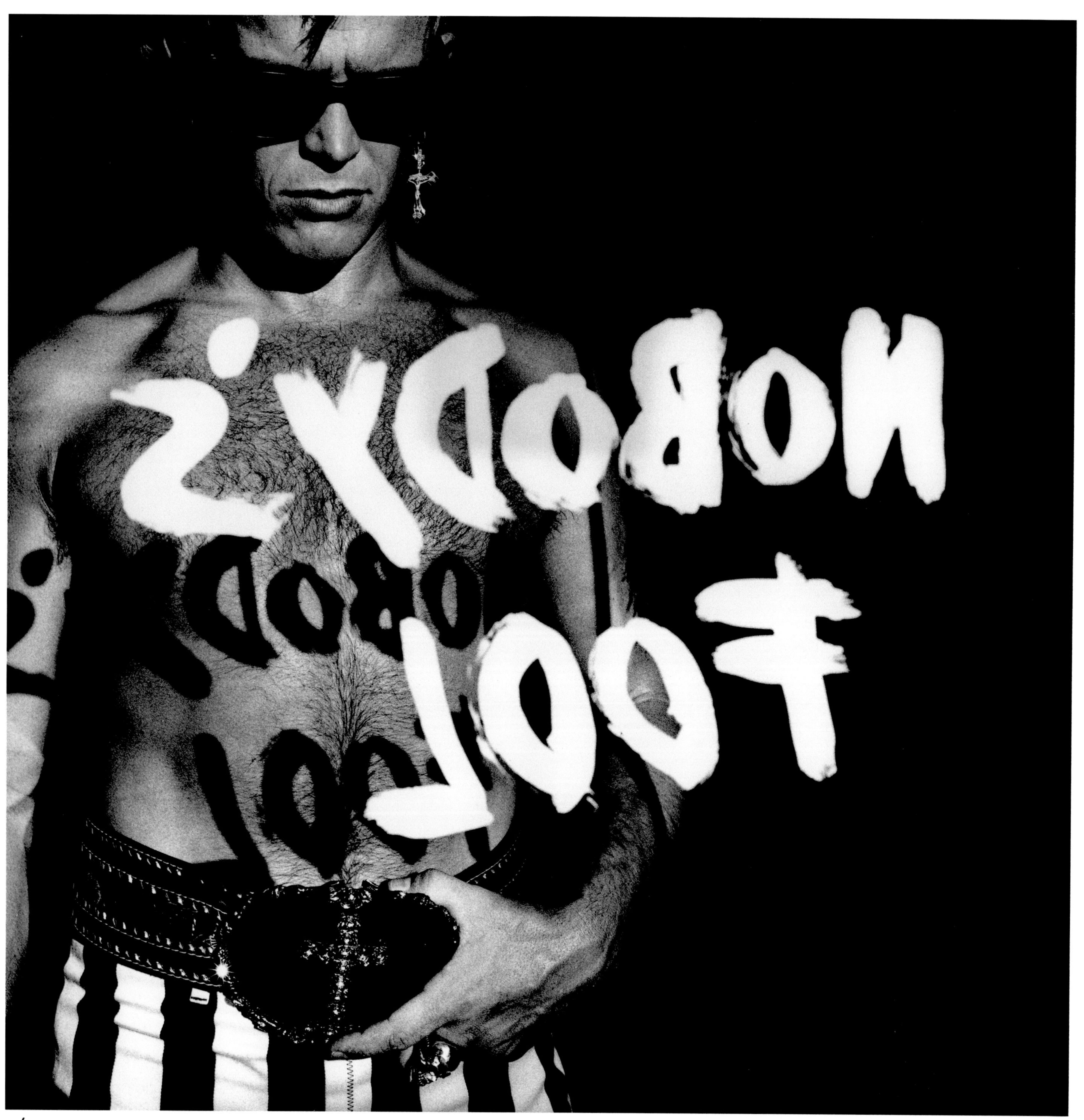

billy idol

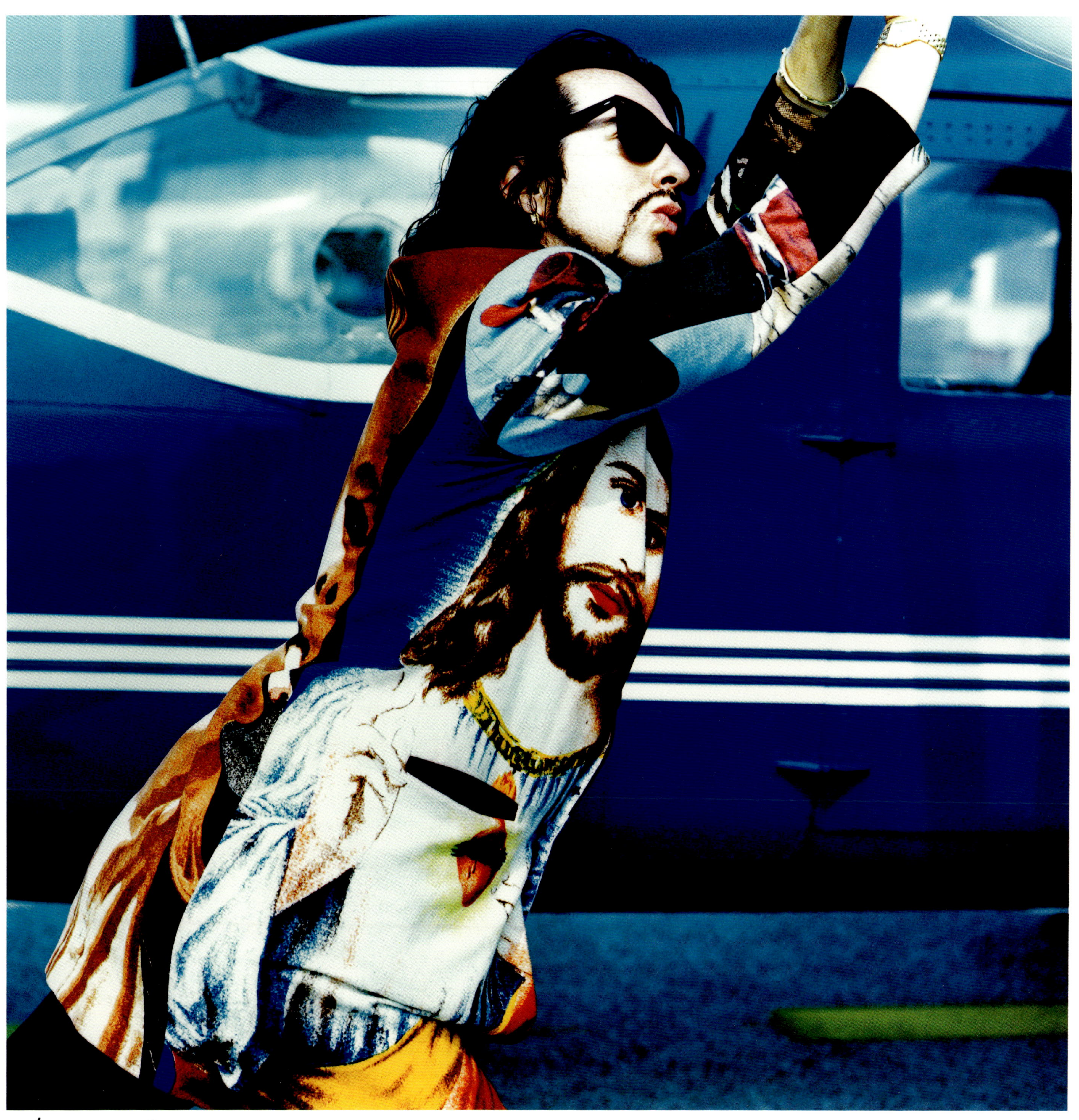

dave stewart

101

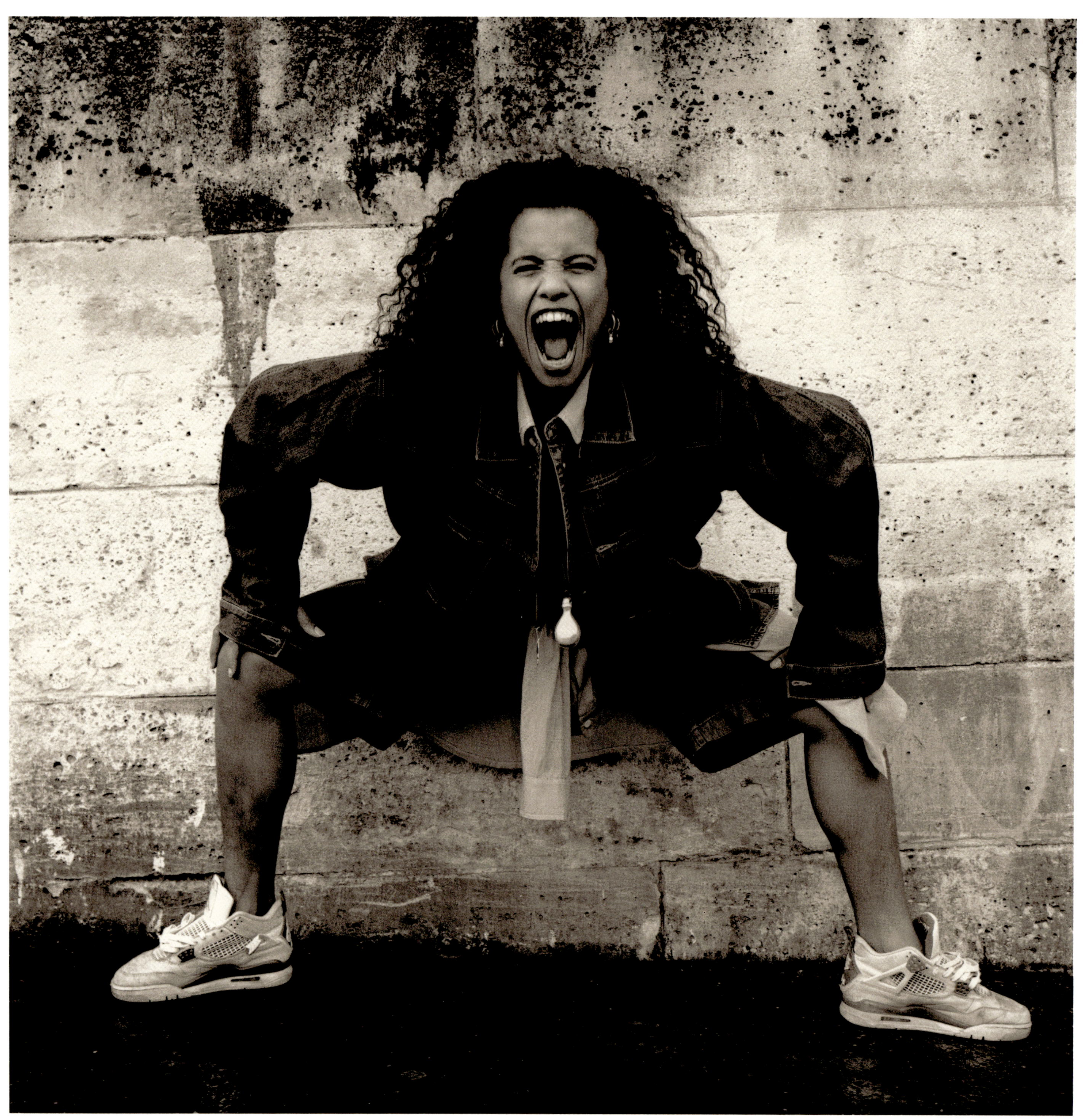

102

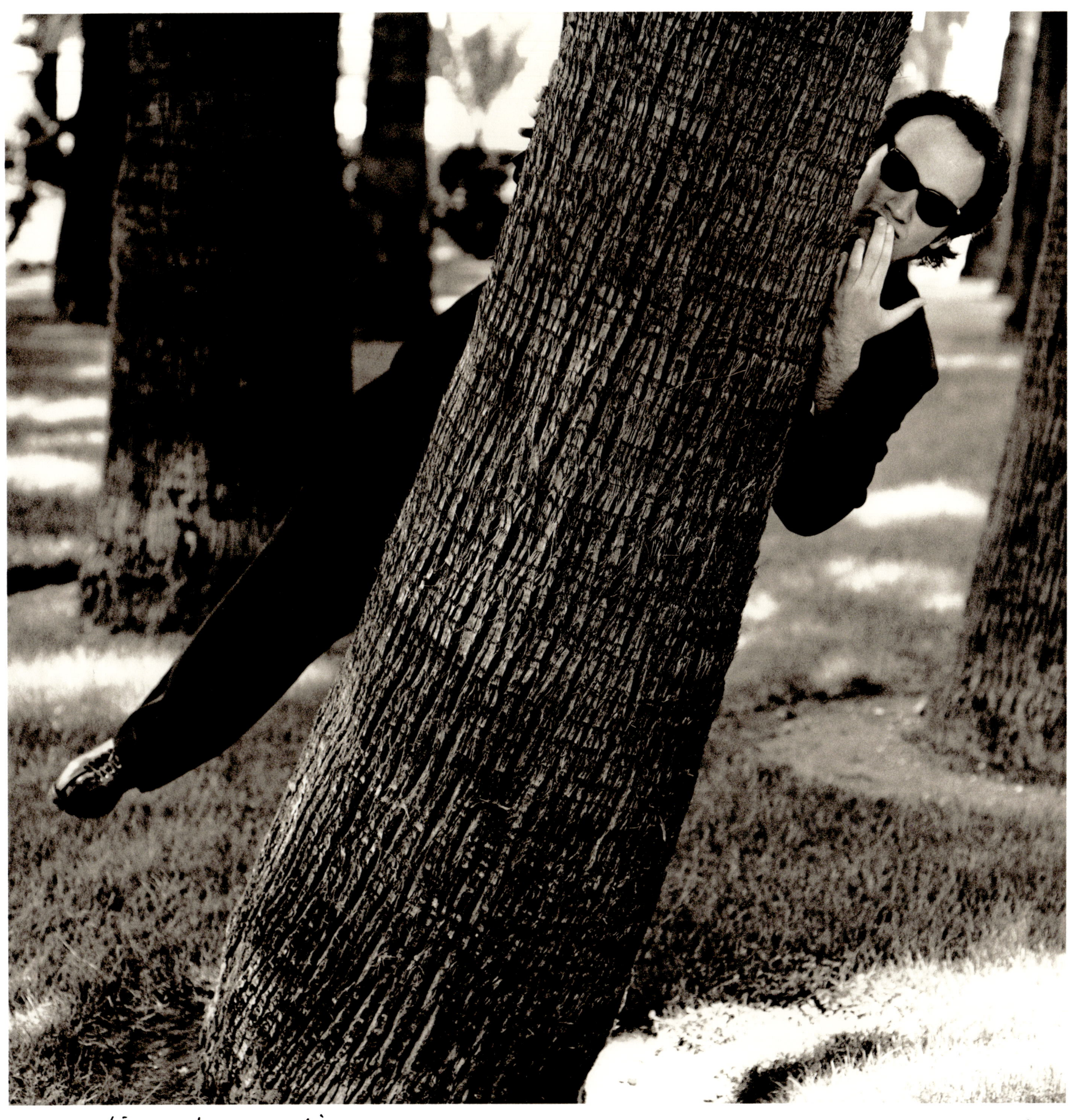

quentin tarantino   103

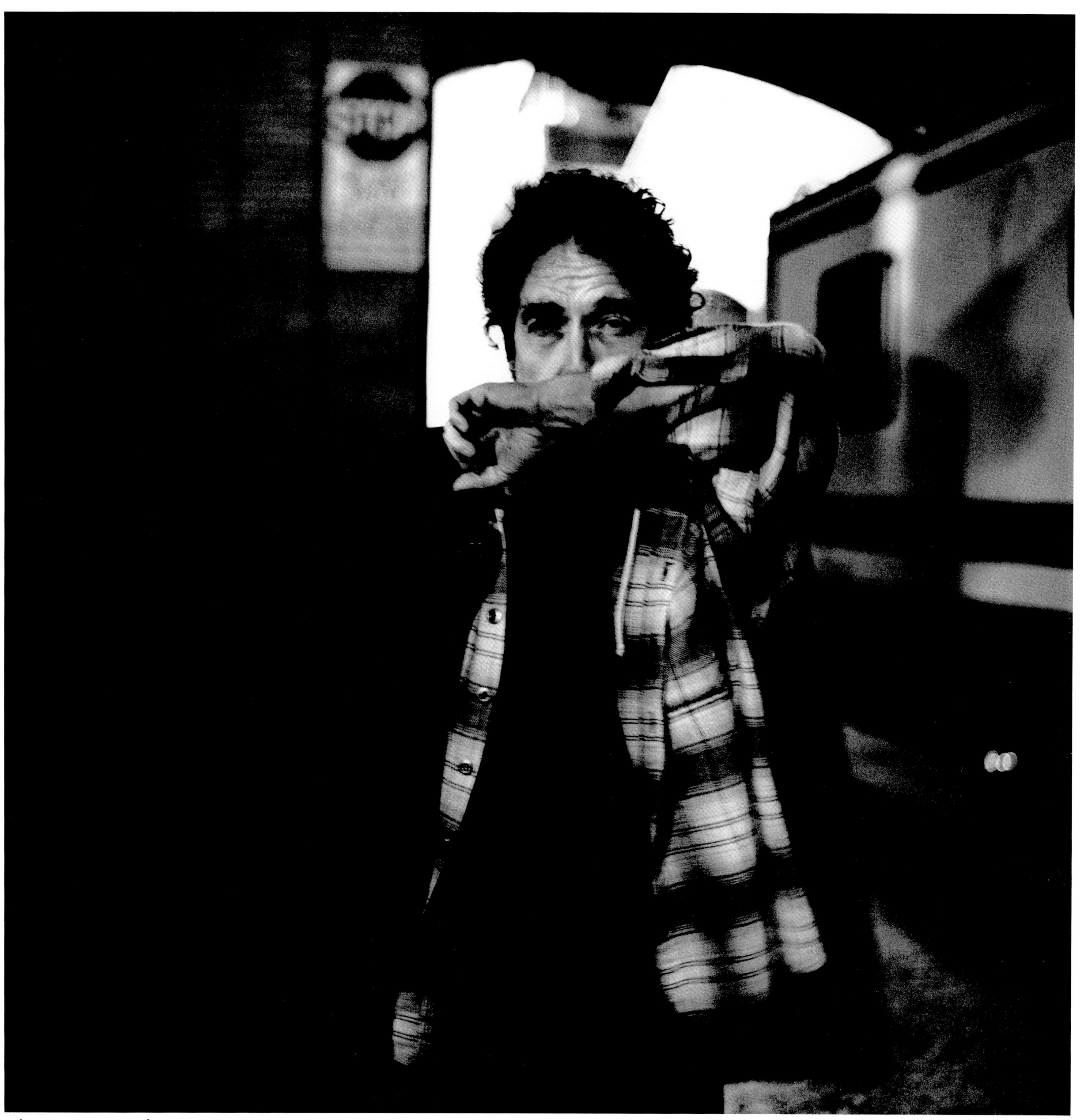

bob dylan   104

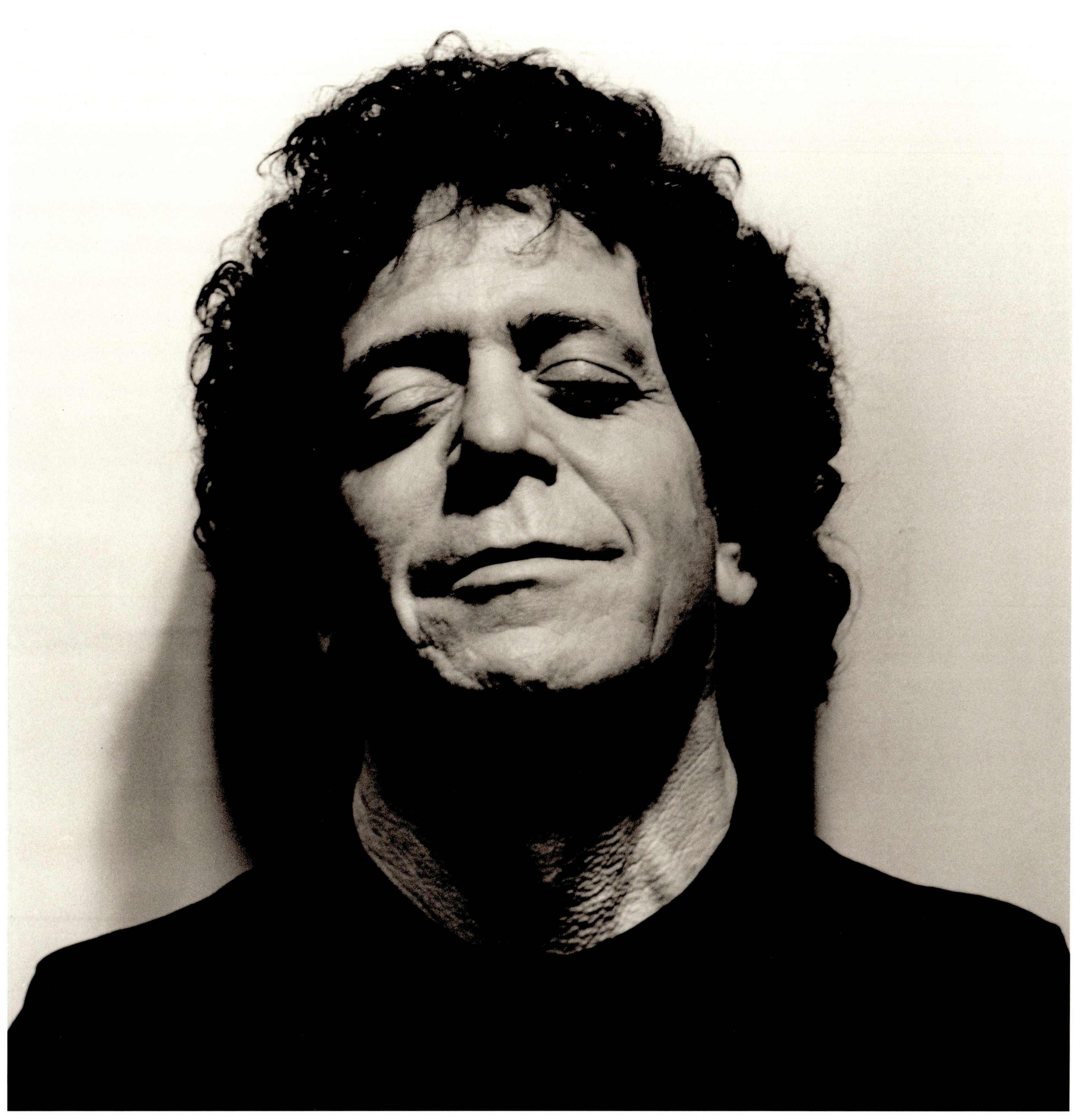

lou reed

105

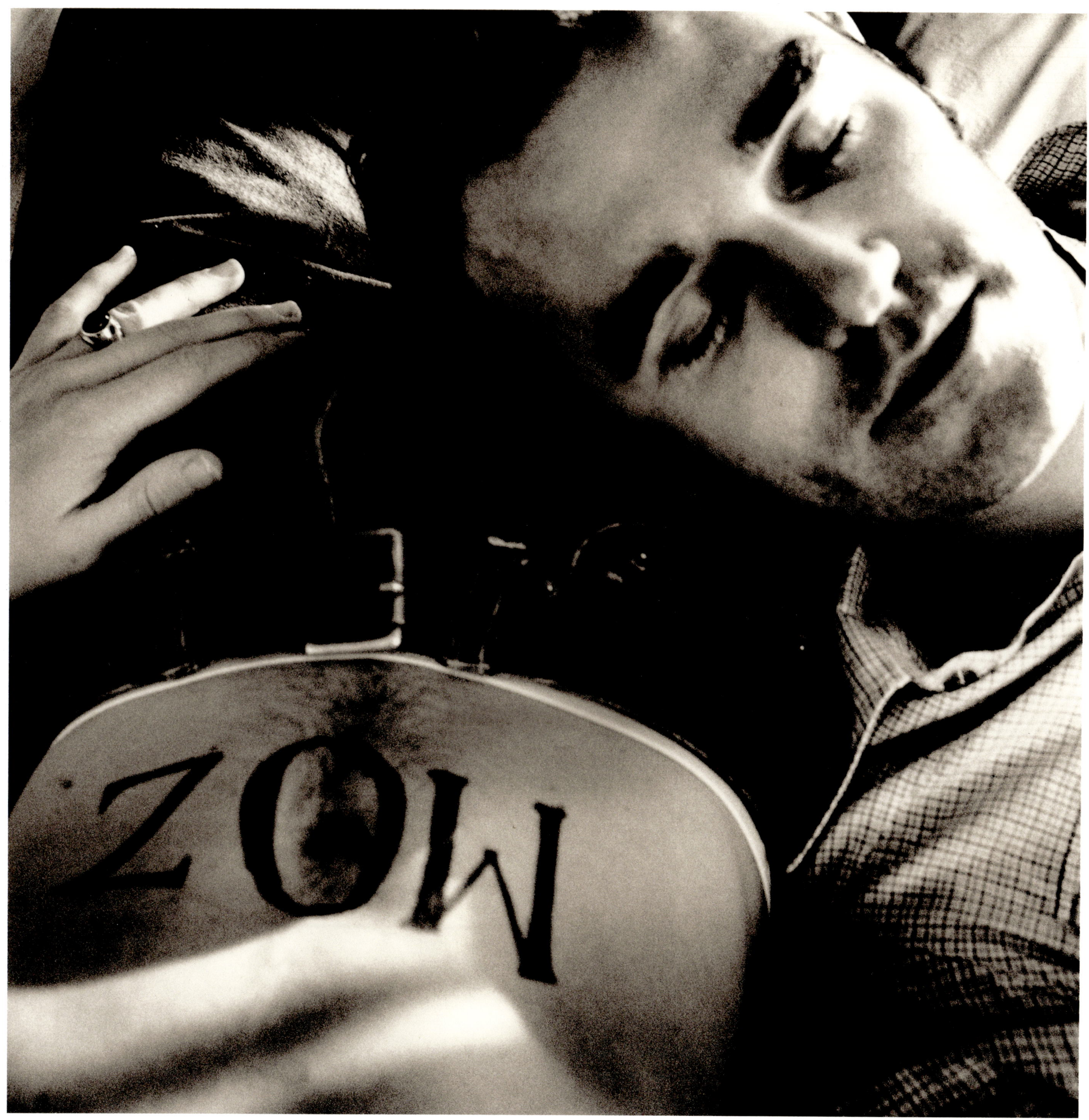

morrissey

106

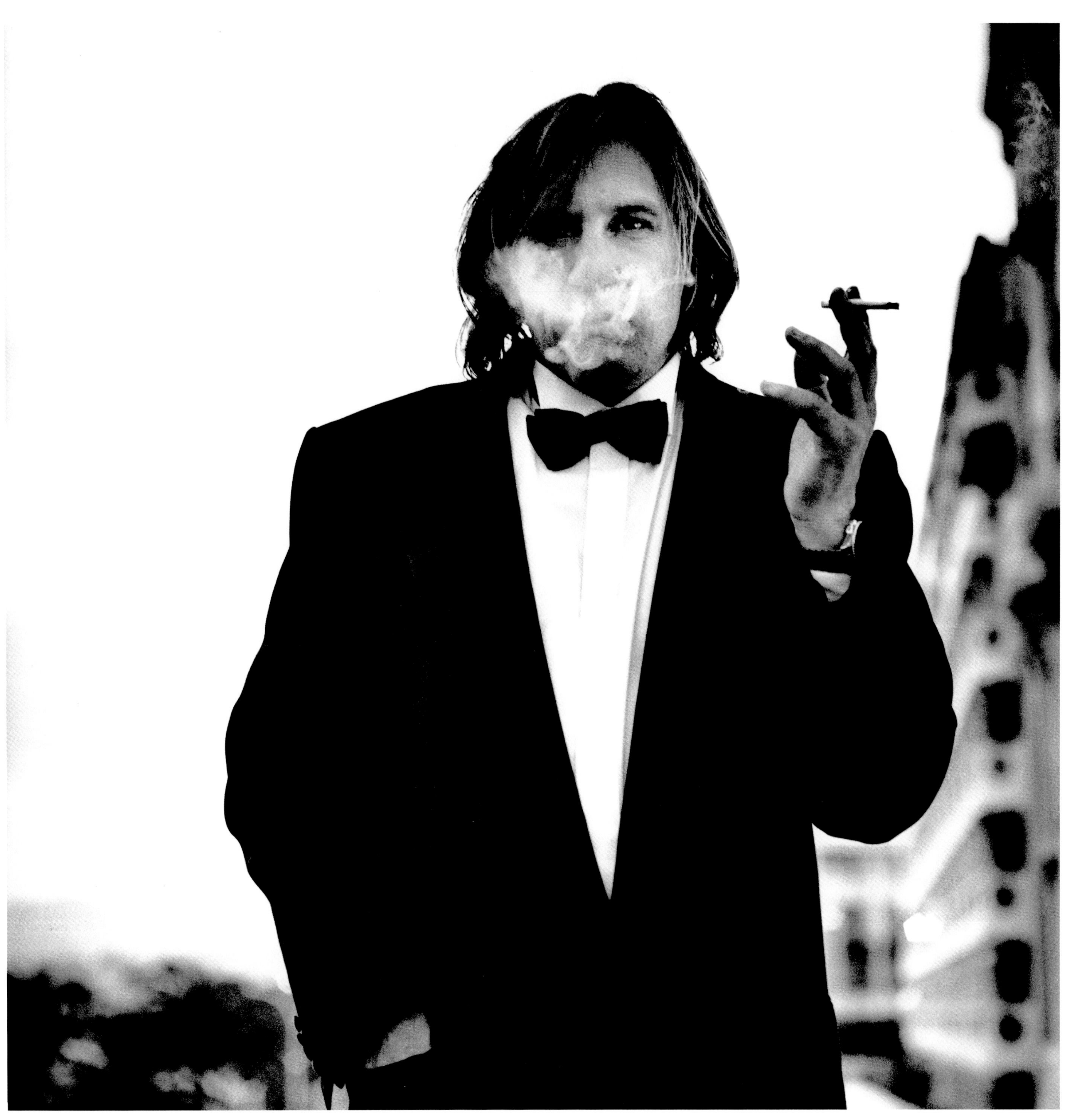

gérard depardieu

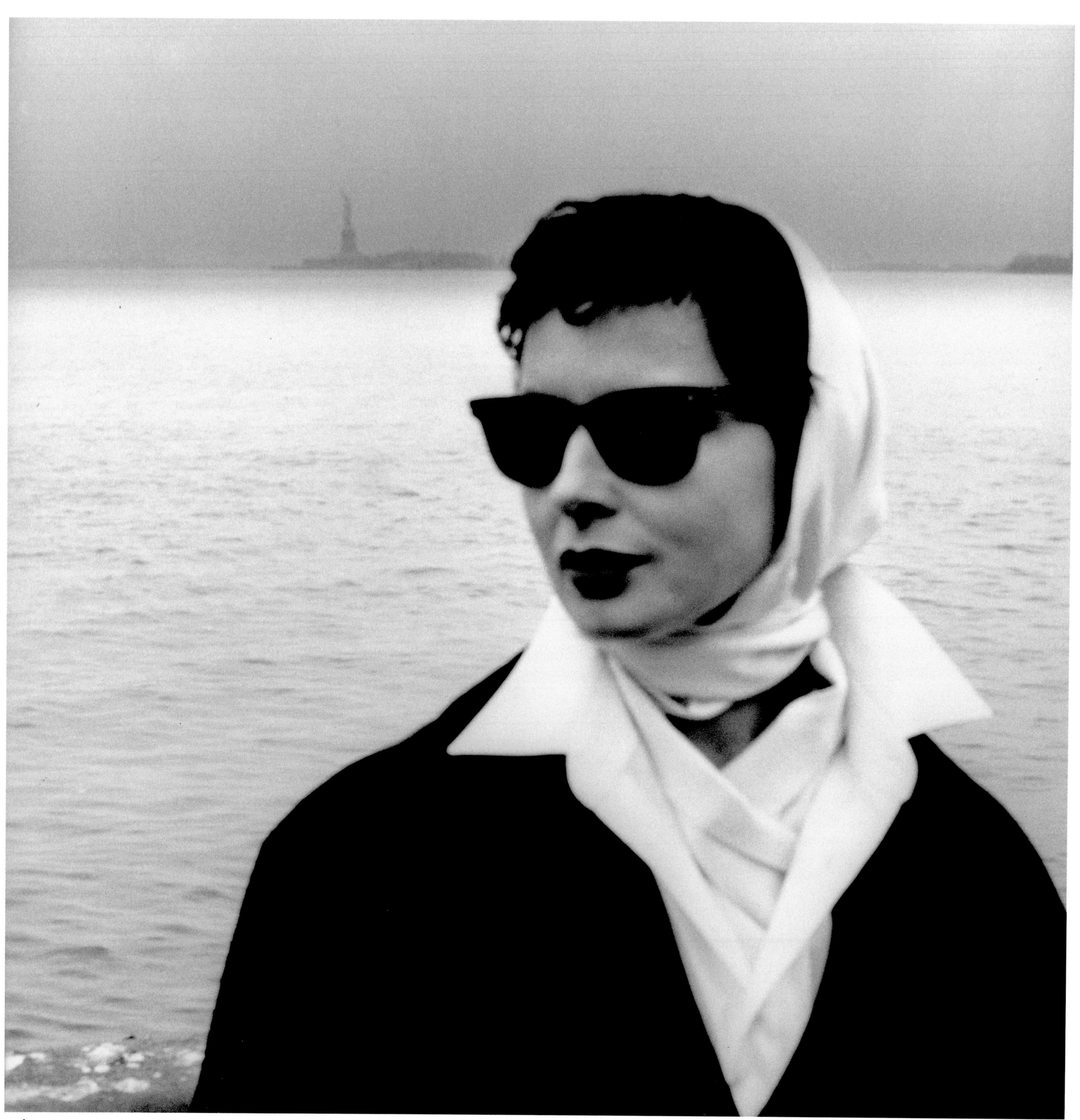

isabella rossellini

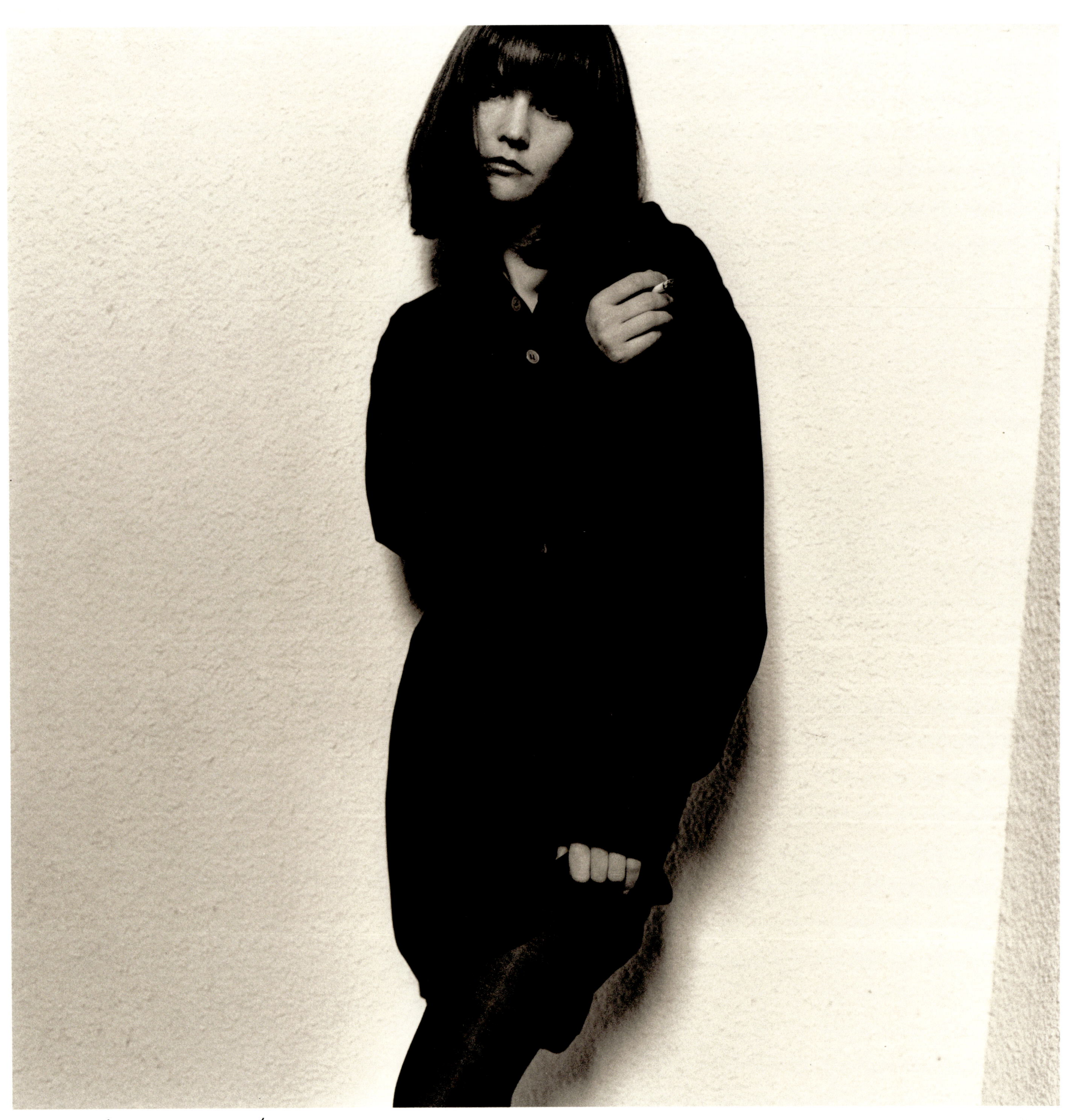

jennifer jason leigh   109

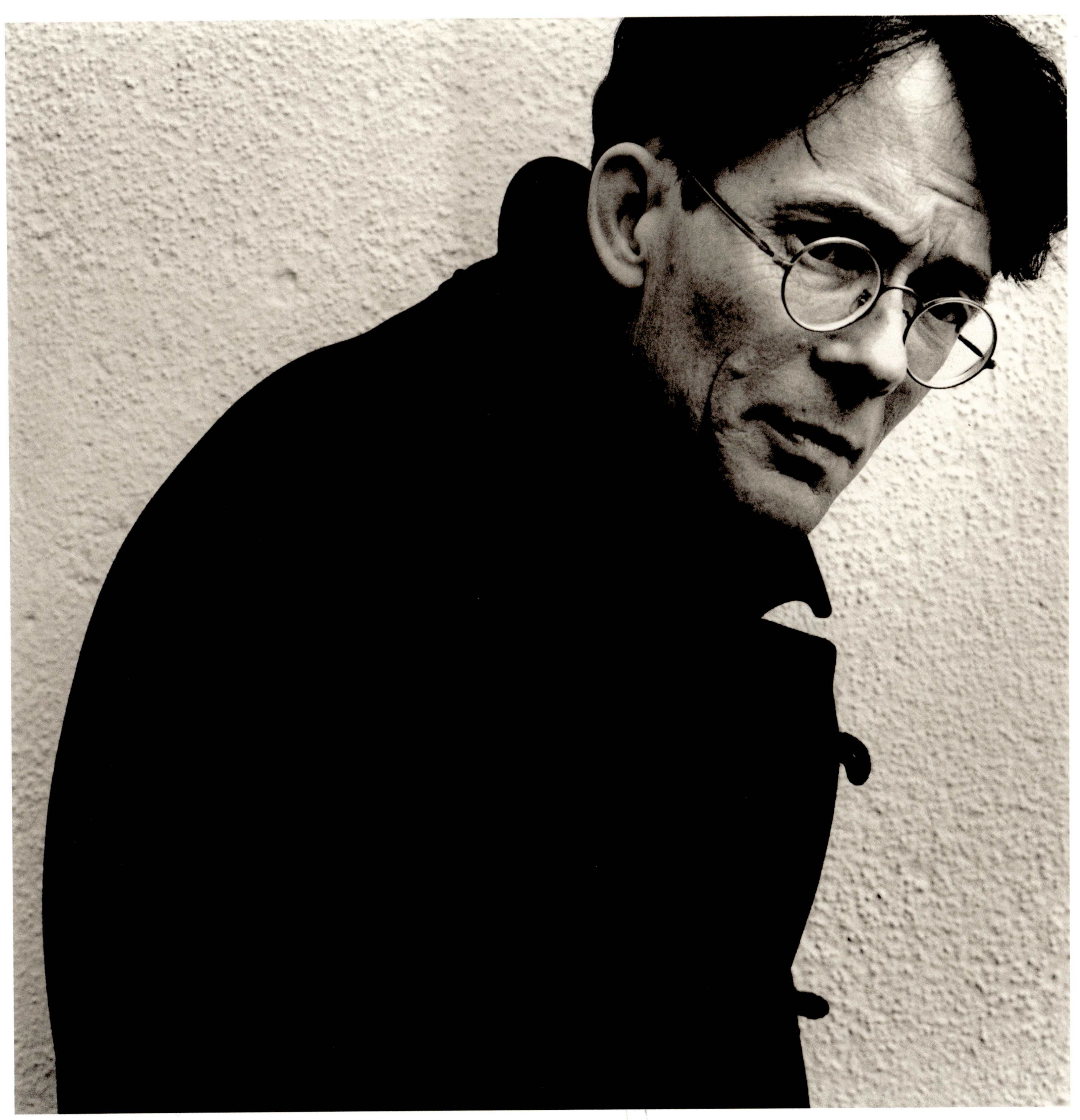

william gibson

110

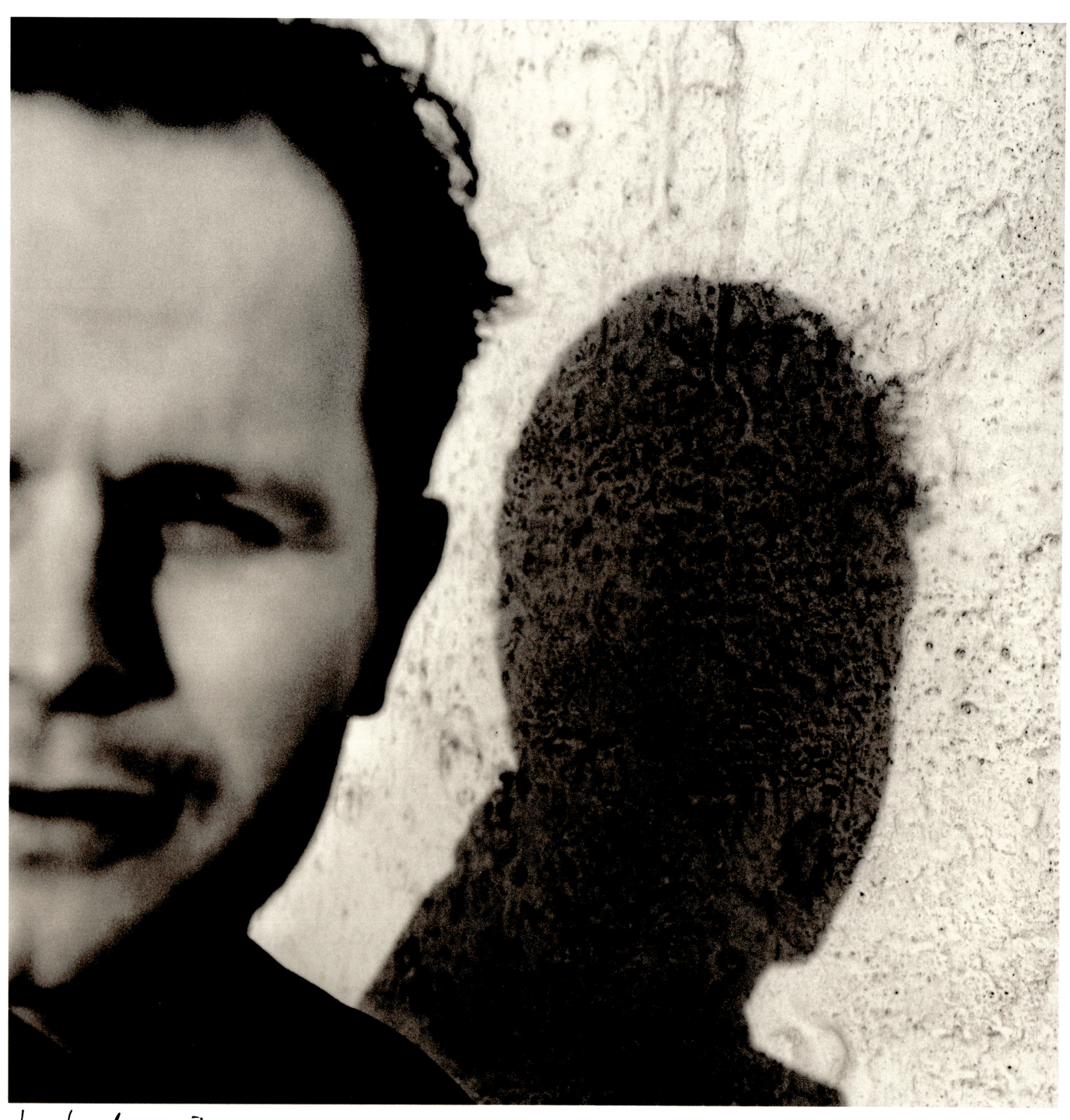

111

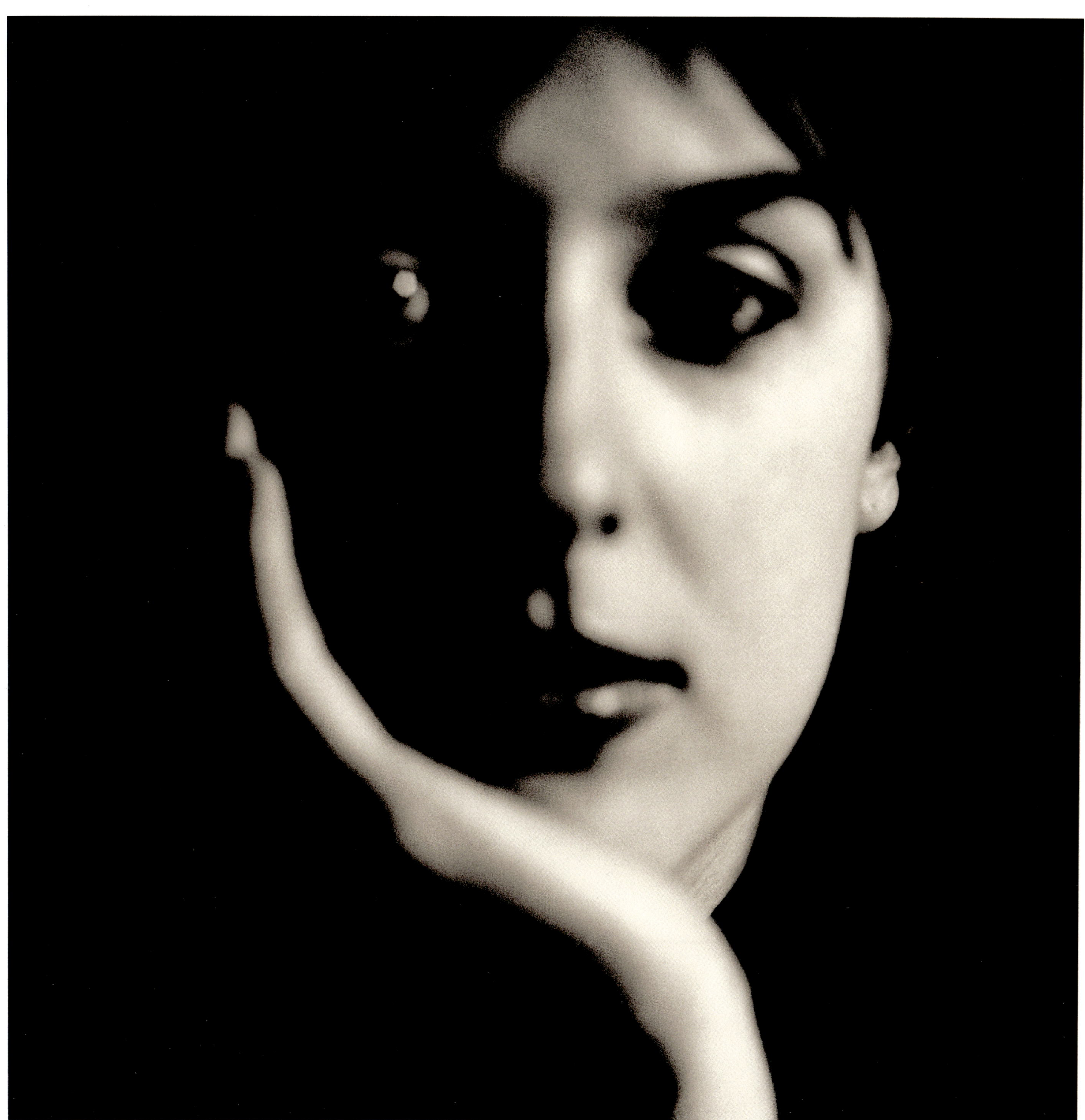

julie burchill

112

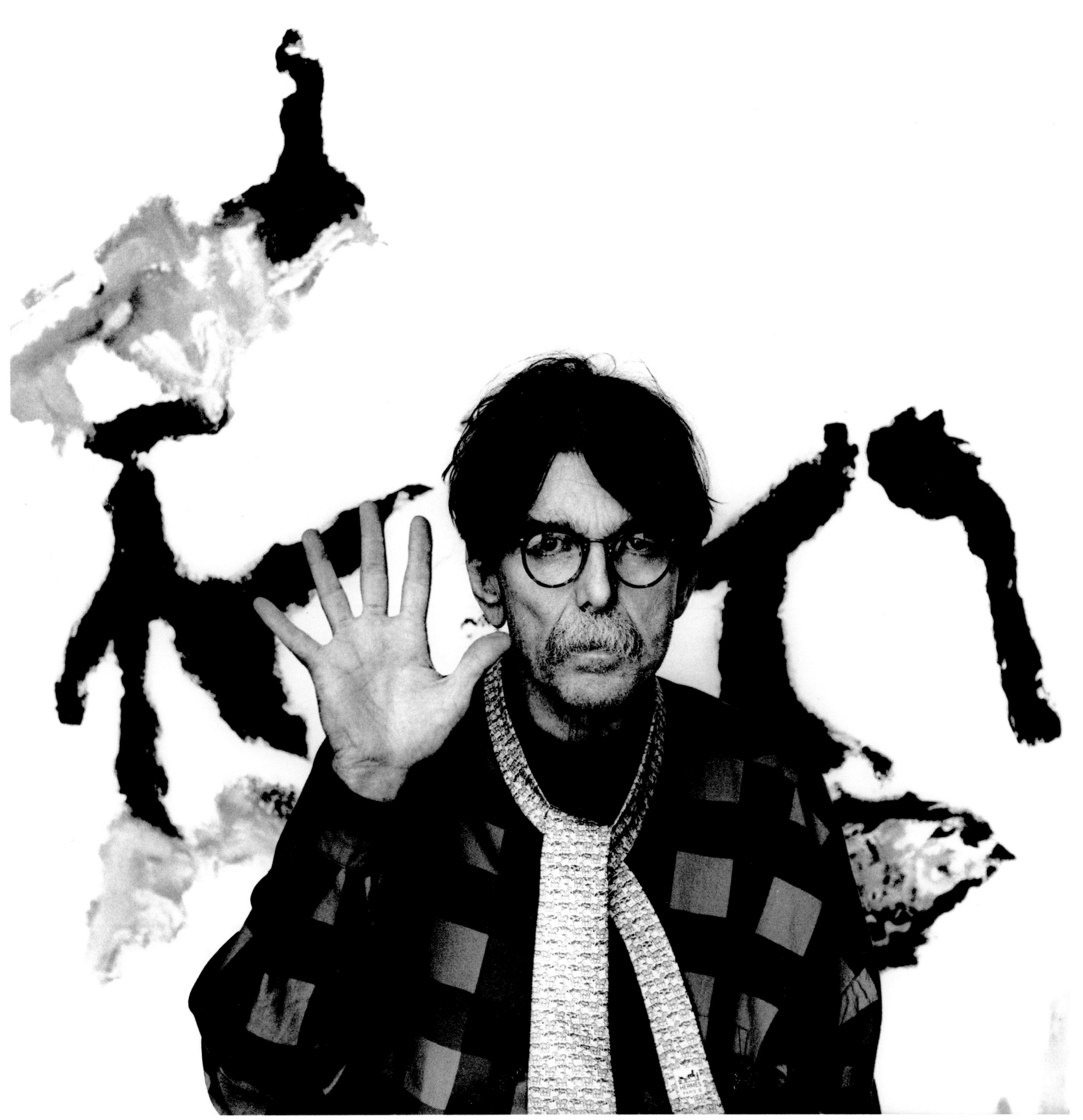

113

ANNEX

PHOTOGRAPHS

1. ALLEN GINSBERG New York 1996
2. Hand of JOHN LEE HOOKER
   Los Angeles 1994
3. HENRY ROLLINS Lancaster 1994
4. EAZY-E with bodyguards
   Los Angeles 1991
5. TRICKY London 1995
6. AIMEE MANN Boston 1992
7. MICHAEL STIPE Hollywood 1994
8. DAVID BOWIE London 1993
9. WILLIAM S BURROUGHS
   Lawrence 1993
10. DENNIS HOPPER Beverly Hills 1995
11. RUTGER HAUER Los Angeles 1992
12. MARTIN SCORSESE New York 1995
13. BRUCE SPRINGSTEEN Cleveland 1995
14. TOM JONES Las Vegas 1995
15. JON BON JOVI Vancouver 1992
16. PET SHOP BOYS London 1993
17. JERRY LEE LEWIS Cleveland 1995
18. U2 Dublin 1991
19. FRANK SINATRA Palm Springs 1993

20. HELENA CHRISTENSEN
    New York 1996
21. LIAM and NOEL GALLAGHER
    Long Island 1995
22. JIM SHERIDAN Eze 1994
23. BONO and SALMAN RUSHDIE
    London 1993
24. STEPHEN DORFF Malibu 1995
25. MICHAEL STIPE
    Saint Paul de Vence 1994
26. TRENT REZNOR Aqua Dulce 1994
27. CHRISTY TURLINGTON Dublin 1993
28. SINÉAD O'CONNOR Dublin 1990
29. BOY GEORGE London 1993
30. JODIE FOSTER Hollywood 1995
31. STEVEN SPIELBERG Los Angeles 1995
32. LARRY MULLEN Jr and BONO
    Berlin 1990
33. MICHAEL STIPE Miami 1992
34. DON VAN VLIET Eureka 1994
35. KEITH RICHARDS Toronto 1994
36. JEFF BUCKLEY Woodstock 1994
37. LEONARD COHEN London 1992

38. HAL HARTLEY Cannes 1994
39. JJ CALE San Diego 1994
40. JIMMY PAGE and ROBERT PLANT
    London 1994
41. NICK CAVE Santa Monica 1991
42. BRYAN FERRY Newcastle 1992
43. FRANK ZAPPA Los Angeles 1991
44. PJ HARVEY London 1994
45. KATE MOSS New York 1996
46. LUCIANO PAVAROTTI Turin 1996
47. BONO Tokyo 1993
48. GLENN DANZIG Green Bay 1990
49. RICK RUBIN Los Angeles 1990
50. DWIGHT YOAKAM Beverly Hills 1992
51. PETER MURPHY London 1992
52. DAVID BYRNE Hollywood 1991
53. DAVE GAHAN Hamburg 1992
54. TIM ROTH Hollywood 1995
55. BRIAN ENO London 1990
56. ISAAC HAYES London 1995
57. ANTHONY KIEDIS Los Angeles 1995
58. LENNY KRAVITZ New Orleans 1995
59. MICK JAGGER Toronto 1994

60. NASTASSIA KINSKI Bel Air 1995

61. NEIL YOUNG Half Moon Bay 1990

62. JACKSON BROWNE London 1993

63. ANNIE LENNOX London 1992

64. KURT COBAIN Seattle 1993

65. VANESSA PARADIS London 1992

66. JOHNNY DEPP Paris 1995

67. MARIANNE FAITHFULL
Los Angeles 1990

68. MICK JAGGER Toronto 1995

69. BONO Santa Cruz 1991

70. NAOMI CAMPBELL London 1993

71. BRYAN ADAMS Puerto Banus 1995

72. BRUCE COCKBURN Toronto 1991

73. COURTNEY LOVE Orlando 1995

74. KURT COBAIN Seattle 1993

75. HENRY ROLLINS Hollywood 1993

76. IGGY POP New York 1995

77. LL COOL J Brooklyn 1990

78. ELLIS, BRANFORD, WYNTON and
JASON MARSALIS New York 1990

79. DAVID LYNCH Hollywood 1994

80. JOHNNY CASH Los Angeles 1993

81. WILLEM DAFOE New York 1995

82. CLINT EASTWOOD Cannes 1994

83. HAL WILLNER London 1989

84. BJÖRK Los Angeles 1994

85. HORACE ANDY London 1991

86. SLASH Santa Fe 1992

87. STING Amesbury 1996

88. JOHN LEE HOOKER with model
Hollywood 1994

89. MICK HUCKNALL Paris 1995

90. ZZTOP Minneapolis 1990

91. CHRISTY TURLINGTON and NAOMI
CAMPBELL Dublin 1993

92. GARY LUCAS New York 1990

93. GRANT LEE PHILLIPS
Santa Paula 1994

94. MICHAEL SCHUMACHER Estoril 1995

95. MICHAEL STIPE Miami 1992

96. NICOLAS CAGE Santa Monica 1990

97. WIM WENDERS Munich 1993

98. HARRY DEAN STANTON
Beverly Hills 1993

99. BRYAN FERRY Miami 1992

100. BILLY IDOL Beverly Hills 1990

101. DAVE STEWART Amsterdam 1991

102. NENEH CHERRY Paris 1992

103. QUENTIN TARANTINO Cannes 1994

104. BOB DYLAN Cleveland 1995

105. LOU REED New York 1996

106. MORRISSEY and friend
London 1994

107. GÉRARD DEPARDIEU Cannes 1994

108. ISABELLA ROSSELLINI
New York 1993

109. JENNIFER JASON LEIGH
Cannes 1994

110. WILLIAM GIBSON Dublin 1993

111. HERBERT GRÖNEMEYER
Almeria 1992

112. JULIE BURCHILL London 1989

113. DON VAN VLIET Eureka 1994

SELECTED EXHIBITIONS

SOLO EXHIBITIONS

1982   SHEFFIELD Untitled Gallery

1989   AMSTERDAM Torch Gallery
PARIS Fnac Gallerie
VIENNA Galerie Gawlik & Schorm
TOKYO Parco Gallery
NAGOYA Kirin Building
BRUSSELS Fnac Gallerie
COLOGNE Galerie Torch-Onrust

1990   DUBLIN City Centre Gallery

1991   PARIS Institut Neerlandais
AMSTERDAM Vrije Universiteit
Exposorium
MUNICH Galerie Mosel &
Tschechow

1993   LEVERKUSEN Museum Morsbroich

1994   AMSTERDAM Stedelijk Museum
ROTTERDAM Kunsthal

1996   AMSTERDAM Torch Gallery
ANTWERP Zeno X Gallerie
DARMSTADT Galerie Beckers
HAMBURG Deichtorhallen

GROUP EXHIBITIONS

1980   AMSTERDAM Dutch Photography,
Canon Gallerie

1987   GRONINGEN Groninger Museum

1989   BOSTON Photographic Research
Center

1992   ESSLINGEN Fototriennale Esslingen

TORCH Gallery in Amsterdam represents
Anton Corbijn's work.

ACKNOWLEDGEMENTS

I would like to thank all the persons appearing in this book and also express my gratitude to the following for either their direct involvement and/or their continuous support: Bryan Adams, Richard Bell, Steve Berkowitz, Robin Betts, Bono, Adam Clayton, Joe Dolce, Sarah Doukas, Brian Eno, Dr Zdenek Felix, Fintan Fitzgerald, Dagmar Forelle, *Studio* Magazine France, Cara Gallardo, Martin Gore, James Grauerholz, Andrea Griminelli, Adriaan vd Have, Roland Hepp, Susan Jacobs, Mike Kappus, Nassim Khalifa, Lane von Kories, Kristine McKenna, Maryam Malakpour, Bill Mullen, Jodi Peckman, Greg Pond, Tessa Posnansky, Principle MGMT, Susan Reynolds, Robbie Robertson, Michelle Romero, Michelle Rosenblatt, Bob Rosenthal, Eric Schaub, Lothar Schirmer, Richard Smith, State Ltd, Sophie Stolberg, Stoya, Michael Stipe, James Truman, Jann Wenner.

Some of the photographs have been commissioned by: Beggars Banquet Records, Columbia Records, Delabel, *Details, Elle* (Germany), EMI Electrola GmbH, *Entertainment Weekly, The Face, HP, The Independent Magazine, LA Style, Live!, Max* (Germany), Mute Records, Nothing Records, *OOR,* Polygram Records, REM Athens Ltd, *Rolling Stone, Spin, Studio* (France), *US Magazine, Vogue Homme,* U2, Virgin Records.

Very special thanks to Mike Spry at Downtown Darkroom for all the b/w printing, Brian Dowling at BDI for the colour work, and Anja Grabert and Elizabeth Lewis for being such a great team.